TEXAS
ICONOCLAST

To Susan Dangle,
It has been a
great pleasure working
with you. Keep
up the good work
with teachers.

Allan Koumsber

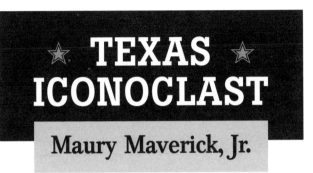

TEXAS ICONOCLAST

Maury Maverick, Jr.

Edited and with a preface by
Allan O. Kownslar

TEXAS CHRISTIAN UNIVERSITY PRESS
FORT WORTH ★ TEXAS

New material © 1997 Allan O. Kownslar

Library of Congress Cataloging-in-Publication Data

Maverick, Maury, 1921-
    Maury Maverick, Jr., Texas iconoclast / edited by Allan O. Kownslar.
    p.   cm.
    ISBN 0-87565-172-0 (alk. paper)
    1. Texas–History–Anecdotes. 2. Texas–Biography–Anecdotes.
    3. Heroes–Texas–Biography–Anecdotes. 4. Heroines–Texas–
    Biography–Anecdotes. 5. Civil rights–Anecdotes. I. Kownslar,
Allan O. II. Title.
    F386.6.M36   1997
    976.4–dc20   96-31443 CIP

Editor's Note: Unless otherwise designated, all excerpts are from columns written by Maury Maverick, Jr., and published in the San Antonio *Express-News*.

All columns are essentially as Maverick wrote them, although minor editing has been done to regularize spelling and punctuation.

Design by Margie Adkins

Acknowledgments

Thanks to Marguerite Louise Hanicak Kownslar and Donald Edward Everett for excellent editorial suggestions and Eunice Herrington and Evelyn Luce for typing the manuscript.

★ CONTENTS

Maury Maverick, Jr., is opinionated, disgusting, a racist, a crackpot, bigoted, biased, unpatriotic, decadent, psychotic, unrealistic, not operating with a full deck of cards, and full of sentimental baloney.

Maury Maverick, Jr., is a true-blue American, a free agent, a gadfly, devoid of racism, provocative, entertaining, an effective historian and educator, and a first-rate philosopher. Above all he is a champion defender of civil liberties.

—A compilation of opinions from letters about Maury Maverick, Jr., that have been sent to the editor of the San Antonio *Express-News*

Few people who know him or read his Sunday column in the San Antonio *Express-News* are neutral about Maury Maverick, Jr., not only one of the twentieth century's most outspoken iconoclasts but an individualist who helped shape American constitutional history. Many of Maverick's columns continue his efforts to achieve civil rights guarantees for the disadvantaged. They draw heavily on what he learned from his previous professional careers as a politician, a teacher, and, more significantly, a successful civil rights lawyer.

Maverick was born on January 3, 1921, in San Antonio to Maury Maverick, Sr., and Terrell Louise Maverick. Maury, Sr., was one of the most outspoken and well-known liberal Democrats of the mid-twentieth century. Maury, Jr., spent his childhood and early adult years witnessing almost daily heated debates between his father and his father's opponents and supporters during the 1920s, the Great Depression, and the beginnings of the Red Scare.

Maury, Jr., left home to further his formal schooling and enter the professions for which he is so well known. He received the B. A. degree from the University of Texas at Austin, attended Loyola Law School in Los Angeles, and was graduated from St. Mary's School of Law in San Antonio. In World War II he served in the U. S. Marines, achieving the rank of major. From 1951 to 1957 he was a liberal Democratic member of the Texas House of Representatives and in 1960 was an unsuccessful candidate for the U. S. Senate seat vacated by Lyndon B. Johnson. In the meantime he taught political science at Incarnate Word College and St. Mary's University and was co-chair of the National Advisory Council of the American Civil Liberties Union, also serving on the board of directors of the Texas Civil Liberties Union.

As a member of the Texas House, Maury repeatedly fought against overwhelming odds during the McCarthy era to preserve rights guaranteed in the U. S. and Texas Bills of Rights. Although he was seldom successful as a legislator, his actions represented great courage.

As a lawyer, Maverick followed the civil rights tradition of noted attorney Clarence Darrow, who did not hesitate to put on trial a law he deemed unconstitutional or to defend a client whom he felt was being denied due process. Maverick has said that practicing law "is like pecking manure with chickens—nine chunks of dung to one good kernel of corn." He added: "I've always been taken with something my local attorney friend, Gerry Goldstein, said. He said he'd rather represent dope pushers than businessmen because at least dope pushers don't ask you to go to lunch."[1]

Despite his negative comments about the legal profession, in 1991 Maverick received the prestigious John Minor Wisdom Public Interest and Professional Award from the American Bar Association. He was one of seven recognized for exemplary *pro bono* (public interest) case work. As a lawyer, Maverick has handled over 300 *pro bono* cases since 1949.

During most of his legal career, Maverick earned between $10,000 and $13,000 annually. Often, he wouldn't cash checks given him by clients. When reminded of this, he responded: "I feel sorry for young lawyers who run off to Wall Street or to the big-money law firms and never have excitement in their lives or contribute much to the country in the area of the Bill of Rights. I used to get upset that people would think that [I was rich], but now I think it's a good idea because people are afraid of you if they think you have money.[2]

His legal career suffered even more financially when he represented draft-eligible protestors to U. S. military involvement in Vietnam. He credits

Julia Isabella Orynski, his artist wife whom he married at age forty-two, for helping him through those hard times. As he has often noted: "For about nine years during the Vietnam War, I was a lawyer for poor-as-churchmice conscientious-objector applicants, making slim pickings for a living. Julia spent her conservative Republican oil inheritance keeping us afloat. We walked through some fire together. Julia and I argue like hell, and I'm impressed that she has always stuck by me. I owe her."

The legal issues that most deeply interest Maverick are free speech, due process of law, separation of church and state, world peace, and preservation of human dignity. Maverick's feelings are evident in his lifetime support of guarantees of civil rights. For example: his insistence that working people deserve both decent wages and working conditions; his support for public schoolteachers against the activities of McCarthyites and other censors of public education; his commitment to equality in all endeavors; his support of the right of individuals to protest U. S. involvement in any war they deem unnecessary or immoral; his call for an independent Palestinian state; his opposition to arbitrary, hypocritical or power-hungry politicians or bureaucrats; his legal assistance to Madalyn Murray O'Hair, the renowned atheist; and his insistence that the so-called "little woman or man" get an adequate chance to succeed in society.

Maverick is significant in Texas and American history not only for his legislative and legal accomplishments but as well for his widely read newspaper columns. At age fifty-nine he launched a new career— writing a Sunday column for the San Antonio *Express-News*.

His colorful career as a journalist compares favorably with an earlier one in San Antonio's history, that of James P. Newcomb. The latter arrived in Texas as a three-year-old with his Amherst, Nova Scotia, family. By the outbreak of the Civil War, Newcomb had already published several papers in San Antonio, one being the *Alamo Express*. In his editorials he argued: "We are for the Constitution, the Union, and the enforcement of the laws, a platform broad enough to hold every American citizen within the borders of our great republic." Dale A. Somers related how Newcomb continued to espouse his Union views in print even after secession. This caused him great trouble, because on the night of May 13, 1861, a mob of Confederate Rangers and members of the Knights of the Golden Circle (the future Ku Klux Klan) broke into his newspaper office, destroyed everything in it, and then set the place

3

ablaze. When Newcomb heard rumors the next day that some secessionists planned to lynch him, he left town and eventually made his way to California by way of Mexico. He returned to San Antonio in 1867, published another newspaper, the San Antonio *Express*, served as secretary of state under Reconstructionist Governor Edmund J. Davis, was a radical Republican defeated for a state congressional seat at the end of Reconstruction, remained a staunch Unionist, and began the San Antonio *Light*, which he published until his death in 1907.[3] Fittingly, Maury would become a columnist for the *Express*, which later purchased the *Light*.

Like Newcomb's, Maverick's newspaper columns have provided a means for him to continue his crusades, and he wants people to think about what he writes whether or not they agree with him. He might well paraphrase the words of nineteenth-century Texas iconoclastic journalist William Cowper Brann: "Don't imagine for one moment that my . . . column is always published expressly to please you!" Indeed, as Maverick has often observed: "People write and tell me all sorts of different ways to go to hell. Of course, most of them don't sign their names. They usually can't spell too well, but they make it real clear what they think of me."

Sometimes Maverick has his facts wrong or fails to acknowledge those who disagree with him, but he refuses to keep quiet about what he regards as a wrong that needs to be righted. Indeed, using the press as an avenue to express his political, economic, social, and religious views has kept Maverick active in public life. He has observed: "Every person as he begins to get old, as I have, needs a new adventure in life. Journalism has done that for me. Besides, I like journalists. Journalism gives me a kinship with sculptors who start out with a big blob of nothing and try to make it into something. That's what writers do. Because of journalism, I feel that artists, poets, and musicians are my spiritual cousins. I never had that feeling about the law."[4] But occasionally Maverick admits: "I get tired of writing about a steady diet of politics. Now and then I like to write about pinto beans, poetry, music, birds, abandoned dogs, and gardening so I can slip the friendly five to retired colonels around town who, much of the time, would like to boil me in oil." [5]

Maverick has a special fondness for stray dogs, many of whom he adopts, and purple martin shelters, which he urges people to build.

More often than not, his more than 900 *Express-News* columns have focused on controversial topics. They illustrate vividly the opinion of the late

D. B. Hardemann, journalist and aide to U. S. House Speaker Sam Rayburn, campaign worker for Lyndon B. Johnson, and one of Maverick's soulmates: "Now, when Maury Maverick, Jr., gets an idea about something, he runs his friends absolutely to the asylum, and his enemies up over the wall!" [6]

With a preachy, stubborn, bulldog mentality, Maury finds redemption in becoming enraged about issues and takes to heart folklorist J. Frank Dobie's warning in *The Voice of the Coyote*: "Conform and be dull!"

Maverick approaches his controversial columns much as a trial lawyer tries to convince a jury to vote a certain way. His long-time friend, Ronnie Dugger, publisher of *The Texas Observer*, criticized Maverick for this. Maury relayed that criticism in a 1987 article he did on Dugger, who told him: "I have never liked it when you seem to say in your column, 'Look, this is what you should be raising h—- about, and if you don't you are morally faulted.' Everyone has to decide what he or she wants to do, and the decision can be complicated and personal." Yet, to Dugger: "One of the things that is most endearing about Maury is also one of the things that is most aggravating about him: his will to be outrageous about taboos. He is not a puppet of the American Dream as formulated by J. P. Morgan. He's himself. It's as simple as that." [7]

Fortunately, Maverick can laugh at himself. Maybe this was said best by Willie Morris, another iconoclast, editor of *The Texas Observer* and *Harper's Magazine*, and author of *North Toward Home* and *New York Days*: "In truth Maverick is one of God's last angry men with a sense of humor." [8] An example of his early use of humor occurred while he was a student at what is now called Texas Military Institute. Maury felt he should have received a letter for playing football. Because Maury, Sr., had told him not to use foul language in correspondence, Maury, Jr., wrote "that in regard to the football letter he had been 'sexually intercoursed.'"

On more than one occasion, however, Maverick's humor and blunt speech has embroiled him in public embarrassment. In 1960, when John F. Kennedy was campaigning for the presidential election, Maverick took JFK on a tour of the Alamo. Kennedy had the usual crowds following him, and as Maverick related: "He turned to me and said, 'Get me out the back door of the Alamo. I've got to get on my airplane for Houston.' A reporter was standing behind me, Jim McCrory of the *Express-News*, but I didn't see him. I said, 'There is no back door. That's why they were all heroes.' Kennedy, with his

Irish sense of humor, began roaring with laughter and called over the Irish Mafia, and still I didn't see that damn reporter. The next day, the headlines were: 'Maverick Says No Back Door to Alamo!'" For that, Maverick had to sheepishly go hat-in-hand to the Daughters of the Republic of Texas. "It was like going before the North Korean People's Court," he said. "I profusely apologized for that lack of dignity."[9] On another occasion, when he campaigned to fill Lyndon Johnson's vacated U. S. Senate seat, the plane that took Maverick to Houston developed a malfunction in its landing gear, and the pilot lost radio contact with the Houston Hobby Airport tower. The plane finally touched down at Hobby and skidded to a halt near a hangar. Willie Morris was there and dashed over to the disembarking passengers. Maverick got out first, and Willie asked: "How are you, Maury?" To which Maury answered: "I just switched from a low Episcopalian to a high Episcopalian."[10]

Maverick's impulsive behavior has also brought him trouble. Once, for example, when a teenager, Maury was in one of San Antonio's theaters when his well-known father appeared in a "March of Time" newsreel. Upon seeing this, Maury, Jr., shouted loudly, "That's my pop!" For that, the manager almost threw him out on the street.[11]

Maverick continues to rise several hours before dawn, complaining to himself about what he regards as all kinds of injustices. With his dogs and any strays that happen by, he walks his usual two and a half miles in Brackenridge Park and returns to his home which is nearly buried amid a jungle of trees, plants, and birdhouses. His office is where he goes to turn on his telephone answering machine. He claims he is now "deaf as a post," but friends notice that he manages to hear what he wants to. In the office he does research for future columns and then pounds them out on an old manual typewriter. (Anyone trying to read his handwriting is thankful he does type.) The remainder of the day he spends doing more research, having lunch with either a friend or someone he wants to interview, and trying to decide whether to become a vegetarian. Years ago his doctor prohibited him from having more of his "Episcopalian sherry."

Currently, Maverick calls himself an independent liberal seeking opposing viewpoints. As several people have observed, he is a liberal who speaks from the right side of his mouth, but he maintains: "If everybody in the country got to be an independent liberal, I would become an independent conservative. I couldn't stand being in the majority."[12] Maury's determination to afflict the comfortable and comfort the afflicted is evident in the selected *Express-News* columns which follow. Some topics are dealt with in more than one column, each designated by its original headline and date. The topics illustrate how Maverick is intrigued with individuals of both sexes and all races who take unpopular stands. Maverick uses stories about such persons to express his belief that this country has not progressed to its present position through mass conformity but instead through the efforts of dissenters who have not been content with the status quo.

This, then, is a look at important events in history and selected individuals through the eyes of one of the twentieth century's most outspoken iconoclasts. ★

Individualism is a characteristic of the Maverick gene pool. The very word "maverick," according to legend, became part of the English language after Maury, Jr.'s great-grandfather, Samuel Augustus Maverick, arrived in Texas when it was still under Mexican rule. By the middle 1850s Samuel had become mayor of San Antonio and a prominent businessman. He owned a ranch but paid little attention to cattle raising and seldom if ever had identifying marks burned on the hides of his herd. He sold his Longhorn cattle in 1856, and cowboys began rounding up the herd for the new owner. Because barbed wire had yet to appear in Texas, Maverick's cattle were scattered around the Matagorda area. As the roundup got under way, cowboys started calling any stray "one of Maverick's." Soon, an unbranded cow came to be labeled a "maverick." Because Longhorns were obstinate, independent, and hardy animals, the word "maverick" gradually came to incorporate those synonyms.

Samuel, however, had been a "maverick" long before he arrived in Texas. His father, for whom he was named, had married Elizabeth Anderson, daughter of General Robert Anderson of American Revolution fame. The couple settled in Pendleton, South Carolina, and built a home named Montpelier to honor a French Huguenot grandmother. Their son was born July 23, 1803, and by age twenty-seven had graduated from Yale University and become a member of the bar.

During South Carolina's quarrels with President Andrew Jackson over the tariffs of 1824 and 1828, both Samuels thought John C. Calhoun's opposition to the tarriff laws exaggerated. Samuel, Jr., in particular presented arguments against secession, state nullification of federal laws, and "extreme states' postures in general." When the elder Samuel joined his son and made a speech against secession, a man in the audience heckled him. Samuel, Jr., challenged the man to a duel, wounded him, and took him to the Maverick home to recover. Young Samuel's opposition to secession and the duel did serious harm to any political advancement on his part in South Carolina, so he went to Alabama to live with his widowed sister.

On a business trip to New Orleans, he learned about possible opportunities in Texas and decided to investigate further. He landed at Velasco on the Texas coast, contracted malaria, and, to recover, went to San Antonio, arriving there on September 8, 1835. He was thirty-two.

Maverick fell in love with San Antonio and was soon involved with the Texas Revolution. He fought with Ben Milam in defeating the forces of Mexican General Martín Perfecto de Cos during December 1835, was a signer of the Texas Declaration of Independence, and helped to draft a constitution for the young republic.

With the Texas Revolution a success, Samuel had time to complete his courtship of Mary Ann Adams, whom he had met earlier while on a visit to Tuscaloosa, Alabama. The couple married in August 1836 and two years later settled in San Antonio, she then nineteen years of age with a young infant, the first of their six children.

At one of Mary's famous parties during an 1841 hard freeze in San Antonio, she made some ice cream. At least one of the guests had never eaten such a delight and consumed so much of it that she became ill and had to be taken home. A few other guests left with roast chickens hidden in their coats while others elected to stay the night uninvited.

However, life for the Mavericks was certainly not a parade of parties. Their lives in Texas during the days of the Republic embodied the hardships that many people endured in settling a new frontier. They lived through fights with Indians and the occasional invasion by Mexican forces. During one of the latter, Mexican troops under the command of General Adrian Woll attacked San Antonio in 1842. Samuel and some others fought back in defense of their homes, claiming they thought the Mexican soldiers were outlaws. Woll did not believe them, had them made prisoners of war, promised them good treatment, and marched them to Mexico City, where they were moved to the stench and filth of the nearby castle prison of Perote. Mexican authorities finally released Samuel, and he resumed his political and business careers in Texas.

By the time Texas became a state of the Union, Samuel had become one of its greatest landowners. As a member of the Texas legislature from 1853 to 1862, he also had to help decide whether Texas would secede from the Union and join the Confederate States of America. Although he was a Unionist, his first loyalty was to Texas. This forced him to support secession, and in February 1861 he was one of the secessionist commissioners who forced federal authorities to relinquish all their munitions in the state. Four sons—Lewis, Sam, George, and William—served in the Confederate Army and survived the war.[1]

Mary, in the meantime, began to write the diary and other correspondence that after her death would be edited and published privately in 1921 by Rena Maverick Green, her granddaughter. Of the events during 1861-1865, Mary Ann Maverick in her memoirs recalled:

> The Civil War . . . came on and Mr. [Samuel] Maverick and my sons did not shrink from what they conceived to be their duty. Mr. Maverick had always been a Union man in sentiment, he loved the Union of the states, and although he may have believed (before the question was settled) that we had the abstract right to withdraw from the Union, he thought the Union was sacred, and that the idea of a dissolution of the Union ought not to be harbored for a moment. Having such ideas and convictions, he found life to be uncongenial and unpromising for him in South Carolina, where the doctrines of nullification and ultimate secession were aggressively espoused by an overwhelming majority of the ruling class. He came to Texas, but all doctrines and issues of the former time bloomed into life about him when Texas became a member of the Union. Creeping beneath the shadow of the manifold blessings of the Union, came the bitter and unceasing strife. At last he came to believe the quarrel was forced upon us and that

11

there was before us an "irresistible conflict" which we could not escape, no matter where we turned.

The Secession Convention of 1861 met—there was intense excitement and, need I say, deep gloom—the hour came at last when he was compelled to take his choice for or against his kith and kin. The question was no longer whether secession was right or wrong, wise or unwise, the question was now narrowed down to this—Even if you could sever your fate from that of your people, would your heart permit you to do it?

Thus it appeared to him, and he did a simple, straightforward unselfish act, and an act which nevertheless gave him deep pain, when he cast his note for secession. . . .

Neither [my sons] nor I can ever be ashamed of the sense of honor which led them to battle for the Lost Cause. When the war was ended, the sentiment was unanimous in our family, that all the old issues had been settled, and that the result of the conflict was right.[2]

Samuel Maverick died in 1870, eighteen years before Mary. Biographer Paula Mitchell Marks noted that when Mary went through her deceased husband's personal effects, she "found a piece of the green muslin dress she had worn on the spring day over thirty-four years earlier when a [first] chance meeting on horseback [between Mary and Samuel] led to a life of Texas pioneering."[3]

The last son of Mary and Samuel, Albert, called "Allie," was too young to serve with Confederate forces. After the war, he enrolled in the University of Virginia but after a year of exhibiting Maverick independence was advised that "his professors had given him passing marks on the condition that he not return."[4] Albert next did some traveling, a journey which eventually took him to Paris. He fell in love with the city but decided to return to the United States in 1877, whereupon in Virginia he met and soon afterward married Jane or "Jenny" Lewis Maury, a descendant of Reverend James Maury, who was Thomas Jefferson's first teacher. The couple moved to Texas, where Albert held a variety of jobs and acquired real estate, but he was not always a good businessman because he refused to collect rent from financially distressed tenants.[5]

Jane had her own independent characteristics, too. As a young girl in Virginia, she had sympathy with the Confederate cause but always regarded President Abraham Lincoln as a nice man. She and Albert had eleven children, the youngest being Fontaine Maury Maverick, later known as Maury, Sr. He would continue the family's iconoclastic tradition.

Born in San Antonio on October 23, 1895, Maury, Sr., spent much of his youth at the family's Sunshine Ranch northwest of downtown San Antonio, where he had freedom to roam about. He also became an avid reader of various authors. Biographer Richard B. Henderson noted that "Albert and his son read and discussed together the works of Thomas Paine and Thomas Jefferson, and the elder Maverick taught his son the lessons of free enquiry and freedom of expression. The atmosphere in the home was conducive to the development of liberal views on most subjects."[6]

Maury, Sr.'s formal education did not stop with his graduation from San Antonio's old Main Avenue High School. He studied at Virginia Military Institute for a year and then enrolled in the University of Texas at Austin. He often neglected his university studies to write for *The Daily Texan* and even distributed his own underground newspaper, the *Blunderbuss*, "which appeared on the University of Texas campus each April Fool's Day. It had the primary objective of lampooning and even slandering members of the faculty."[7]

After graduation, Maverick worked for a brief time as a reporter for the Amarillo *Daily News*, returned to Austin to attend the University of Texas School of Law, and passed the state bar exam in May 1916. Throughout his career as an attorney, however, he was never very enthusiastic about being a lawyer. He once said he had a tendency to empathize too much with opposing sides in a case.

Maury, Sr.'s stubbornness, evident as a child, became even more so as he emerged into adulthood. In 1916, for example, just after he had become an attorney, he tried to get a U. S. cavalry officer's commission so he could go to Mexico to help try to capture Pancho Villa who earlier had raided Lincoln, New Mexico. Maverick saw his opportunity when General John J. Pershing made a stopover in San Antonio. Maury saw the general at a dance, and he and his date rushed over to meet Pershing. Maury then had his date dance with the somewhat unnerved general. The next day Maury and his date took Pershing on a tour of historic San Antonio—in a car for which Maury had to borrow money from Albert to rent. At the end of the tour, Maury asked Pershing to help him get that commission. Pershing replied, "Son, I'll tell you what to do. You go out to Fort Sam Houston and enlist, and you can tell them you have my recommendation." [8]

Maury, Sr., did not get to join Pershing's Mexico expedition but did become a second lieutenant in the army when the United States entered World War I. As a young officer stationed in the States, he held English classes for Hispanic soldiers deficient in the language and even defended two of them when they deserted to Mexico and were returned to face charges. Maverick, with the threat of a court-martial against himself, defended the deserters by arguing that not only were they not certain why the United States was going to war, but also neither was he. The commanding general then commended Maverick for his English classes, dismissed charges against the deserters, and placed them under Maverick's care.

Once in Europe, Maury saw more action than he cared to see. During the Battle of the Argonne, he was badly wounded and for his gallantry in action received the Silver Star. He was discharged as a first lieutenant in February of 1919.

The following summer he met the woman who was to become his wife. The initial meeting between Terrell Louise Dobbs and Maury occurred at a party held on the Texas Military Institute campus. Terrell was then living with an aunt and uncle in San Antonio. Maury immediately became interested in Terrell and had his mother invite her to a party that the clan was to hold at Sunshine Ranch. Terrell declined the invitation and wrote her sister that Maury "thinks he is going to marry me, but he is not." [9] She then went with her aunt and uncle to Port Aransas. The day after the Maverick party at Sunshine Ranch, Maury called Terrell and told her he was coming to Port Aransas to visit her. She met him at the ferry landing, and he immediately proposed marriage. She politely refused, but that made Maury even more determined. Thereafter, he often went to see her uncle, allegedly to discuss politics, and sent Terrell flowers at every opportunity. She finally relented, and the couple married on May 22, 1920, less than a year after their first encounter. They had two children, Maury, Jr., born January 3, 1921, and Terrelita, born January 10, 1926. [10]

During most of the 1920s, Maury, Sr., and Terrell appeared to live the usual kind of domestic life, he practicing law and she trying to control two headstrong children. Then, in 1929 Maury, Sr., began his public career. He organized the Citizen's League of San Antonio and became tax collector of Bexar County, being reelected in 1931. After taking on the Ku Klux Klan, he served in the U. S. House of Representatives from 1935 to 1939. There he supported increased U. S. air and sea power, creation of the Tennessee Valley Authority, conservation of natural resources, and legislation for federal housing construction and slum clearance. In 1937 he introduced the bill which created the National Cancer Institute. As mayor of San Antonio from 1939 to 1941, he was instrumental in getting federal aid to beautify the downtown area of the San Antonio River and to restore La Villita, the original San Antonio Spanish settlement. He also tried to triple the wages of Tejano pecan shellers and established housing projects for the poor or homeless.

Maury, Sr.'s tenure as mayor only accented his outspoken ways. The late historian Joe B. Frantz, for example, felt that sometimes Maverick

walked a thin line between crude honesty and complete courage. Some of us have long felt that one of his greatest achievements was choosing a wife who could smooth over the crosspatches he had scuffed up. Sometimes he seemed to irritate just for the sake of keeping people stirred up. He did not function in an atmosphere of serenity. For instance, to get street sanitation under control and to ensure clean food, the city fathers of San Antonio once banned all outdoor eating places except under the most stringent conditions, an action that resulted in the banishment from the streets of the city's famed and colorful "chili queens." So Maury Maverick was elected mayor, and as mayor had to be accepted as the town's first citizen by people who, though they had known him and his family in perpetuity, nevertheless abhorred Maury's free-wheeling politics. Eventually the mayor attended one of the fancier garden parties, breathed graciousness itself through the receiving line, and then turned to his host and bellowed (there was not another word nearly so precise), "You-all know that it's against the law to have outdoor eating places. You bastards passed the law yourself. I'm giving this party fifteen minutes to get these tents down and all this food indoors, or the police will be called!" For the remainder of the party he was hardly the most popular guest present. [11]

His colorful political career also included being indicted and later acquitted on charges of purportedly conspiring to pay the poll taxes for some Mexican Americans.

Maverick was active in the work of the San Antonio Public Library and in 1953 helped form a group to halt book censorship. It was his earlier determination to combat censorship and to adhere literally to the First Amendment that eventually helped end his political career. In 1939 he was almost lynched by a mob that violently opposed his decision as mayor to grant a permit to a group of communists to hold a forum at the city auditorium. The communists were led by Emma Tenayuca, a local labor leader. Before the Tenayuca group could speak, the mob hanged Maverick in effigy. The Mavericks fled their home and escaped to the safety of the home of John Wood, Sr. Some members of the Ku Klux Klan, expecting the Mavericks to go to their Sunshine Ranch, went there and were disappointed. Of the incident Maury, Sr., told his son that the behavior of the mostly Christian mob with a few Jews signified how "destruction of civil liberties can come from any direction."

Biographer Richard B. Henderson noted that Maverick's "support for the ultimate in freedom of expression and procedural guarantees for the communists (as well as his support for equal rights for racial minorities) derived from intellectual convictions. He heartily disliked the communists and their tactics, perhaps even 'despised' was often the more correct word, and he was quite sensitive to the northern liberals' complaints about conditions in the South; he opposed social equality for the Negro until about 1950, and even then he had some misgivings about it. In his usual pungent style, Maverick once wrote to his son: 'Lord God, I have spent my life fighting for minorities. But what have they done for me? They have shit on me, but I hasten to say, having washed, I am ready to go on defending them. But every now and then I get tired of that stuff. . . . Prejudice is inherent in every religion, race, creed, or nationality. We Protestants have it, as others do. The thing to do is to try to level it down as much as we can.' Maury, Jr., [remembered]. . .that his father had said at a later date, after a particularly trying bout over civil liberties: 'Don't do anything for minorities with the hope of getting something in return, even if it's just gratitude; if you do, they will break your heart. Do for them because it's the right thing to do and for no other reason.'" [12]

The Tenayuca episode, however, resulted in Maury, Sr.'s, changing his mind about too much freedom of expression. In June of 1940 some Jehovah's Witnesses asked for a permit to have a similar meeting at the city auditorium, and Maverick refused their request. The British-French disaster at Dunkerque had just occurred, and Maverick used the U. S. Supreme Court case of *Minersville School District v. Gobitis* as a basis for that refusal. The High Court had ruled that the state could require public school students to salute the U. S. flag even if it was contrary to the children's religious beliefs. In turning down the request by the Jehovah's Witnesses, Maverick wrote that "society cannot exist without authority." Three months later, with Japanese forces threatening much of Asia, Nazi planes bombing cities in Great Britain, and the signing of the nonaggression pact between Adolf Hitler and Joseph Stalin, Maury rejected another request from the Tenayuca group to use the city auditorium. Of Maverick's actions, Richard Henderson concluded: "War seems to have a corrosive effect upon even the stoutest of defenders of civil liberties." [13]

Although the mob episode at the city auditorium coupled with the decline of support for New Deal liberalism in Texas would keep

Maverick, Sr., from being elected to public office again, he did continue to serve his country in other ways. When the United States entered World War II, he headed the Bureau of Governmental Requirements of the War Production Board and a program for the production of needed goods in prisons. At the request of President Harry Truman, in 1945 and 1946 he went on fact-finding missions to Europe, China, Japan, Korea, many Pacific islands, Australia, and New Zealand.

After World War II, he joined a law firm in Los Angeles but continued his outspoken ways. He failed to comprehend that "if you call somebody a son of a bitch out here, he thinks you are insulting him!" [14]

Homesick, in 1947 he and Terrell returned to San Antonio, where he again entered politics, running for mayor. His opponents attached the "Red lover" label to him, and he lost the contest. Maverick made one last attempt to gain public office in 1951 by seeking a Texas Congress-at-large seat, but while campaigning he suffered a heart attack and had to withdraw from the race.

His office-holding years were over but not the legacy he left in his iconoclastic writings. He was the author of many articles in national magazines and of two books, *A Maverick American*, published by Covici-Friede in 1937, and *In Ink and Blood*, Starling Press, 1939.

He also introduced a word into the English language—"gobbledygook." In a 1944 *New York Times Magazine* article, he elaborated on his invention of the word:

> People ask me where I got "gobbledygook." Perhaps I was thinking of the old turkey gobbler back in Texas who was always gobbledy gobbling and strutting with ridiculous pomposity. At the end of his gobble there was a sort of gook.
>
> In Washington I soon realized that the double-talkers and long-winded writers were moving in on us, creating in their wake confusion, dullness, and a slowdown. . . .
>
> What is it that brings this long-winded, heartbreaking wordiness? I have a hunch that a writer, feeling defeat in

advance, gets lengthy and vague in self-defense. Then, if defeat comes, he can ascribe it to the ignorance of the people addressed. . . .

A man's language is an important part of his conduct. He should be held morally responsible for his words just as he is accountable for his other acts. Let us be orderly and brief. Slovenly disorder in speech and writing is not only a reflection upon a person's thinking but an insult to the person addressed. Anyone who is thinking clearly and honestly can express his thoughts in words which are understandable, and in very few of them.[15]

Maury, Sr., could also use words to ridicule. Richard Henderson, for example, related that when Maverick became president of the San Antonio Bar Association "he created and edited a little paper, *The Whereas*, for which he wrote a piece entitled 'Koo Klucks Kondemned.' Maverick, as the self-appointed 'Imperious Gizzard,' had held a 'called meeting' attended only by himself at which the 'Koo Klucks' had been judged as 'wearers of nightgowns who were fully as mentally developed as an ape.'" [16]

The Mavericks through their Maury ancestors in Virginia also added "lynch" to our language. Maury, Sr.'s fourth great-grandfather, Charles Lynch of Ireland, came to America as an indentured servant. After he was treated badly by owners, a Quaker family obtained him and later freed him from his almost-slave status. His son, Charles, Jr., became a well-known patriot judge during the American Revolution and issued harsh penalties against those supporting King George III. The younger Lynch never ordered anyone hanged, but the word "lynch" came to mean severe punishment and ultimately the horrible connotation it has today. Characteristically, Maury, Sr., when in the U. S. House of Representatives, was the only southern member of Congress to vote for a federal antilynch law, true to his reputation of being an unreconstructed rebel.

Outspoken to the end, Maury, Sr., died on June 7, 1954, survived by Terrell, Terrelita, and Maury, Jr. Terrell would later marry Walter Prescott Webb, the noted historian. Maury Maverick, Jr., as a politician, lawyer, and journalist would actively continue the family's outspoken legacy. Samples of that appear in the following columns that he used to provide readers with stories about his relatives. ★

EARLY REBEL RELATIVES

"Sons of Liberty Inspire Patriotism,"
April 8, 1984

On March 5, 1770, the first five men who gave their lives for this country were killed in what has come to be known as the Boston Massacre. They were: Crispus Attucks, a black man with an American Indian heritage, Samuel Gray, Patrick Carr, James Caldwell and my distant cousin, Samuel Augustus Maverick. They are buried in a common grave about four feet from the grave of Samuel Adams.

A protest meeting was held by the colonists at the Old South Meeting House, where one orator proclaimed that every March 5, in that very same meeting place, "discontented ghosts with hollow groans appear to solemnize the anniversary of the Fifth of March."

By pure accident I was in the Old South Meeting House, March 5, 1984, to be with the "discontented ghosts with hollow groans." You may not believe it, but my cousin, Sam Maverick, began talking to me. This is the exchange we had:

"Cousin Maury, I see that you visited our single grave next to the grave of Samuel Adams, the 'great agitator' who led this nation at Boston into revolution. It is an unusual burial ground. To the rear of us is the grave of Paul Revere. Beyond that are the graves of the parents of Benjamin Franklin. Nearby is the grave of the woman who wrote the famous Mother Goose rhymes."

"What happened that day when you were killed, Sam?"

"I was only seventeen years old and an apprentice carpenter. About 150 of us young people were gathered before the Custom House. Samuel Adams called us the 'Sons of Liberty' and stirred us up to make trouble. A solitary Redcoat sentry—we called them Lobsterbacks—was walking his post. There were taunts. Crispus Attucks threatened the sentry with a stick. A nineteen-year-old bookseller, Henry Knox, who was later chief of [George] Washington's artillery and our first secretary of war, warned the Lobsterback not to fire his rifle."

"What happened next?"

"The sentry shouted, 'Turn out the main guard.' And with that, officer-of-the-day Captain Thomas Preston came running at us with nine soldiers. We were a mob by then, swinging clubs, throwing pieces of ice. It was then the British killed us."

"What about the funeral, Cousin Sam?"

"We were killed on March 5, and the funeral was on the eighth. It was a propaganda bird nest on the ground for Samuel Adams, who, with Paul Revere's drawings, turned Boston into a city of manifest frenzy. All shops were closed and the bells of the community were tolled. Our bodies were taken to the very spot where we were shot. Five hearses came for us and we were brought to the middle burial grounds and all put in a single grave. That day, although the British issued a proclamation saying we were street ruffians, Samuel Adams scattered about Boston shouting patriotic verses that stirred the colonists up even more."

"What about Samuel Adams?"

"Adams lived from 1722 until 1803 and was considered a failure in life as a businessman and lawyer. His cousin, John Adams, who later defended the Lobsterbacks who shot us, was embarrassed on occasion by Sam, but Samuel Adams was a profound force for liberty and revolution. . . . The British governor called him the 'greatest incendiary in the empire.' That was the equivalent of calling him a 'terrorist' in those days. The word 'incendiary' caused the otherwise sensible Englishmen in London to quit thinking, just as the word 'terrorist' causes you living Americans to be dumb about the current world revolution."

"What do you mean by that?"

"The British perceived me to be a terrorist. I hope my more than 250 blood cousins in San Antonio understand that, according to British history, they have a terrorist for an ancestor."

"Why, Sam, the other night at a family party I bragged on you, and one of my cousins said you were a 'nice young English gentleman.'"

"No, that's not so. I was a revolutionary, a man of violence. . . . Cousin Maury, you have to accept the truth: You come from people who were called 'terrorists' during the days of the American Revolution."

"Sam, you are asking me to pay too great a price in agreeing I come from terrorists. Why, today all over America, the newspapers, television stations and especially the [slippery] editorial writers put down contemporary revolutions about the world by using the word 'terrorist' as a kind of buzz word to keep the rank and file from thinking. My God, man, I love my cousins, but about half of them are Republicans, and six of them even belong to the San Antonio Country Club. I'll get run out of town if I admit you were a terrorist."

"Maury, be serious. In all of history people have been called terrorists. Take the Texas Revolution when the Mexicans called Stephen F. Austin a terrorist and thought they could put down a great revolution with arms. Do you know what Austin wrote in this regard to the Mexican government?"

"No."

"Austin wrote, 'I have informed you many times and I inform you again it is impossible to rule Texas by a military system. . . . Upon this subject of despotism I have never hesitated to express my own opinion, for I consider [military violence] the source of all revolutions and of the slavery and ruin of free peoples.'"

"What's the point?"

"Maury, the point is that neither the Russians nor we Americans are going to put down the world revolution forever. And get this in your head: It isn't a question of communism or capitalism nearly as much as it is a question of nationalism. For God's sake, Cousin Maury, memorize the words of Stephen F. Austin regarding your own Texas Revolution. You living Americans are not going to win in revolutionary situations by military might. . . ."

"Sam, that is some history lesson. And, yes, you were a terrorist, and I am proud to proclaim that, although I do hope Cousin Barbara McCaughy won't refuse to invite me to her Christmas party come December now that I have let the cat out of the bag."

"Maury, we are running out of time. You tell my Texas relatives hello, and tell the people of San Antonio to have confidence in the spirit of the American Revolution. Let the light of American liberty inspire the world."

"Good-bye, Cousin Sam."

"Good-bye, Cousin Maury."

With that I began walking out of the Old South Meeting House. As I made it to the door, once again, I heard "the hollow groans of discontented ghosts."

Postscript: There is no exaggeration in today's column. It is a true story, word for word, so help me. ★

 ## TEXAS ANCESTORS: MARY & SAM MAVERICK

"The Sweet and Sour of Ancestors,"
June 18, 1989

We cut our cables, launch
into the world,

And fondly dream each wind
and star, our friends;
All in some daring enterprise embark'd,
But where is he can fathom
its event?

Lines recorded by a classmate in
Samuel Augustus Maverick's memory book,
Yale University, 1825.

I am up a creek without a paddle about doing this particular column on a book about my great-grandparents, Sam and Mary Maverick–a book entitled *Turn Your Eyes Toward Texas–Pioneers Sam and Mary Maverick* by Paula Mitchell Marks, Texas A&M University Press, 1989. . . .

By the time I get through with my writing for this Sunday, my cousin, Ellen Dickson, who wanted me to review the book, may wish she had left me alone.

I had decided to refuse to do a review of the book because I first thought *Turn Your Eyes Toward Texas* would be a bootlicking good old Texas family book, but the truth is that although it is generally favorable to my ancestors, it also rawhides Sam Maverick on occasion.

For example, the author quotes one J. David Stern in William Safire's book, *The New Language of American Politics,* as saying: "Old man Maverick, Texas cattleman of the 1840s, refused to brand his cattle, because it was cruelty to animals. His neighbors said he was a hypocrite, liar, and thief because Maverick's policy allowed him to claim all unbranded cattle on the range. Lawsuits were followed by bloody battles and brought a new word to our language."

I question that statement. At least the family version is that he knew almost nothing about cattle, that he had been paid a debt in cattle, cared little about them, did not brand them and let them run at will. None of my aunts and uncles and cousins, including the ones who would take a drink—tell the truth and shame the Devil—ever mentioned cattle.

The word "maverick" got around the world, by the way, through the cattle boats that went to the distant corners of the globe. Rudyard Kipling used the word in his poetry.

What Sam Maverick did do that concerns me is that he was at one time the biggest land speculator in the Republic of Texas and later the United States. "Only the czar of Russia owns more land," was the common expression in San Antonio. . . .

One must take the sweet and sour of his or her ancestors. *Turn Your Eyes Toward Texas* relates: "It was not easy to look down on the many cultured Mexicans living in San Antonio, but Anglo-American newcomers often managed to do so. To Maverick's credit he was to speak out against such prejudice." That's the sweet part. The sour part: My great-grandparents brought the first black slaves to San Antonio after the fall of the Alamo.

Sam and Mary came with their slaves from Alabama. As their party made Cibolo Creek east of San Antonio, Indians threatened an attack. The black slaves, a man named Griffin in particular, saved the day.

A few years ago, when we Mavericks celebrated 150 years in San Antonio, an Episcopal priest at St. Mark's asked us to give thanks.

I gave thanks to those black people, and, as I looked around the church and saw some three hundred relatives, all descendants of Sam and Mary Maverick, it dawned on me that it was at least arguably proper to say that none of us would have been sitting there if it had not been for the bravery of the slaves.

I wonder sometimes if there are descendants of those slaves in San Antonio. I would like to thank them. And apologize.

Sam's wife was a Tuscaloosa, Alabama, girl, six feet tall and eighteen years of age when she married her thirty-three-year-old husband. Formally educated, she was one of the few Anglo women, if not the only one, in the San Antonio of 1838 who could fully read and write English. Her diary of early San Antonio is considered a treasure by historians [Rena Maverick Green, editor, *Memoirs of Mary A. Maverick*, University of Nebraska Press, 1987].

Time and time again she was threatened with death through warfare with the Indians in and around San Antonio. As an old ACLU lawyer, I have guilt feelings about the way the Indians were treated, but during those moments when she faced death, I rather think my great-grandmother would have told me to go to h— if I had been alive and mentioned the ACLU.

Sam and Mary's children began to marry. According to *Turn Your Eyes Toward Texas*: "The younger Sam Maverick married Sally Frost in 1872. That same year George married Mary Elizabeth Vance of Castroville, and in 1873, Willie married Emily Virginia Chilton. The only surviving daughter, Mary Brown, would wed in August of 1874, selecting future ambassador to Belgium, Edwin H. Terrell, and youngest Maverick sibling, Albert, would marry in 1877, taking as his bride Jane Lewis Maury. . . ."

All those Maverick children in turn had more children than you can shake a stick at. My grandparents, Albert and Jane Lewis, had eleven, the youngest of which was my father, Maury. You would have thought those Mavericks were Roman Catholics, they had so many children, but in truth they were passionate Episcopalians.

Warts and all, Sam Maverick had a pretty good throw of the dice. I think about that when I sit by his grave . . . in the cemetery on East Commerce. I go there fairly often.

In 1835 while living in San Antonio he was a scout for [Texas revolutionist] Ben Milam, who died in his arms from combat. Before the battle started [Mexican] General Martín Perfecto de Cos nearly executed Sam, but a local Mexican intervened and saved his life.

The next year he was elected by the defenders of the Alamo to be one of their delegates to Washington-on-the Brazos and there signed the Declaration of Independence of the Republic of Texas. He was, in 1839, the third American mayor of San Antonio and later its senator to the Republic of Texas.

Taken prisoner by a Mexican army in 1842 and marched to Perote prison, halfway between Mexico City and Veracruz, Sam was placed in chains. [When Mexican authorities released Samuel, they gave him those shackles, which are now at the University of Texas at Austin.]

Those chains haunt me. Time and time again when I was a little boy my father, sometimes full of bootleg whiskey, would give me the treatment about them. We would act as if we were in the U. S. House of Representatives, this in Grandpa's barn, the chickens roosting on the rafters and with Beck, the mule, acting as the speaker.

"Will the gentleman yield for an observation on liberty?" Papa would thunder. Then, God Almighty, what a lecture I'd get on the Bill of Rights and Jefferson's need now and then for revolution. ★

GRANDMA MAVERICK
"Pow! In the Kisser, That Was My Grandma," September 14, 1980

"Did I ever tell you grandchildren about the time I fed King Fisher, the bad man?"

"No, Grandma," we instantly lied. The truth was we had heard the story a dozen times, each new version better than the last.

"Oh, Jenny," Grandpa interrupted, "are you going to tell

that King Fisher story again?" With that my grandfather, Albert Maverick, started for the barn. Grandpa always went to the barn when he thought his wife was talking too much. He went there pretty often.

"It was after your grandfather married me in Charlottesville, Virginia. When he asked me to marry him, Mother made him wait a year to see if he was serious. We now have 150 children, grandchildren, and great-grandchildren, so I think he was serious. Anyway, he brought me to Texas, and in early March 1884, we were on a ranch in Bandera County near the headwaters of the Medina River. I had gone to the spring house. In Virginia, we had a spring house where we kept our food cool when we entertained teachers and students from the university. I had your grandfather build me one just like it out on that Bandera ranch. Well, I had come back from the spring house when there was a knock at the door."

"Who was it, Grandma?"

"It was King Fisher, one of the all-time bad men in Texas, standing there with a silver-plated revolver hanging from his belt. He was so handsome."

"Oh, Grandma," I interrupted, "you said that about General George Custer when he captured your home in Charlottesville [during the Civil War]. If the Devil himself came to your house and was handsome, you'd let him in."

"Be quiet, Maury, Jr. You're like your father. You talk too much." With that, Grandma glared at me and went back to her story.

"Mr. King Fisher looked like he was on the run. 'I'm hungry and need food,' the man told me. I invited him in, and he immediately went to the kitchen table. But he pulled it to another part of the room where his back was to the wall so he could look out the window to see if anyone was coming up the road. I'm glad your grandfather didn't ride up on his horse.

Mr. Fisher offered to pay for his meal, but I wouldn't take his money. He was a complete gentleman. He said he would ride on to San Antonio. About three days later he and Ben Thompson were killed by hidden assassins in the Vaudeville Theater near San Fernando Cathedral."

The most famous economist of this century in Texas was the late Dr. Bob Montgomery of the University of Texas. I just have to tell you about the time Grandma ran Dr. Bob off her property.

Every Sunday out on the Babcock Road, we Mavericks gathered at what we called the Sunshine Ranch, really a dairy run by my Uncle Jim.

One Sunday my father showed up with Dr. Montgomery. "Mama," he said, "this is Dr. Bob Montgomery, the famous economist."

"The communist?" Grandma asked, cupping her hand to her ear.

"Mama, I said 'economist.'"

"Yes, I know you said 'communist.' You quit using that word. Get that man off this property."

"Mama, this is Dr. Bob Montgomery, a much-respected economist."

"Maury, if you say that word 'communist' one more time I'll slap your face. Get that man off my property."

So we all got in a car and drove off with Dr. Bob.

The most impressive sex lecture I ever had in my life was from my Maverick grandmother. As you'll see, she didn't moralize. She just wanted some good manners.

I was getting fresh with a girl on Grandma's porch. It was during high school days.

"Maury, Jr.," she said, "you quit that."

"Oh, Grandma, you used to do the same thing back in Virginia behind shutters."

Pow! I got it in the kisser in front of everybody.

"What do you think shutters are for, you young fool?" Grandma asked.

Grandma never let me forget our ancestors back in Virginia. They included an overabundance of Episcopal preachers, army and navy officers, the most important military person being Commodore Matthew Fontaine Maury, the oceanographer, who lived out his last days as commandant of cadets at Virginia Military Institute.

Then she would say: "You come from French Protestants. Your people were run out of France by the Roman Catholic Church."

"But, Grandma, that happened more than three hundred years ago."

"I don't care," Grandma would always reply, "it was terrible what those Catholics did."

Well, when she was in her upper nineties, she began to talk about death. One day while in bed she brought the subject of death up with the comment, "Maury, Jr., I don't have much time left. I think you should get a priest to talk with me."

"Grandma, do you want a Roman Catholic priest or an Episcopal priest?"

Total silence. Her eyes were completely closed.

Had Grandma died of a heart attack?

Suddenly, both eyes opened, saucer big. She propped herself up on her elbows. Pow! I got it in the kisser.

I went to the door, turned around, and waved at my grandmother. She shook her fist.

Grandma was the cop in the family. She had to be because on those Sunday reunions we Mavericks would go after one another like Kilkenny cats. Those were the great cats of Ireland that fought one another so hard there was nothing left but their tails.

She was self-educated, a victim of the Civil War. There were no schools when Grandma was growing up. Her older sister, Ellen, later a society columnist on this newspaper, was formally educated, dated Woodrow Wilson and decided he was a stuffed shirt. But Grandma never saw the inside of a school. She never bragged on the Civil War as if it had been a good thing, and I was always proud of the fact that she used to tell me: "President Abraham Lincoln was a decent man."

A beautiful young woman when young, she had eleven children, the youngest of which was my father, whose real name at birth was Fontaine Maury Maverick. Although my father dropped his first name when in high school, Virginians insist on using it, and so when I go back to Charlottesville, the old-timers will say, "This is Fontaine's boy."

By the time I grew up, Grandma, worn out with so many children, looked a little like Benito Mussolini, and on occasion acted like him a lot to keep the family discipline. She remains one of the most powerful influences in my life.

On the tombstone for my grandparents it reads: "They lived together for seventy-two years and made many people happy. . . ." Brothers and sisters, [Grandma] was the cat's meow. ★

MOMMA MAVERICK

"Momma Gets a Purina Dog,"
November 27, 1988

Here's a salute to the Humane Society for being so kind to my mother, Terrell Maverick Webb, by giving her an abandoned little dog under the Purina Pets for People program.

Any person sixty or older can qualify for a dog or a cat. Purina pays the expenses (rabies shots, etc.) for some five to ten cats and dogs distributed each month by the local Humane Society.

31

Although no fee is charged under the Purina program, we made a contribution for my mother.

Most dogs and cats are adopted under a minimum contribution of $35 because a majority of the adopting "parents" are under the age of sixty years.

For older people pets are an antidote to loneliness, lower the blood pressure, and make for bundles of love. For that matter, most older people go on and pay a fee without invoking Purina. I went the Purina route in my mother's case to learn how it works so I could explain it here.

I hope what I am about to tell you can be done in good taste. All of us with parents grown senile, as my mother has become, and as many of us will some day, need to reach out to one another. I would like to think I am reaching out to you and that you in turn are giving me your hand. On this issue, pals, we are all in the same boat.

My mother remembers being married to my father, Maury Maverick, once the congressman and mayor of San Antonio. She does not quite remember her marriage to the historian Dr. Walter P. Webb. (I wish she did because I have Dr. Webb's love letters to her when he was courting her. They are touching beyond belief.)

Momma remembers Groesbeck, some fifty miles east of Waco, where she grew up poor as a church mouse, the daughter of a forty-two-year-old Baptist deacon who married an eighteen-year-old girl who sang in the choir. My good friend, attorney Jamie Clements of Scott and White Hospital in Temple, an expert on Baptists, tells me that forty-two-year-old Baptist deacons always marry eighteen-year-old girls who sing in the choir.

My mother came to San Antonio to live with an aunt and uncle near Berg's Mill, graduated from Brackenridge High School, and never had another day of formal education in her life.

She married my father right after World War I, followed him from army hospital to army hospital, where he sought relief from combat wounds, went to Congress with him, had tea with Eleanor Roosevelt, and stood with him through his many political struggles.

Some years after my father died, she married Dr. Webb, who graciously left her money to live on for the remainder of her days. But now he's gone, and it is downhill. . . .

My mother still plays the piano. I mean honky-tonk jazz. A few months ago she looked up from the piano and asked: "Could I have a dog?"

So I went immediately to Kathleen Walthall, the splendid young woman who [then headed the San Antonio] Humane Society. What a nice place because of the kind and gentle people who work there. . . .

Anyway, they all gave my mother "Chip." I can not tell you how much sunshine "Chip" has provided.

But then this may all be a hoax. At least folk humorist John Henry Faulk said so when I told him the story I am about to tell you. Some six months ago my mother took my hand in her hand and said, "Big brother, you have to help me with Maury, Jr. He's not very bright." That's when Johnny said, "Your momma's mind is clear as a bell. . . ." ★

PAPA MAVERICK

"Writing about My Father: A Risk I Want to Take,"
June 8, 1980

A tempestuous man, my father couldn't open the ice box without getting into a fight with the milk bottle, or so I thought sometimes. He could be heavy medicine, and I had to get away from him now and then, but I knew he was something out of the ordinary. The inscription to him by Carl Sandburg sticks in my mind: "For Maury Maverick—fighter, freeman, fool, poet, zealot of freedom. . . ."

"Maury, Sr.: A Real Fighter"
August 19, 1984

I am well aware of the fact that my father had about as many enemies in this town as friends. One time as a child, when I was worried about him, I went to see my cousin Reagan Houston. . . .

"Maury, Jr.," said Cousin Reagan, "your father is the only politician I have ever known who will deliberately cross the street to start a fight with someone who is minding his own business. He loves this city as few people do, but he feels compelled to fight half the town. Whatever his faults, he is not a person who indulges in self-pity. Maury can take it and so should you. Now get the h--- out of my office."

My father was the youngest of eleven children. Grandma Maverick told me: "The day your father was born, he just walked out wearing a diaper, a stovepipe hat, and with his fists up ready to protect himself from the teasing of his ten older brothers and sisters." That may be how he got his combative personality. . . .

"Writing about My Father: A Risk I Want to Take,"
June 8, 1980

When I was a child, we would play the alphabet game together on Sundays. Starting with the letter "A" he would tell me to think of places we could visit. "A" for Alamo, what else? Off to the Alamo we would go. At the Alamo he would tell me: "Our Anglo ancestors were brave people fighting for liberty, but they also tried to maintain the system of slavery. Get all sides of history and figure out the truth. If you have any sense, it will make you love our country more intelligently. . . ."

"Hookers, Truman, and the Blinding Red Light,"
February 22, 1981

My old daddy was mayor of San Antonio from 1936 to 1938 and was the first mayor in these parts to bring doctors to the City Health Department who were board-certified public health specialists.

The doctors told him, and so did the policemen who had common sense, to let the prostitutes operate in a specific location, have health clinics to help prevent venereal disease, provide police patrols to keep young men from getting their throats slit, and let the military set up their own clinics for its soldiers.

That was done until the preachers stopped it. The prostitutes scattered all over town, disease went up, crime generally increased and so did rape. . . .

"Dad's Old Rugged Cross,"
June 21, 1981

[My father designed] a cross . . . during the worst of the Depression following the last days of Herbert Hoover as president. My father had set up a cooperative camp. Out of that camp came the cross, but let him tell the story as quoted from his autobiography:

I had organized a colony. The Bonus Army [a collection of out-of-work World War I veterans who, at the height of the Great Depression, demanded a bonus promised them in 1945 be paid in 1932 instead were driven on President Herbert Hoover's orders from their Washington, D. C., shantytown and] run out of [town], and some . . . had come to San Antonio. The contingent of veterans and their families camped at the San Antonio Fairgrounds and were starving and sick. I. . .made arrangements with the railroad company to get free freight cars to be used for houses. . . .We had a population of 250 to 300. . . . Here in the new colony some men, or a whole family, would come into camp and ask for something to eat and a place to stay. Quite often they would be alive with lice and weak with

35

fever and disease. . . . I made a deal with doctors to deliver babies at $10 each. . . . We put kids in school. . . .[Maury, Sr., disliked much about the hierarchy of the Roman Catholic Church but, as a symbolist, collected Christian crosses, which he regarded as clenched fists.] With an old friend, Charles Simmang, an engraver, they designed a symbol in the shape of a cross. . . . At the top of the cross there was a representation of the world showing the continents of North and South America, expressing the hope that we might have peace. In the middle there was the Alamo, a symbol of sacrifice. There was a cap of liberty, and also a wheel of industry, and a plowshare, on the basis of equality.

If you will look at the cross, you will also see working tools at the bottom—the dignity of labor—and above that a clenched fist—the right of protest. The lone star stands for independence, and in back of the cross there is a glory.

I am of the opinion my father was a deeply religious person, although I am not sure what the much-abused word "religious" means—it is almost embarrassing to use the term. But I do know with certainty—no "think" here—that he had a general suspicion of organized religion and of "men of the cloth." He would tell me that one of the reasons this is a great country is because under our Constitution you could tell a preacher to go to hell. . . .

Here are some of the things he would say about religion when I was a little boy, things I didn't hear at St. Mark's Episcopal Church: "Maury, Jr., let me tell you about Jesus. He was a loudmouth brave little Jew, a rabbi who put the pants on the stuffed-shirt Romans and stuffed-shirt Jews. If he came back to earth he would get run out of every church and synagogue in town. You know what we people of the New Testament were around the time of the crucifixion? In terms of political reform we were the CIO Jews, and the ones who held to the Old

Testament were the American Federation of Labor Jews. The AFL Jews were the establishment Jews. We were the radical Jews. Since then things have sometimes become reversed. Too often we Christians are the reactionaries. We have needlessly hurt people, and we have shunted aside the radicalism of Jesus."

My father collected [other] crosses and crucifixes, mostly Catholic, by going to Mexico on trips specifically to find them. He did the same thing in Ireland. But his favorite cross was a simple wood one made out of the original timbers of the Episcopal church in Richmond, Virginia, and over which Patrick Henry uttered the spine-tingling words: "Give me liberty or give me death!" He asked for that simple cross when he went into the hospital to die.

"You remember this, Maury, Jr.," he told me from under an oxygen tent. "Part of the cross must always be a clenched fist against economic and social injustice."

After he died, the nurses packed everything but the cross next to his bed. There it was by itself, the old rugged cross. . . .

"Maury, Sr.: A Real Fighter,"
August 19, 1984

During his last eight years of his life, Maury, Sr., never touched a drop of alcohol, but he had his share in his younger days.

One time he told me, laughing as he said it, for he loved Roman Catholic Archbishop Robert Lucey: "Maury, Jr., I saw you drinking one of those sissy cocktails at that party last night. You are a disgrace to the Maverick family. Son, don't you know the only way to drink is to drink a pint of whiskey as quick as you can and get in a fistfight over the Catholic Church? . . ."

"Writing about My Father: A Risk I Want to Take,"
June 8, 1980

As I remember it, my father especially gravitated to three

37

clergymen: Rabbi Ephraim Frisch of Temple Beth El, Jesuit Father Carmen Tranchese of Our Lady of Guadalupe, and Archbishop Robert Lucey, who told me one time: "Maury and I got into a lot of trouble together. When I'd open my mouth your father would stick his foot in it. . . ."

When my father did participate in organized religion, it sometimes would turn out to be a disaster. The worst was one day across from Travis Park at St. Mark's Episcopal Church. After services were over and while he was shaking hands with the preacher, one of San Antonio's most important "high society" women came up and in a loud voice accosted him with the comment: "Why, Maury Maverick, what are you doing in church? I've heard talk around town that you were a communist, but I guess you couldn't be if you go to the Episcopal Church."

Poor old Papa's face went livid. With the voice that would have been the envy of a drill sergeant, he said back to the woman: "I hear talk around town that you are an old whore, but I guess you couldn't be if you go to the Episcopal Church." Episcopalians began to scatter like chickens, the preacher rolled his eyes in back of his head, and I damn near wet my pants. God Almighty, that was a nightmare.

Speaking of nightmares, my old man was criminally indicted one time for purportedly conspiring to pay poll taxes. In the old days, thousands of Mexican-Americans were in effect disenfranchised through the poll tax. The jury came back with a unanimous verdict of not guilty. His lead lawyer, Carl Wright Johnson, was a magnificent trial attorney. If you want a lesson in life, try standing by your father waiting for a jury to come in and tell you it might send him to the pen. . . .

"A Moment to Cherish," *Texas Observer*,
January 30, 1981
Then there was the episode noted by Don Carleton in his

book *Red Scare!* Texas Monthly Press, 1985, when Maury, Sr., agreed to let Emma Tenayuca, then a communist and labor organizer, and some of her colleagues speak at the Memorial Auditorium. Carleton wrote: "The Communist Party in Texas decided to hold its 1939 state convention in San Antonio and applied for a permit to meet in the Municipal Auditorium on August 25. Mayor Maury Maverick's decision to grant the permit unleashed a whirlwind of protest in the city from Catholic leaders, American Legion spokesmen, the Ku Klux Klan, and others. . . . [The] city auditorium was surrounded . . . by a hostile mob of an estimated five thousand people. The mob descended on the building, heaving bricks and swinging clubs. The . . . police estimated that seventy-five percent of the rioters were between the ages of seventeen and twenty-five. . . ."

"Writing about My Father: A Risk I Want to Take,"
June 8, 1980

I saw my father's career come to an end [that] night when, as mayor, he [did indeed] let a handful of communists and sympathizers gather at the Municipal Auditorium. For days every newspaper in town whipped up an air of hatred. [The night of the riot] my entire family hid out . . . at the home of John Wood . . . to keep from being murdered. Parts of the mob came to our home looking for us; others went out to intimidate my grandparents.

My father understood the mob, made up mostly of blue-eyes like he was, but he never got over the mob being led by a Jew, a Catholic priest, and a Lebanese-American.

"Those are all three minorities who have suffered and ought to be the first to stand up for free speech," he said.

Life was never the same for him or anyone in our immediate family after that riot. Even today that is true. Have you ever had a mob trying to find you to kill you? . . .

"Maury, Sr.: A Real Fighter,"
August 19, 1984

My old man knew he had rung the bell pretty good with the help of his wife, Terrell: He was the only congressman from the South to vote for the Anti-Lynching Law, co-author (inspired by Dr. Dudley Jackson) in establishing the National Cancer Institute, one of the prime movers in beautifying the San Antonio River and La Villita, and the first mayor to bring modern municipal government to San Antonio.

The last time I saw him on the streets of San Antonio was in the morning at La Villita, where he would go several times a week to see if the place was being cleaned up from the night before.

"I'm washed up in San Antonio politics, but I'm still the mayor of La Villita," he would tell me now and then, as he did that day. . . .

[But while still mayor, Maury, Sr., continued to battle. There is the story that began]: "Mayor Maverick, this is Elizabeth Graham calling you from the Conservation Society, and I want you to know that we are not going to permit you to put flush toilets in the Governor's Palace."

"Why not?" my father asked.

"Because it would not be authentic. They did not have flush toilets in the days of the Spanish governors."

"Yes, that's right, Elizabeth, and in the days of the Spanish governors they didn't have children of tourists urinating in the back patio. It smells bad, and the Health Department says I have to do something."

"Maury, we grew up together as children, and I'm telling you there will be no flush toilets."

A few days later house painters began to put up scaffolding in front of the Governor's Palace. Elizabeth Graham, Floy Fontaine, and all the dear ladies wanted to know what was going on.

"The mayor told me," said Juan Rodriquez, the foreman of the job, "to paint the Governor's Palace fire-engine red if you don't let him put in flush toilets."

Wanda Ford, Graham's daughter and my wife's first cousin, claims a different version, but I have just told you the truth, so help me God, as to how flush toilets came to the Governor's Palace. . . .

"Writing about My Father: A Risk I Want to Take,"
June 8, 1980

During World War I Maury, Sr., served as a first lieutenant, Twenty-eighth Infantry, First Division, where he won the Silver Star for gallantry, captured twenty-six German soldiers single-handedly, and was severely wounded in the shoulder. Judith Doyle, one of his biographers, wrote: "On November 16 (1934) the nurses at the (Mayo Brothers) clinic wheeled (Lieutenant Maury Maverick, Sr., U.S. Army retired and congressman-elect) into the operating room, where he remained under anesthesia for over five hours. . . . The surgeons removed the large tumor (caused by shrapnel) and sawed off the backs of five of his vertebrae from his skull to his shoulders. At one point someone rushed out of the operating room and warned the anxiously waiting Terrell to prepare for the worst. But Maverick pulled through, and the nurses rewarded him with a medal of St. Jude, the saint of impossible causes. . . . By New Year's Day, he was stumbling along a chilly Washington alley, leaning on Lyndon Johnson's arm. . . . Two days later he stood on the floor of the House and took his oath (as U. S. Representative from Bexar County). . . ."

My father was horribly wounded from World War I combat and remained a partial cripple to his death. My first memory was to hear him cry out in pain at night. My mother would fill the tub with hot water, and I'd go sit with my dad. We had big talks about war, and he would tell me: "You must never be for war. Never."

He took all his medals and pasted them to a death's head as a protest against war.

But then, years later, Hitler began to move.

We would listen at night over the transatlantic radio to Ed Murrow, who had the spine tingling sign-on, "London Calling!" One night there had been an especially cruel bombing of London. You could hear the fires burning and the screams of Englishmen. My father's back was turned to me. It was hot and the sweat was running down those crevices in his body where the German shells had ripped away his flesh and bone.

Murrow signed off.

Slowly my father turned around, and for the first time in my life I saw him crying. Great tears were rolling down his face. "Maury, Jr.," he said, "we have to go to war. We have to kill that son of a bitch Hitler. . . ."

"Maury, Sr.: A Real Fighter,"
August 19, 1984

But even his combat wounds got Maury, Sr., into trouble, as he explained in his autobiography, *A Maverick American*, Covici Friede Publishers, 1937, which Heywood Broun thought as good as Erich Remarque's *All Quiet on the Western Front* regarding the chapters about war.

On a hospital ship going home, a chaplain held a prayer meeting and proclaimed that the German soldiers were such cowards that they had to be chained to their machine guns.

"If they were cowards," interrupted Lieutenant Maverick, "then it didn't take any courage for us to whip them. What do you know about combat?" He called the chaplain some words that [*Express-News* publisher] Charlie Kilpatrick, a southern gentleman, will not let me repeat in this family newspaper.

Lieutenant Maverick, twenty-two years old and a former cadet at Virginia Military Institute, was placed under arrest. A wireless was sent to New York to have him investigated for a possible court-martial. Upon the ship's docking, an investigation was conducted, but nothing came of it.

In World War I, reserve officers were retired in rank for serious injuries. So, until the day he died, my father was "Lieutenant Maverick . . . ."

My father also hated to have a voter come up to him and say: "I bet you don't know my name." He equally hated having people slap him hard on the back because he had been brutally wounded there in World War I.

Anyway, we were out pressing the flesh one election time in a German-American community in Bexar County. A big, beefy guy came up and hit my father on the back and knocked him down. While he was down, the man yelled at him in front of many people: "I bet you don't know my name."

Papa got up, swung from the ground, and knocked out the beloved voter, and then shouted, "No, you German son of a bitch–I don't know your goddamn name, and I don't want to know your name."

We lost that box three hundred to one, but it was a moment to cherish. . . .

"Maury, Sr.: World War I Years,"
February 1, 1987

I have the obituaries about my father from the major newspapers of America and even some from London and Paris, but what might be a real treat is to quote from World War I combat letters he wrote to his father, Albert. . . .

I never saw the letters myself until about a year ago when my cousin, Jane Welsh Reyes, gave them to me. I have given the letters to the Barker Historical Center at the University of Texas-Austin. . . .

Without further ado here are excerpts from some of those

war letters, all written in 1918 and 1919:

"Dear Papa: The First Division always gets the real fighting. The First never fights except to win a battle. When we travel we are placed from point to point on weak spots of where offenses are contemplated."

"Dear Papa: A score and three ago, my forefathers brought forth upon the great continent of America a lad none other than myself, born in liberty, and dedicated to the proposition that all men are created equal.

"And now, as the world is in the throes of gripping battles, he, the lad born in the very shadows of that immaculate building, the Alamo, finds himself in France in order that those who have no conscience (the Germans have none) may die, and those who have may live."

"To tell the truth, Papa, I really should not let you know, but I have been wounded. *Tell no one!*

"For suppose, Papa, that you should say so and a spy should hear it (and spies are everywhere). The spy would tip the imperial government of Germany off, and the Germans would then be unafraid, and would probably advance instead of retreating.

"Papa, be careful. *Must democracy die?* I say no, it shall not. *Keep Quiet.* No great victory was ever built upon unbridled license of foolish talk."

"Dear Papa: The Germans claim 'Gott Mit Uns' (God is with us), but we Americans have got mittens which keep our hands as warm as Germans. George (his brother) came to see me (in the hospital). . . . I have some grapes, chocolate, dried fruit, chewing gum, and tobacco.

"When I came here I could not move; now I can get out of my bed and stay on my feet a few seconds. When I came I looked out the window and all was green and beautiful, but now the leaves are yellow and falling to the ground.

"I am some sixty miles from the front, but starting on the

minute with my birthday (October 23) the heavy guns talked. . . . Well, I am tired and I guess I will lay my head down. Love."

"Dear Papa: Not too many moons will pass and Maverick in a flashy suit . . . will get in a palatial taxi and say, 'Home, James.' I will see a major general in the path of my motor and I will say, 'James, run over the general.' Then I will see an 'old buck private' and I will say, 'Enter my limousine and ride.' I shall know no rank, I shall curse my enemies and love my friends. Again I will be human.

"Well, Jerry [the Germans] has given in. . . . I cannot describe it, and if I should tell you all I saw . . . you would think me sentimental. But suffice to say every Frenchman and Frenchwoman was out on the streets.

"The veterans of 1870, with rather oldish voices, collected on the streets. In one bunch, some twenty or thirty, some with guitars, sang 'Madalone,' a happy, jolly song.

"Then the old Frenchmen stopped. They sang the 'Marseillaise' . . . the Frenchmen stopped laughing; they took off their hats and cried.

"That night (in Paris) the Frenchmen swelled into the thousands. . . . A band began playing the 'Marseillaise' again. Of course, the Frenchmen all started crying again. Then the band played 'The Star-Spangled Banner' but there was no singing for we Americans don't know the words. But it meant more to us than ever before. I know where my thoughts were–to America, to Bexar County, Sunshine Ranch on Babcock Road and home."

"Dear Mr. Maverick: The Red Cross wishes to notify you of the return to this country of First Lieutenant Maury Maverick, Twenty-ninth Infantry, Company M., who landed at Staten Island, New York, December 28, 1919."

"Dear Papa: At the Lambs, 130 West 44th Street, New York. . . . This club is composed of the most brilliant actors in the world along with playwrights. I have met [Fatty] Arbuckle, world-famous comedian. He was born on the Cibolo Creek, eighteen miles from San Antonio. I have also met Gene Buck, playwright for the follies, John Barrymore, John J. McGraw [baseball player] and other men equally famous. . . ."

In his autobiography, *A Maverick American*, my father wrote of going "over the top" and of the time he was wounded. . . . I leave you with a few excerpts from those chapters:

". . . into the Argonne we marched. . . . Frank Felbel, a little Jew, was commander of my company. He was shy. He spoke of art and the opera. 'Maverick,' said Felbel, interjecting like a professor, 'did you ever read Le Bon's *Psychology of War?*'

". . .[A] great shrieking noise came, then a dull explosion. Gas! Gas! Soon we marched on. . . . We were getting lost. I stumbled. It was the body of a dead man, and he was soft and rotting and slippery. . . . It was near the village of Exermont."

"We started to advance again. A shell burst over my head. It tore away part of my shoulder blade and collarbone and knocked me down. I looked at my four runners, and I saw that the two in the middle had been cut down to a horrid pile of red guts and blood and meat. Felbel was dead, and there was no officer to take my place. I got up and reformed the lines again.

"But I was losing so much blood. . . . I finally got to a field hospital. I passed out. But when I did wake the Germans were shelling. . . . I was in the ward for severe cases. There were ten of us, three Germans and seven Americans. A German close to me had most of his face shot out. From him I first learned of pensions and social insurance. He said they came from German Chancellor Otto von Bismarck. . . ."

"Writing about My Father: A Risk I Want to Take,"
June 8, 1980

I hesitate to describe the deathbed scene because my old friend, Herschel Bernard, claims that my father never would have had time to die if all the death scene stories I tell really happened.

But this is a true story, a story Willie Morris made famous in his book *North Toward Home*, Yoknapatawpha Press, 1967, and one LBJ loved to tell.

My father looked like death that last day of his life as I sat by him trying to make small talk. Finally, I couldn't take it any longer and started to walk out of the hospital room to regain my composure.

"Maury, Jr.," he called out just as I made it to the door, "come back here. I want to give you a compliment."

"What is it, Papa?"

"Son, I want you to know you didn't turn out to be as big a horse's ass as Elliott Roosevelt."

"Oh, Papa!" I said. We embraced and both started laughing. Thirty minutes later my father was dead. . . .

> Maverick Quoted in "Life as a Maverick,"
> *Dallas Morning News,* July 8, 1995

Some years later, [President Lyndon B.] Johnson got mad at me 'cause I was defending [Vietnam] war resisters. He had one of his aides call me up and tell me my father was wrong. Johnson said I was a horse's ass. I'll never forget that. ★

 ## STEPFATHER: WALTER PRESCOTT WEBB

"A Scholar Grown on the Range,"
August 10, 1986

On December 14, 1961, in the original Episcopal Church of Fredericksburg (which Lady Bird Johnson helped to restore), an Episcopal clergyman asked the widower Walter Prescott Webb, a country boy from Stephens County (Breckenridge, the county

47

seat), and the widow Terrell Dobbs Maverick, my mother, a country girl from Limestone County (Groesbeck, the county seat), if they took one another as husband and wife.

The clergyman was Bishop Everett H. Jones, who had been Webb's student at Main High School of San Antonio, the school from which Webb went in 1918 to the University of Texas. Bishop Jones' presence was the icing on the cake; a lot of love was in the air that day.

On March 8, 1963, while driving back to Austin, my mother and Dr. Webb were in an automobile accident. Dr. Webb was instantly killed; my mother was seriously injured. So much so that the owl came close to calling her home.

The doctors told me to lie to my mother and say that Dr. Webb had survived, while they fought to keep her alive. I went into intensive care and whispered the lie into her ear. Later she told me: "I knew you were lying." Mother knows everything.

I often think about the contrast in the two marriages my mother had. With my father it was a roller coaster ride past fistfights with constituents, a rampaging riot when my father, the mayor, let a communist [Emma Tenayuca] speak at Municipal Auditorium, a year in a hospital while my father recovered from war wounds and I was sent off to Utica, New York, to live with relatives.

Then after, when he was a congressman, folks such as Hugo Black and Vito MarcAntonio, the famous radical, plus artists and writers and musicians, Huey Long and Archibald MacLeish, the poet and librarian of Congress, visited our home.

There was nearly always a question of money. My father paid his bills, but if he got a dollar ahead, he would get me and off we would sneak to buy a rare book. That gave my mother nightmares.

My father as a young lawyer worked for a famous old-time lawyer of San Antonio by the name of John Boyle. Boyle told him: "Maury, the only way to make money is to think about money and nothing else. You not only won't think about money, but in addition you are going to be in trouble all your life. Get life insurance for your wife."

Alistair Cooke wrote in the *Manchester Guardian* of England about my father, when he died, that he never let his fists down as long as he could draw a breath of air. And, yes, John Boyle turned out to be a prophet with honor, for the bulk of my father's estate at death was insurance money. It was guns blazing the entire marriage for my parents.

My mother's marriage to Dr. Webb was the exact opposite of what it was with my father. I remember the courtship, for every day a special-delivery letter arrived for my mother from Dr. Webb. I have a whole cabinet drawer full of those letters. Some are of astonishing intellectual depth and excitement. . . .

Dr. Webb and my mother had a serene and affectionate marriage with gentle people from the academic community around them. All over Texas there are history teachers, high school and college, interesting people who studied under Dr. Webb. They were marvelous friends.

But, looking back on it, I knew almost nothing of Dr. Webb's childhood in Stephens County, which is in North Central Texas, leaning to the west. Now, thanks to Mike Kingston, [author of *Walter Prescott Webb in Stephens County*, Eakin Press, 1985, and] editor of the *Texas Almanac,* who was himself a boy in Stephens County, I have found out all there is to know about Dr. Webb's days as a boy.

I could tell that my stepfather had a lot of country boy in him, although profound intellectuals from around the world paid homage to him. Of his West Texas country-boy roots, Dr. Webb wrote this: "A friend asked me about when I began preparation to write *The Great Plains* [first published in 1931]. I answered that I began at the age of four when my father left the humid East and set his family down [in Stephens County] in West Texas, in the very edge of the open arid country which stretched north and west farther than a boy could imagine. There I touched the hem of the garment of the real frontier; there I tasted alkali. I was not the first man, or boy, but the first men, Indian fighters, buffalo hunters, trail drivers, half-reformed outlaws and Oklahoma boomers were all around, full of memories and eloquent in relating them to small boys. There I saw the crops burned by drought, eaten by grasshoppers, and destroyed by hail. I felt the searing winds come furnace-hot from the desert to destroy in a day the hopes of a year, and I saw the trail herd blinded and crazy from thirst, completely out of control of horse-weary cowboys with faces so drawn they looked like death masks . . . ."

Larry McMurtry, a distinguished modern writer, insists that Dr. Webb was overrated as a writer, but what I just quoted to you is pretty good writing, I think. . . .

Dr. Webb's father, Casner Webb, was a country schoolteacher, first in Rusk and Panola counties in East Texas after leaving Mississippi, then in Stephens County. He kept the attention of his students, as Dr. Webb remembered it, not only by intellect, but also by the fact he was a boxer and would give a strapping son of a rancher a good whipping if necessary.

Way out in an isolated part of Stephens County, the post office became Dr. Webb's best friend. He would send off for things to read and would write years later as an old man: "I have all my life loved a post office, and with good reason. Ever since I was a boy I have kept a box, and I still get a thrill looking through the little glass window to see what chance has brought. You can always speculate on what lies there, a message from a distant friend, a publisher's check, or some other demonstration of the magic of living."

As a country boy he must have been a bit of an outsider. He wanted books, books and books, and said of his days as a youngster: "There was a delicious odor about a new book that is

50

indescribable. I loved the soft paper, still with fresh ink, and the delightful crackling sounds that a virgin book gives off when opened for the first time. . . . My father brought me a four-volume encyclopedia. . . . Here was the spiritual world in which I was living far removed from the physical and social world around me."

Then something happened to Webb as a young boy that was so electrifying that the late Jack Fischer, editor, gave it great play in *Harper's Magazine.*

A wealthy man in Brooklyn, William Hinds, wrote Webb that he had read one of his letters to the editor in *Sunny South.* That was the beginning of a friendship that resulted in Hinds, a person Webb never met in his life, underwriting much of his expenses so Webb could go to the University of Texas.

The late Robert Lee Bobbit, a lawyer in San Antonio and a former attorney general of Texas, told me that Webb and he were in the same freshman class of the University of Texas and that "Webb was so country he wore a high celluloid collar and bow tie and looked like a turkey gobbler peeking over a fence."

In time Dr. Webb went on to write *The Great Plains* (1931), *Divided We Stand* (1937), which touched Franklin Roosevelt's life, *More Water for Texas* (1954), and *The Texas Rangers* (1935), among other books. Mexican-American intellectuals feel the book on the Rangers was too praiseworthy of those frontier lawmen, seeing that they were so hard on the poor of Mexican descent. At the last, according to my mother, Dr. Webb was considering a revision of *The Texas Rangers.*

My mother, now eighty-four [in 1986], does not, alas, remember much of this anymore.

But now and then, if but for a fleeting moment, the clouds part and we talk about cabbages and kings. On such occasions I tell her: "Mama, for a country girl with only a high school education, you did pretty good when it came to husbands."

And my mother will look at me and say: "You are right, Maury, Jr., and I'll tell you something. Your daddy was exciting, but Dr. Webb was nice."★

MAVERICK WRITES ABOUT RED SCARES & LEGISLATIVE MEMORIES

Maverick's three terms in the Texas House of Representatives occurred during the height of communist advances in many parts of the world and during a national Red Scare.

During the immediate post-World War II era, the Soviet Union had seized control of most of eastern Europe, including Poland, Czechoslovakia, Rumania, Hungary, and Bulgaria. In 1947 President Harry Truman proclaimed a corollary of the Monroe Doctrine to keep Greece and Turkey from falling into Soviet hands. That same year the United States helped rebuild war-torn western Europe under provisions of the Marshall Plan. During 1948 Soviet forces blockaded West Berlin, forcing Truman to implement an airlift of supplies to that city. With the end of the Soviet blockade of Berlin, the United States created the North Atlantic Treaty Organization to halt any further Soviet advances in Europe. (The Soviet Union in 1955 would respond with its own military counteralliance, the Warsaw Pact.) In Asia in 1949, Mao Tse-tung's forces defeated those of the nationalist government of Chiang Kai-shek. A year later, the Korean War began, lasting until well into 1953. That was followed by Ho Chi Minh's Vietnam forces defeating French troops at the crucial battle of Dien Bien Phu.

On the domestic scene all was not well, either. Truman's order for American loyalty oaths in 1947 caused about five hundred U.S. citizens to lose federal jobs, and another five thousand left such work voluntarily. Alger Hiss, a civil servant in the Franklin D. Roosevelt and Truman administrations, faced accusations of communist subversion and would later receive a prison term for perjury. Three years later, in 1951, the federal government put to death U. S. citizens Julius and Ethel Rosenberg, convicted of atomic espionage for the Soviets. All the while, FBI Director J. Edgar Hoover was ordering his staff to continue to compile data on suspected subversives, one of them being Maury Maverick, Jr.

Also on the home front several federal and state laws were passed to deal with the communist threat. The Smith Act of 1940, for example, made it illegal for any American to advocate the overthrow of the U. S. government by force or to belong to any such group that did so. The law was not in force during World War II because of the U. S. alliance with the Soviet Union, but the U. S. Supreme Court case of *Dennis et al. v. U. S.* upheld the constitutionality of the act and led to imprisonment of some leaders of the American Communist Party. The McCarran Internal Security Act of 1950 made it illegal "to combine, conspire or agree with any other person or perform any act that would substantially contribute to the establishment . . . of totalitarian dictatorship." The act also made it unlawful for any "communist-front organization," not really defined in the law, to fail to register with the attorney general of the United States, established the Subversive Activities Control Board to monitor the activities of communists in America, and forbade entry into the U. S. of anyone who had ever been a member of any totalitarian organization. President Truman vetoed the act on the grounds that it would "put the government into the business of thought control." He also stated that the act was "about as practical as requiring thieves to register with the sheriff." Nevertheless, Congress overrode his veto. (In 1965, the U. S. Supreme Court ruled the act unconstitutional on the grounds that the government could not force a person to register as a communist because under the law as written that amounted to self-incrimination.)

Another law, also passed over Truman's veto, called the McCarran-Walter Immigration and Nationality Act of 1952 (rescinded in 1990), required foreigners to pass a series of complicated loyalty checks before gaining entry into the United States. The act permitted certain exceptions. The United States, for example, continued to allow entry of selected Nazi scientists in the field of rocketry or atomic weaponry. Some Nazis even worked for the United States in counter-intelligence roles against the Soviet Union.

All these events and laws, coupled with the Korean War, increased tensions on both sides during the Cold War and helped feed the hysteria so dominant during the Red Scare in the United States.

Yet, perhaps more inflammatory than anything else was a speech that Joseph McCarthy, the junior and Republican U. S. senator from Wisconsin, made on February 12, 1950, in Wheeling, West Virginia. He produced a piece of paper that he described as containing a list of communists working in the State Department. Holding aloft the paper, McCarthy told his West Virginia audience: "I have here in my hand a list of 205 names known to the secretary of state as being members of the Communist Party and who nevertheless are still working and shaping the policy of the State Department." The next day, McCarthy spoke in Denver, Colorado. He said that he had the names of 205 "security risks." The day after, in Salt Lake City, Utah, the 205 security risks turned into "fifty-seven card-carrying communists." Ten days later, in the Senate, the fifty-seven communists became "eighty-one cases." The fact was that McCarthy had no names of any communists. What McCarthy held in his hand that night in West Virginia was a three-year-old letter from former Secretary of State James Byrnes. It stated that permanent employment might be denied to 205 unnamed State Department employees on various grounds, including drunkenness. Six months after the Wheeling speech, a U. S. Senate subcommittee concluded that Senator McCarthy had carried off a "fraud and a hoax." But few people listened until McCarthy's Senate subcommittee held hearings from April 22 to June 17, 1954, on alleged communist influences in the U. S. Army. It was then that Joseph Welch, representing the U. S. Army, along with CBS newsman Edward R. Murrow and U. S. Senator Margaret Chase Smith, a Republican from Maine, finally managed to expose more fully McCarthy's ruthless methods.

In Texas, tense political battles between liberals and conservatives dated back to 1938. At that time the influence of the Texas New Deal Democrats was on the decline. Maury, Sr., then a leader of the group, in his campaign for reelection to the U. S. House of Representatives had the endorsement of the Congress of Industrial Organizations, which supported a federal wages and hours act, but he lost to Paul Kilday, who won with the goal of the "elimination from Congress of one overwhelmingly shown to be the friend and ally of communism." [1]

At the same time, Martin Dies of Texas became chair of the U. S. House Committee on Un-American Activities, a prelude to the McCarthy Senate subcommittee, and W. Lee "Pappy" O'Daniel, owner of the Hillbilly Flour Company, became governor of Texas, a term of office he held from January 1939 to August 1941 at which time he became a U. S. senator.

O'Daniel hosted a folksy radio program, with the Lightcrust Doughboys playing country music, and campaigned for governor on the Ten Commandments. Historian George Norris Green noted that O'Daniel's 1938 bid to become governor signaled the "deterioration of liberalism in the state . . . when conservative, corporate interests took over [Texas], once and for all, perhaps permanently. They launched the Establishment, a loosely knit plutocracy comprised mostly of Anglo businessmen, oilmen, bankers, and lawyers. These leaders—especially in the 1940s and 1950s—were dedicated to a regressive tax structure, low corporate taxes, antilabor laws, political, social, and economic oppression of blacks and Mexican-Americans, alleged states' rights, and extreme reluctance to expand state services. On federal matters they demanded tax reduction, a balanced budget, and the relaxation of federal controls over oil, gas, water, and other resources."[2]

So things went in Texas until Maury, Sr., again emerged into the political spotlight by organizing the liberally oriented Loyal Democrats in 1951. His goals included condemning McCarthyism and forcing what biographer Richard Henderson labeled the "anti-Truman, antiadministration Shivercrat forces of [Texas] Governor Allan Shivers" to sign a loyalty pledge to support whomever the Democratic Party nominated on its national slate in 1952. The scene was set for a confrontation between the conservative Shivers forces and the Loyal Democrats at their state convention held in San Antonio. The latter group lost its bid to have the loyalty pledge accepted and held its own rump convention at La Villita Assembly Hall, where they selected their own delegation to the Democratic National Convention in Chicago.

Thus, at that convention the Shivers and Maverick forces each had contested seats. After much debate on live television, the

Credentials Committee voted thirty-six to thirteen to seat the Shivers group, and the full convention, fearing a southern revolt, followed suit when some in the Shivers delegation promised to try to get the top Democratic nominees, Adlai Stevenson and John Sparkman, on the Texas ballot that November. However, at another Texas Democratic convention in September, the group by a voice vote endorsed the Dwight D. Eisenhower-Richard Nixon Republican ticket.[3] As a result, Governor Shivers solidified his hold on Texas politics, which continued until he left that office in 1957.

Maury, Sr., however, did not give up his efforts to oppose Shivers and the McCarthyites. The most active among the latter were members from the Minute Women and the American Legion. They urged Texas to ban from public schools any study of the United Nations Declaration of Human Rights as well as any mention of Quakers (who opposed war) or the National Education Association (which urged passage of comprehensive civil rights legislation). Primary targets of book censorship included Albert Einstein's *Theory of Relativity*, all writings by D. H. Lawrence, Magruder's *American Government*, Thomas Mann's *Joseph in Egypt*, Norbert Wiener's *Cybernetics*, Louis Untermeyer's *The Treasury of Great Poems*, plus "books on sculpture, the mentally ill, alcoholics, child care, architecture, and mystery novels."[4]

Shortly before his death in 1954, Maury, Sr., responded to such tactics in a speech in which he declared:

> The urge to persecute, to make inquisitions, to punish, to make people squirm, to find out everybody else's business or sex life, and to humiliate, may seem strange, but it is strong in some. Throughout history these inquisitors want to force one to break silence, to confess publicly, and thus embarrass, persecute, cause public pain, torture and hurt—and this country is passing through such a phase now. . . .
>
> History repeats itself. My [Huguenot] ancestors fled from the religious persecution of Louis the XIV in France, some from England. Now we all live in what amounts to civil persecution, fear, malice, Romanesque TV circuses and modern electric

57

inquisitions. . . .

I ask you, do women and men have to be brought before legislative committees to give affidavits as to whether they slept with certain people? Do you get brought before the city council or a committee of the city council, to be asked whether you were drunk and disorderly on a certain night? The city council, a legislative body, has as much right to do that within its own sphere, according to present-day theories, as Congress to put you before inquisitorial procedures. Imagine your mayor and city council calling you and questioning you on your sex life . . . and then asking you who were the participants of these drinking parties, sex offenses, or other misdemeanors. This sounds ridiculous, of course, but Congress has such rights, so have other bodies within their own spheres.[5]

The McCarthy era and battles between the Texas liberals and conservatives made Maury, Jr.'s tenure in the Texas House of Representatives one of the most frustrating episodes in his life. Writer-humorist Larry L. King declared that the state legislature was then "controlled beyond belief by vested interests and showing the ideological instincts of early primates."[6]

During a videotaped interview with Robert Davis at Trinity University, April 30, 1985, Maverick talked about his legislative career from 1951 to 1957. For him, his lawmaking experiences were defensive. "I'm an expert on defeat," he said and added: "I would have liked to have built some things. . . . It is one of the sad things in my life. . . . I was one of the four people who voted against outlawing the Communist Party in Texas. But, I finally realized that some conservatives weren't looking for communists in Texas. Governor Allan Shivers knew there weren't really any communists in Texas. What he was trying to do was to keep the budget down and not tax corporations and not tax rich people, and not pay schoolteachers and not have three meals a day that were adequate for people in insane asylums. I introduced a bill to raise daily appropriations for food in San Antonio's Mental State Hospital from about seventy-five cents to a dollar and ten cents. That is a thirty-five-cent increase. And the headline in the *Dallas Morning News* said 'Liberals Run Amok.' That was after I was trying to get some poor devil to eat three meals a day. What the hell has that got to do with being liberal—someone having enough food to eat three meals a day? Those conservatives are fools for calling everything like that 'liberal.' But why call every reformer a liberal? He isn't necessarily a liberal. However, there are some decent conservatives in this country that have got a healthy, admirable attitude about life."[7]

Because Maverick served as a major with the U.S. Marines in the South Pacific during World War II, he was asked which was the most frightening experience for him—being a marine, a lawyer, or a politician. Maury, downplaying his time as a soldier, replied: "I had some combat as a marine, but not a lot. I didn't have a tough time with the marines. But I would say in the legislature, when the so-called anticommunist bills were coming across the speaker's desk, that was far worse than the marines. I don't know that I could physically stand it anymore. It would kill me, I think, now. The anticommunist era in Texas and in the Texas House of Representatives was worse than everything else that's happened to me and everything else put together—compounded, multiplied four or five times. There was nothing like that. As I have written and said, in the final analysis the worst thing about it wasn't the bad guys, but the good guys. Everybody was terrified. I mean the Texas State Teachers Association. The damned teachers' lobby came in on a bill to censor books and libraries, to take books out of the libraries, like Hitler did in Nazi Germany, and the damned teachers endorsed the bill for a pay raise. I remember the day when that happened. I went to their chief lobbyist, and I said, 'Jesus Christ, man, what are you doing? You're a goddamned schoolteacher, and you're endorsing that bill. What are you doing that for?' And I walked home to my apartment. I got halfway to my apartment, and I vomited so much that bile was running down the side of my face. I thought I was going to die. I said, 'Jesus Christ, damned schoolteachers doing that.' When that starts happening, that's the beginning of the end. That's when someone is going to start killing Jews, or Presbyterians, or Methodists, or conservatives, or liberals, or whatever. Somebody's going to get killed if that doesn't stop. That was the thing that almost finished me off. It was the nice people that either capitulated to it or kept quiet. Not a teacher in Texas said a word for a couple of years. Not a one that I remember right now."[8]

Equally frightening to Maverick was the time when the Texas House considered a bill to have membership in the Communist Party U.S.A. punishable by the death penalty. Maverick recalled: "No one will understand this today, but I once offered a left-wing amendment to have membership in the Communist Party punished by life in prison. It sounds funny now, but the McCarthyites were at the time talking about putting people in the electric chair for mere membership. We pulled stunts like that just to slow the goddamned bill down."[9]

This was also the time, as noted by the late historian Joe B. Frantz, that some state legislators decided to launch a McCarthyite attack on University of Texas economics professor Clarence Ayres. They called for an investigation of him because he had dealt in class with what he regarded as some flaws in the capitalist system. A university committee investigated Ayres, concluded that economics is not an exact science, and decided that Ayres was not a communist but instead sort of a classical-modern economist who forced his students to think about all sides of an issue. The Texas House finally agreed with those conclusions. Yet, when the House first voted on the resolution to have Ayres investigated, Maverick and a few of his liberal colleagues sought refuge in the men's restroom. There they hid in stalls with their feet perched upon commodes so that pages could not see them as the announcement for the vote was called and as the House made its formal decision.

Shortly thereafter, Maury, Jr., got a phone call from his father. The elder Maverick wanted to know about the vote to investigate Ayres. As Frantz recounted the event: "I didn't see your name as voting against it," said Maury, Sr. "No, Papa, I was in the men's room," replied Jr. In a very loud voice, Sr. shouted to his son: "Goddamn it, boy, I won't have any shithouse liberals in my family!" He did not, either.[10]

Earlier, his outspoken father told Maury, Jr.: "When you've got a famous name, you ought to use it to speak up for people who can't speak up for themselves. After all, nobody's gonna throw you in jail—they know the Mavericks have been crazy for a hundred years!"[11] On this same subject Maury, Jr., once wrote: "I would be more conservative if others would take my place and be more liberal. Sometimes I am a pain in the ass to myself about being to the left, but I keep remembering what my father said: 'You have a famous name. Speak up, goddamnit, and help the [poor] ribbon clerks.'" Maury, Jr., was quick to add: "I do not think of myself as a smart man. I could not pass the SAT test to get into Trinity University, and therefore, not being smart, I have some doubts about SAT tests, especially when they do not involve motivation. Law schools are outrageous on this."[12]

One of the few successes Maverick did have as a legislator occurred in 1957. He related the experience when asked if he approved of the use of filibusters: "Well, you don't have a true filibuster in the Texas House, but during the McCarthy era and on the last day of one of our sessions, the conservatives brought up the Un-American Activities Committee. It was to get the college teachers in Texas. For the first time in my six years in the House, the speaker told me: 'I'm gonna let you have the microphone. Don't let them knock you off that microphone. If you can stay on there, even if you have a fight, stay on the microphone. I'll give you the gavel.' No one ever the hell gave me the gavel before in my life, and my deskmate, Edgar Berlin, of Port Neches, got on the back microphone. The two of us filibustered to death the Texas Un-American Activities resolution to get college teachers. We were the bullies. The speaker let me be the bully, then. I learned how bullies operated that day because bullies had done that to me for six years. The speaker let me have the microphone, and it's up to [the time] when we were supposed to adjourn for the session. Ed knew that and moved the clock back. I, too, kept pulling it back, and I stayed up there with the gavel, and people would run at me. They'd grab me and pull me away from there. I'd pull back. The speaker finally said: 'We declare this session adjourned, *sine die*.' I literally collapsed on the floor of the House after holding on to that microphone for a number of hours. But the point is I disagree with the liberals from the North on the filibuster because you'll get a rampaging fire coming across a prairie where, for the moment, everybody in the world is for it. A filibuster makes people think and slow down. If people can just hang on another twenty-four hours, then maybe somebody will speak up against that fire. So I kind of like the filibuster. I'm for the filibuster in the Old South. I don't know if I'm for it in Washington, D. C., but I'm for it in the South."[13]

On occasion, however, Maverick did manage to get a laugh by being a member of the Texas House of Representatives. He recalled an exchange of letters at the outset of his time as a state legislator. He received a letter from D. F. Strickland, then a powerful movie theater lobbyist. Strickland had written: "Dear Representative Maverick: I enclose herewith a movie pass to all Interstate Theaters in Texas as you begin your first term in the Texas House of Representatives." Maverick answered: "Dear Mr. Strickland: Thank you for the movie pass which I am returning herewith. It would not be proper for me, a public official, to accept it." Strickland replied: "Dear Mr. Maverick: I have been a lobbyist in Austin for over three decades. In all that time only one other legislator returned his movie pass, and he was a Baptist preacher who later went insane." Maverick quickly wrote back: "Dear Mr. Strickland: Please send me back my movie pass."[14]

The Strickland episode was one of the few times Maverick saw much humor in his legislative experiences. This is evident in the following, in which he describes what life was like for a liberal Democrat and an ACLU lawyer serving in the Texas House of Representatives during the 1950s Red Scare.★

TEXAS RED SCARE

"Red Scare a Study in Liberty,"
June 30, 1985

I think I would have raised an outcry if I had believed my eyes. But I didn't believe them, at first—the thing seemed impossible. The fact is I was completely unnerved by a sheer blank fright, pure abstract terror. . . .

Heart of Darkness, Joseph Conrad.

[Reading *Red Scare! Right Wing Hysteria, Fifties Fanaticism, and Their Legacy in Texas,* Texas Monthly Press, 1985, by Don F. Carleton is] like getting a good horsewhipping, obviously no fun, but if liberty and freedom are serious issues with you, then read it you must as a civic duty and act of civilized patriotism. . . .

Blacks, I suppose, have nearly always lived under one form of McCarthyism or another although for them it has gone under other names. For whites it comes and goes, one of the first such local histories occurring in the 1850s when Know-Nothing candidates took over [San Antonio's] municipal offices.

They were after immigrants, European and Mexican, and I am proud to say that state Representative Sam Maverick, my great-grandfather, denounced the Know-Nothings in a letter to Judge L. A. Paschal dated July 11, 1855. One hundred years later during the Red Scare I was faced with the same thing, being then a member of the Texas House of Representatives.

I cut and ran a time or two, for which I am ashamed of myself, but for those six years in the House, I invite a comparison of my long-haul voting record with any other member during the same period. Babe Schwartz, one of the best fellows in Texas and then a member of the House, might even say a kind word. Ask him if the following items are true, which isn't bragging because once you read them you will know that I am blowing my last chance to be named "Man of the Year" by the Chamber of Commerce.

Item. I was one of thirty-five who voted against the censorship of library books.

Item. One of four who voted against outlawing the Communist Party, which vote was essentially sustained by a later unanimous U. S. Supreme Court decision written by a Republican judge.

Item. One of the two who, on the last day of the session, took the lead in defeating the creation of the Texas Un-American

Activities Committee, where the main purpose was not to get Reds, but to terrorize the teachers of the University of Texas.

Item. When a resolution was introduced inviting U. S. Senator Joe McCarthy to address the legislature, I offered an amendment inviting instead Mickey Mouse, "for if we are going to invite a rat, why not a good rat?"

Dr. Carleton in *Red Scare* describes the day when the House voted on the final passage of the bill outlawing the Communist Party: "Three representatives, A. D. 'Buffalo' Downer, Edgar Berlin, and Maury Maverick, Jr., the son of the former New Deal congressman, dared to speak against the pending legislation. Maverick delivered a defiant speech that others had wanted to give, but, cowering under the shadow of the Great Fear, could not. The San Antonio legislator looked at his colleagues and noted that it had been said that to oppose the bill would be political suicide. 'If it is,' said Maverick, 'let me write my own political obituary.' Maverick warned the representatives that: 'We cannot put the ideology of communism in the electric chair or in prison. You cannot lynch communism. You cannot burn communism. If we in fighting communism adopt totalitarian tactics . . . then we by our own hands will destroy ourselves. Under the broad limitations of this bill a cop can go into your home, knock down the door and see what you are reading. . . .'" (And that precisely is what later happened and which event was ruled unconstitutional [by Justice Potter Stewart] in the U. S. Supreme Court case of *Stanford v. Texas* . . . .)

After the speech and the final vote on the bill outlawing the Communist Party, I walked to my apartment doing all I could to keep from openly weeping. Like the character in Joseph Conrad's *Heart of Darkness,* "I was completely unnerved by a sheer blank fright, pure abstract terror." I wondered that day if the political climate was becoming like that in Nazi Germany just before the various political, racial, and religious minorities were carried away. Texas at that moment was an absolute nightmare for me.

The main thrust of Dr. Carleton's *Red Scare* goes to a description of the Minute Women of Houston and what they did to throw gasoline on the fires of hatred associated with the McCarthy period. Their initial target was Dr. George Ebey, who had been brought to Houston from Portland, Oregon, to be the deputy superintendent of the Harris County School District.

In the end, Ebey, a decent and loyal American, was completely destroyed and forced to return to the West Coast. Some years later he was quoted as saying: "I find it a bit ironic . . . that probably my most significant contribution to education came from being lynched professionally by savages in a community where I was a relative stranger."

Along with what was done to Ebey, there was the Port Arthur story where a phony TV program was produced by the friends of Allan Shivers depicting that city in the grips of the "red CIO." The end result was to destroy [liberal Democrat] Ralph Yarborough in his bid for governor.

Time after time appropriations for the poor were defeated in the name of "communism."

Teachers and librarians were especially kicked around with the teachers' own lobby, the Texas State Teachers Association, supporting a book-censorship bill in a swap-out for higher teacher salaries. After more than thirty-five years, I am still uncomfortable around TSTA. Of course teachers are underpaid, but why sell out liberty for a piece of silver?

The truth of the matter is that a McCarthyite wouldn't have known a Texas communist if he had found one in his bed. That was a racket, a kind of device to keep the poor on the defensive and not have economic reform. It was also a means to keep college teachers from telling the truth. "Maury," Chancellor Jim Hart of the University of Texas told me one time with tears in his eyes, "the lights of liberty are going out one by one for the academic community."

Today Judge Hart is in retirement at Austin. What a brave citizen Jim was to stand by his faculty, including Dr. Walter P. Webb, who might have been destroyed if Judge Hart had looked the other way. Every now and then I say a little "thank you" in my heart to Jim Hart, and, by God, you do it, too. And while I'm at it, dance a little jig for the ghost of [folklorist] J. Frank Dobie, who also fought for academic freedom. . . .

The people who sustained me in those lonely days were the poor, blacks and browns largely. There was that friendly nod now and then from Episcopal Bishop Everett Jones, and out-and-out backing from Archbishop Robert Lucey, an old hero of mine. And a group of liberal Jews, good friends then and now, whose love of constitutional liberty had been nurtured by Rabbi Ephraim Frisch of Temple Beth El.

Those were the days, my friends, and I would ask you to read about them in the book *Red Scare*. It's not easy reading, I must tell you, but neither were the times. ★

POLITICAL NIGHTMARES

"Political Nightmares Continue,"
October 4, 1987

Only four members of the entire Texas legislature . . . voted against outlawing the Communist Party–A. D. "Buffalo" Downer, Doug Crouch, Edgar Berlin, and [myself].

In 1954 in Austin we state legislators were reeling from the hysteria of the Joe McCarthy-Governor Allan Shivers-Chamber of Commerce-orchestrated "Great Terror."

The alleged purpose was to prevent the "communist takeover" of Texas, and especially the city of Port Arthur, where any moment communists by the hundreds would go on a rampage.

That was, of course, a contrived lie.

The real purpose was to bust unions and to keep poor Mexican-Americans and blacks from having decent wages. A side purpose was to intimidate teachers of the University of Texas at Austin. . . .

"American Socialism Helps Rich,"
August 12, 1990

I remember also that as state representative, I had to come home each weekend and as a cowed politician go to lunches where, time after time, business would get up and praise free enterprise.

"Keep government out of business!" the speaker would always say.

But come Monday morning those same businessmen, including the luncheon speaker, would be in Austin asking me to vote them a statutory edge over their competitors; that is, give them a state-created cartel.

The idea of having competition in a free market was the last thing those fellows had on their mind. . . .

"Political Nightmares Continue,"
October 4, 1987

The specific legislation outlawing the Communist Party provided, when first introduced, for the death penalty. Mere membership was enough. No other act was required.

When I spoke against the bill on the day of final passage, it was then and remains to this day the most terror-filled moment of my life.

No John Wayne when it comes to courage, I had to hold on to the podium because I was shaking so hard. Usually when a House member is on the microphone the other members chatter among themselves, but on that day there was a deathly silence.

Those three self-made men, all graduates of law schools, who voted "no" with me—Downer, Crouch, and Berlin—I'll never forget.

I had an easy time during the Depression, but they had a hard time and their working fathers had a worse time. . . .

"Where Are Doug Crouches of Today?"
July 30, 1995

Doug Crouch . . . came from economically oppressed working people of the Great Depression. He was the kind of fellow who could have walked out of this line by Carl Sandburg: "In the night, and overhead a shovel of stars for keeps, the people march." As a fourteen-year-old boy during the Depression, he was a hobo riding the rails all over America. Even as Tarrant County district attorney, he slipped off and rode the rails "to find out what's going on in the country."

One day on the floor of the House when we were voting on the general appropriations bill, Crouch noticed money going to something like "Texas Southern University for Negroes." He turned to me and said, "That sounds like Jim Crow," whereupon he offered and got adopted an amendment changing the name to Texas Southern University. That's forgotten history.

My old friend was capable of being a first-rate barroom brawler and had been one in hobo jungles and in the army, where he saw combat in the South Pacific, but he was also a quite good painter in oils, Grandma Moses style. He was shy about that.

When my deskmate, Representative Edgar Berlin, and I filibustered to death legislation to establish the Texas Un-American Activities Committee, designed to destroy college professors, it looked like I would be jerked from the microphone in the hysteria. Crouch came and stood by me, made his hands into fists and whispered to me from time to time, "Keep talking." It was a cliffhanger, and we won for the teachers.

When I listen to some of the radio talk shows around town, I wonder if there is any hope for the country. Sometimes the meanness and ignorance of the plain people on such shows is worse than that of a professional politician.

The answer is to have political leaders who will speak up by going against the mainstream and who will demonstrate the intellectual honesty and independence of a Doug Crouch. . . .

Downer, Crouch, and Berlin . . . inspired me.

When will people with big money quit using the communist smear tactic to destroy poor people and the cause of liberty?

The Joe McCarthy period was nothing new. It went on with the rise of Nazi Germany. Look at these words William Shirer wrote in his book, *The Nightmare Years: 1938-1940*, Little Brown, 1984: "I was rather puzzled that our American businessmen and our rich tended to sympathize with fascist countries. I wondered if it was because the right-wing dictatorships claimed to be anticommunist. . . ."

"Legislative Memories both Bitter and Sweet,"
March 6, 1983

In 1950 Beeville was represented in the House by John Barnhart, today a first-rate and high-minded lawyer in Houston.

But in 1950 that unconstitutional bill outlawing the Communist Party was to be used as a device to intimidate loyal American teachers and librarians.

We legislators told one another: "Our careers are too important. After things cool down, let the judges declare the law unconstitutional." Only one person in the entire legislature had the monumental courage to vote against the bill: John Barnhart. And how he suffered for it!

I know now why a . . . Sam Houston or a John Barnhart makes us angry. It's because they remind us we were not as brave as we should have been. After all these years, although we are close friends, I still inwardly wince when I see Johnny Barnhart for he reminds me of the day I ran out on the Bill of Rights. . . . ★

OLD FOGIES

"Old Legislators, a Sight to Behold,"
May 5, 1985

When I die I hope they bury me
On the Pedernales River 'neath a
live oak tree,
No place but Texas
My home sweet home.

From the song written for the old legislators' reunion.
April 22, 1985

How do you like those lyrics? In 1985 that's what they sang for us old former legislators in the Texas House of Representatives at our reunion.

Around two hundred one-time state representatives were there, some having served in the House nearly fifty years ago. It was a sight to behold: wheelchairs, crutches, pot bellies, the lame and the blind. As I stood there with my hearing aid turned up, I thought funeral director Porter Loring would show up any minute with a fleet of hearses to take us over to the state cemetery, where we all have the right to be buried a stone's throw from Stephen F. Austin's grave.

After the ceremonies we had grilled steaks on the Capitol grounds, thanks, I bet, to the lobbyists whom Governor Jim Hogg once described as the "knights of Congress Avenue who have done more to injure Texas than all the highwaymen combined."

When I was in the House from 1951 to 1957, I did the then-rare thing of running with country legislators more than with the big-city legislators. In those days, before individual legislative districts and before there were black and Mexican-American legislators, liberalism, such as it existed, came mostly from the sticks.

Big cities were largely controlled by big businessmen. In San Antonio it was done through the manufacturers association and the city public service board. At our delegation luncheons, financed, I suspected, in part by city funds, a famous strike-breaker was often there along with other powerful honey-money boys to keep you in line. As a result, I was a loner in my own delegation.

Loners get lonely, so I headed for the boys from the forks of the creek. A few of them were honest-to-God heroes who stood up for the Bill of Rights, opposed racial injustice, and fought for the poor. But nearly all of those country boys, good and bad, could spin a yarn. Especially the ones from the Piney Woods. When the time came to swap a good yarn, I even like the scoundrels.

Well, at the legislators' reunion the other day, the country boys I hadn't seen in twenty years were dusting off those yarns. Want to hear a few? Listen.

"The chair recognizes the distinguished gentleman of Czech descent, Mr. Spacek of Hallettsville, to urge passage of his bullfrog bill." (I was there the day this happened.)

"Mr. Speaker, those darn restaurant owners in Houston are sending commercial hunters to Lavaca County to get all our bullfrogs. It's getting so bad we country folks don't have frogs legs anymore. My bill will prevent the hunting of bullfrogs by those commercial guys."

We passed Spacek's frog bill, and he became the statesman of Hallettsville, but the next session he was back calling for the repeal of the bullfrog law.

"Mr. Speaker, fellow members of the House, I am asking you to take that bullfrog law off the books. You know what hap-

71

pened? Since you can't hunt bullfrogs anymore, they croak so loud at night we can't sleep anymore."

My deskmate, Edgar Berlin of Port Neches, decided to have some fun, and so he spoke in opposition to Spacek's new bill.

"Mr. Speaker, I rise for the bullfrogs of Lavaca County. Do not vote for this bill."

The House caught the spirit of the occasion, and we voted overwhelmingly not to repeal the bullfrog law.

Spacek never spoke to Berlin again.

Want to hear a dog bark in your heart in memory of a grand old lady? To the rear of the speaker's podium in the Texas House of Representatives is a huge painting of Sam Houston standing there with a hound dog. Legend has it that whenever a truly honest legislator speaks, the dog will bark.

It was 1936, and a young woman legislator, a former schoolteacher and by then a lawyer, rose to speak. That woman, Sarah Hughes, died recently.

In the House she was a fighting lieutenant of Governor Jimmy Allred, who is described by liberals as "the last great governor of Texas." Sarah was fearless and honest. After leaving the House, she became a state district judge and then a U. S. district judge.

When Sarah was recommended to the federal judgeship, Bobby Kennedy, then the U. S. attorney general, would not approve her because she was "too old." But something happened. All of a sudden the good old Irish boys the Kennedys wanted appointed as judges in Boston were unable to secure committee approval in the Senate.

"Lyndon," asked President Kennedy, "what's the matter?"

"Mr. President, I think you better send Bobby over to talk to Mr. Sam." [Lyndon being then-Vice President Lyndon Johnson and Sam being Sam Rayburn, a fellow Texan and U.S. Speaker of the House of Representatives.]

So Bobby went to see Speaker Rayburn and told him, "I've got word you asked your buddies in the Senate not to let the Boston appointments out of committee."

"Oh, Bobby," replied Mr. Sam, "I wouldn't say that, but maybe things will get better for all of us if you approve Sarah Hughes to be a federal judge."

Bobby, understanding hardball politics, pulled down his red flag, and that, my friends, is the inside story on how Sarah made it to the federal bench.

Let every person who loves liberty and honesty hear old Sam Houston's hound dog bark as a memorial for Sarah Hughes. Above all, let every woman in Texas, black, white, brown or polka dot, remember Sarah with the deepest of affection. She was in the vanguard to those who fought for the dignity of women. . . .

Former state Representative Bob Mullen of Alice drove me to the legislators' reunion and back. . . .

On the way home Mullen and I went by the state cemetery, where we sat on the tombstone of [old legislator friend] D.B. Hardeman and told lies to one another. When Bobby wasn't looking, I emptied one of those airline dry martinis at the head of D.B.'s grave.

With Beefeater gin, of course. ★

MAVERICK WRITES ABOUT BASIC CIVIL LIBERTIES

Maury Maverick, Jr.'s role in changing American constitutional history began during the civil rights revolution of the late 1940s and the 1950s. It was a time of "separate but equal" fostered in the 1896 *Plessy v. Ferguson* case. This situation began to change during the presidency of Harry Truman. In 1947, Truman made several important recommendations for civil rights reform, based on a study done by his Committee on Civil Rights. Among other things, he recommended (1) that a special government office be set up to prevent civil rights violations, (2) that Congress pass laws protecting the right to vote in federal and state elections, (3) that laws be passed outlawing discrimination in employment, public and private education, housing, public and private health facilities, transportation, and all other public services, (4) and that the government begin a campaign to inform people of the civil rights to which they are entitled and which they owe one another. U. S. Senator Hubert H. Humphrey of Minnesota was responsible for including many of the committee's recommendations in the election platform of the Democratic Party in 1948. That year, Truman took additional action to guarantee equal rights to many Americans. He ordered the desegregation of the armed services. However, it took ten years for this to be fulfilled completely.

In the 1950s, another branch of the federal government became involved in the movement to secure civil rights for black Americans. In 1950 and in 1954 the Supreme Court decided two important civil rights cases. Each involved an attempt to abolish segregated facilities for blacks and whites.

The first case, decided in 1950, was that of *Sweatt v. Painter*. Herman Sweatt, an African-American, had applied for admission to the University of Texas Law School. The university denied Sweatt's application for admission and instead set up a separate school for blacks—the Texas State University Law School. Sweatt then took his case to the U. S. Supreme Court which decided in Sweatt's favor and said it was Sweatt's constitutional right to have a legal education equal to that offered by the state of Texas to students of other races. Because the education offered to Sweatt at the all-black law school would not be equal to the one offered at the all-white University of Texas Law School, Sweatt was being denied his constitutional rights. Therefore, the court ruled that Sweatt should be admitted to the University of Texas Law School. In making this decision, the Supreme Court referred to the Fourteenth Amendment: "No state shall . . . deny to any person within its jurisdiction the equal protection of the laws."

Another landmark decision in civil rights occurred with the 1954 case of *Brown v. the Board of Education of Topeka*. The U. S. Supreme Court overturned the decision made in *Plessy v. Ferguson*, declaring the doctrine of "separate but equal" unconstitutional. Specifically, the Court ruled "that in the field of public education the doctrine of 'separate but equal' has no place. Separate educational facilities are inherently unequal. Therefore, we hold that the plaintiffs are, by reason of the segregation complained of, deprived of the equal protection of the laws guaranteed by the Fourteenth Amendment. This disposition makes unnecessary any discussion whether such segregation also violates the Due Process Clause of the Fourteenth Amendment."

A year after the *Brown* decision, a young Afro-American woman named Rosa Parks refused, as required by law in Montgomery, Alabama, to move to the back of a city bus in order to make room for whites to have the front seats. Police arrested her, and that evening many blacks in Montgomery met in a Baptist church to protest the law. They also selected a new minister in the community to serve as leader of the protest movement. He was the Reverend Martin Luther King, Jr., then in his mid-twenties. He and Rosa Parks would soon make history.

Maury Maverick, Jr., also began to make history. He joined in a civil rights crusade not as a "street protestor" but as a lawyer in a courtroom. For his efforts he received in 1991 the American Bar Association's John Minor Wisdom Public Interest and Professional

Award for handling over three hundred pro bono cases. Among those cases, several stand out as most significant in American constitutional history.

One of the first occurred while Maverick was still a member of the state legislature. The *I. H. "Sporty" Harvey v. Morgan* case of 1954 allowed Maverick, with Carlos Cadena as co-counsel, to have the Texas Court of Civil Appeals overrule a lower court's order and declare unconstitutional a 1933 Texas law that would not allow whites and African-Americans to box professionally against one another, even though amateur boxing and professional baseball, basketball, and football games were already desegregated. Maverick said the state trial judge of the lower court told him he would have ruled in his favor if he had not been up for reelection. But according to Maverick: "Someone in our society must be in a position to say no to churches, labor, big business, and popular ideas that may not really be good without being thrown out of office the next day by a popularity poll."[1]

Maverick eventually won the case by doing his homework and by using plain English—not fancy lawyer talk—to argue that the law denied Harvey the opportunity to make a living. To quote his legal brief: "Point of Error No. 1: this is a case about Sporty Harvey not being able to pick up his grocery money. . . . He wants to fight in Technicolor!"[2]

Another case that Maverick would take all the way to the U. S. Supreme Court began when he was only one of seven Texas House members to oppose the state's Loyalty and Subversive Communist Party Acts of 1954. The Texas House vote was 107-7; the Senate, 29-0. As noted by Don Carleton in *Red Scare!*, the acts eliminated loyalty boards and did not outlaw the Communist Party, but they did make illegal the "advocacy, conspiracy, participation, or assistance in any other way in the overthrow of the government by force." They also allowed judges, if one witness urged, to order a search and seizure in any place of business that supposedly had subversive literature. Search and seizure in a private residence required two witnesses. Punishment for conviction carried a maximum fine of $20,000 and twenty years in prison.

Maverick, who had risked his political career by opposing such legislation, would finally gain personal and professional redemption. By 1963 he was long since retired from the state House and involved full-time with his law practice and ACLU activities. It was then that Texas law enforcement officers, deriving authority from the 1954 acts, raided the San Antonio private home of John W. Stanford, Jr. An alleged communist at the time, Stanford operated a bookstore at his residence. The police took all writings and books from him, including his marriage certificate, insurance policies, bills and receipts, personal letters, and publications by such individuals as Karl Marx, Jean-Paul Sartre, Pope John XXIII, C. Wright Mills, Hans Bethe, Eric Fromm, Fidel Castro, Earl Bowden, Theodore Draper, Linus Pauling and a dissenting civil rights opinion by U. S. Supreme Court Justice Hugo Black. The take totaled fourteen boxloads.

Maverick entered into the fray, arguing that law enforcement authorities could not use a general search warrant to seize all writings and documents belonging to a person believed to be a communist. Willie Morris, in *North Toward Home*, noted that Stanford at his district court trial caused Maverick some rather tense moments, even more so than did his Marine Corps days in World War II: "Plainclothesmen and detectives were planted about in the courtroom to keep Maverick and his client from being hurt. In the middle of the trial a somewhat sinister man walked in wearing large black eyeglasses. At that moment Maverick was at the bench, directly in front of the judge, whose name was Solomon Casseb. The judge told Maverick, 'Mr. Maverick, please move to the left or right a few feet. If you get shot at now, I will get it right between the eyes.' 'This so unnerved me,' Maverick said, 'I had a paralysis of my vocal cords and had to go in a conference room and lie down to recover my voice.'"[3]

On appeal, the U. S. Supreme Court, during 1965 in *Stanford v. Texas*, ruled unanimously that the 1954 Texas law violated the Fourth and Fourteenth Amendments and declared that no official of the state could "ransack [Stanford's] home and seize his books and papers under the unbridled authority of a general warrant. . . ." Prior to the decision, each side made oral presentations before the High Court, and Justice Potter Stewart asked Maverick if the seized dissenting opinion of Hugo Black had been returned to Stanford. Maverick replied: "No, sir. I have high hopes [those who seized it] will read that opinion and grow in stature."[4]

On a more serious note, Maverick argued that "this business of playing havoc with a mail-order bookstore in a citizen's private residence under a vaguely worded search warrant, based on an application and affidavit which did little more than spread a rumor, and where no specific violation or any crime was alleged, was as contrary to the ways of a civilized state as it was to the Constitution. It was tyranny. It was a monkey-see, monkey-do reminder of a dictatorship. It was unworthy of the great state of Texas. It cannot stand before the Constitution of the United States of America."[5]

Of Maverick's many public interest or civil rights cases, several others are particularly noteworthy. In 1951 he used the Austin Court of Civil Appeals (the Texas Supreme Court denied error) to win *Elder v. Aetna Casualty and Surety Company* by representing a child, Billy Elder, who requested worker's compensation after being injured while delivering newspapers. In *Flower v. U. S.* in 1972, Maverick acted for John Flower, a Quaker, whom police arrested for offering literature on the grounds of a San Antonio military base. The U. S. Supreme Court overruled a lower court decision and declared that the base commander had the right to limit public access but not to restrict the exercise of free speech after people were on the property. Thus, Flower, on the base legally, had a First Amendment right to distribute his material.

Maverick served also as co-counsel with Gus Garcia and Carlos Cadena in having the U. S. Supreme Court declare unconstitutional the exclusion of Mexican-Americans from juries. Maverick claims he did little work on that case and recalls how Garcia made the justices laugh when he called Sam Houston "that wetback from Tennessee."

Another of his more interesting cases concerned Madalyn Murray O'Hair, the celebrated atheist. While Maverick served as an ACLU local counsel, she was busy challenging the use of any aspect of religion as part of civil government. She had been forced to leave Mexico, and the FBI had placed her in a San Antonio jail. Maverick was assigned to represent her while she was in the Alamo City, and he recalled that when some journalists inquired where he was while O'Hair went behind bars, he replied: "I was on the banks of the Llano River having a drink of sherry like a good Episcopalian should on a Saturday in solemn contemplation of the Sabbath."

When asked in 1985 what he remembered about representing O'Hair, Maverick answered: "Well, it was because other people wouldn't do it. I think a person ought to have his or her day in court. I don't remember going to her because I particularly like the atheists or didn't like the atheists. The New York ACLU office called me and said will you go down and help her. . . . The morning paper had a headline story front page, 'Atheist Calls for Maverick. . . .' I went down to see Madalyn Murray. She said something to me. I said: 'That's wonderful, Madalyn! Let me go talk to the people from the [San Antonio] *Express-News*. I want to tell them a little about what you just said, and I'll come back.' She'd been in jail about three days, and the boys at the paper over there had a sense of humor, and that afternoon in the same paper the headlines said: 'Atheist Tells Maverick, Thank God the ACLU Is Here!' I represented her because New York asked me to do it. She's an interesting woman. She's hell to represent. She's tough, but she's funny. The press would kick her around, and she'd kick them right back. Some young reporter would come up to her and ask her a smart-ass question, and she'd let him have it right between the eyes. The reporters thought she was pregnant without benefit of a husband. The FBI had picked her up in Mexico. The American FBI had more power in Mexico than it did here. They picked her up like a dog, threw her on an airplane, and then they threw her off here in San Antonio. Then I went down to see her. Many called her a communist. Most called her an atheist, which she repeatedly admitted that she was. Then the press was getting ready to ask her if she was pregnant. And I told her that she had better get ready for that question. They had all the cameras ready. She said: 'Don't worry, Maury. I know what to do.' So the press asked: 'Are you pregnant? You're a single woman. Are you pregnant?' And she said: 'Boys, if I'm pregnant, there's gonna be a new star in the east. You see, I had a hysterectomy.' And you could hear all those kids turning off their TV cameras. I mean, she was tough as hell. I kind of liked her, but I wouldn't want a steady diet of representing her. It's kind of like drinking Tabasco sauce with a milk shake. A little of her goes a long way. But she's an important person to American society. [When her son as] an eight-year-old atheist [was asked by] the press: 'Little boy, why are you an atheist?' he said, 'Because we have ten percent less cavities.'"[6]

Some of Maverick's other battles for guarantees of civil liberties took other approaches. In one, the Texas legislature wanted textbook authors as well as teachers to declare their noncommunist beliefs, and some of the ultraconservative legislators even sought to ban any public school textbook that would "discredit the family as an institution, ridicule the Constitution on freedom of religion, scorn American or Texas history, and advocate the violent overthrow of the government." Ironically, the latter would have meant taking the American and the Texas Declarations of Independence out of the textbooks.

To counter such opinions, Maverick entered the fray as a private citizen in 1963 when the state legislature had a special committee conduct hearings on textbooks that many McCarthyites alleged were full of communist theory. He thought such claims were hogwash and prepared to defend one of the attacked textbookss during a San Antonio hearing. Right-wing extremists learned of his plans and sent out leaflets that condemned "two generations of Mavericks for serving the cause of communism." The right-wingers packed the auditorium where Maverick was to speak and jeered, booed, or laughed as he testified, but he spoke anyway. He soundly condemned censorship of books as fascist, communist, totalitarian, and antidemocratic and insisted that a democracy allows for a variety of views.

The testimony Maverick presented to that special committee of the Texas House is included in the following selections in which he also focuses on a variety of other civil rights issues which remain controversial even to this day. ★

RIGHTS OF "THE PEOPLE," AS INDIANS CALL THEMSELVES

"America Loses by Ignoring Indian Heritage,"
May 2, 1982

Most Mexican-Americans of Indian descent do not know who they are. Stop any ten such persons and ask: "What do you know about your Indian ancestry?" You will get a blank stare nine times. . . .

Why this lack of knowledge?

There are all kinds of unhappy reasons for this, "thanks" significantly to the Spanish—secular and religious—and later to us gringos. It is the kind of demeaning thing that caused Porfirio Díaz, the mostly Indian former president of Mexico, to send off to Paris for a cream that, he thought, would lighten the color of his skin. It is reflected in all the school systems of Bexar County by the lack of textbooks or courses which adequately tell students at Alamo Heights and Sidney Lanier about the people of Indian heritage.

The school authorities of Maine have come out with a textbook that I think is one of the most exciting books I have ever read: *Maine Dirigo, I Lead,* produced by Maine Studies Curriculum Project, Down East Books, Camden, Maine. I found out about it from the Quakers.

The chapter on Indian history begins with an Indian by the name of "Moomoom" who tells the junior high school students of Maine about himself and his people. Let's pretend we are sitting around a campfire. Brothers and sisters, you be quiet now, you hear me? Listen to the old man talk: "I am Moomoom of the Penobscot Nation. 'Moomoom' in my language is a nickname for "grandfather." . . . I have seen many changes in my lifetime, but only one thing hurts me very much. It is the way many people still 'see' me and my people. This story I have to tell is a painful one for me. It is true that nearly everything written about my people has been written by non-Indians. When Europeans first came to the area now known as Maine, they wanted our land, and they even fought to take it away from my people. What they wrote about us was not always true. Some things were lies. Others were just misunderstandings. To begin, let me say that many Native Americans do not like the name that Columbus gave us. We are not really Indians and this is not India. We are Sioux or Seminole or Wabanaki. . . . One thing that history books often say is that the Europeans 'discovered' the Americas. I must tell you that it was my people who discovered this land. . . . By the time Columbus stumbled upon the West Indies, there were at least fifteen to twenty million native people in North and South America. . . ."

Our Indian friend Moomoom then criticizes the use of the term "prehistory." Once again, let's listen to the Indian grandfather: "Another thing we do not like is the way a part of our history is called 'prehistory' just because it happened before Europeans came here. In our view, everything that has happened to us is part of our history. Our history was not written; it was oral history passed down by word of mouth. . . . Unfortunately, "prehistory" is an English word which means that part of history which happened before there was anyone who could write it down or record it. . . . From our point of view, however, this word "prehistory" seems to say that our legends and oral histories of what happened before the Europeans came here are not history. . . . When explorers arrived here, they did not understand us. What they said about us showed only the European point of view and not our point of view. Since everything written about us was written by Europeans, nearly everything said about us was biased from the European point of view. "Bias" is an important word for you to know when you study history. It means seeing events from only one point of view and forming an opinion before looking at all the facts. . . . As an excuse for what they were doing, most Europeans said their people were better than ours. Many called us 'savages. . . .' Puritans in Massachusetts, especially, said we were 'children of the Devil.' Seeing us in those biased ways made it seem right for them to treat us badly. Indeed, most Europeans had the same opinions of native people in South America, Mexico, and elsewhere. . . ."

We folks of European descent have devastated the land and nature, and Moomoom doesn't think much of that. He went on: "Until the Europeans came here, we depended on the land for everything. . . . We could not afford to damage [the land] as the Europeans often did. . . . In the early spring, we moved to the hills to tap the maples for their sweet sap. Later we moved down to the streams . . . to catch fish. . . . To us, the whole of nature was sacred. Our survival depended on the survival of everything else. In fact, we thought of animals as our relatives. . . . We did not kill young animals and took only what we needed. We gave thanks to the spirit of every animal and plant we needed to kill for our use."

And on the subject of religion, Moomoom has his doubts about Christianity: "Most early writers could not see the spiritual side of our lives. When they saw some of our spiritual practices, they called us . . . 'pagan,' just because we were not Christian. Because we saw everything as sacred, the Europeans thought we worshipped many gods. In fact, we recognize only one force of good in the world: the Creator or the Great Spirit. When missionaries tried to convert us, they felt they had to tell us that our Great Spirit was the Devil."

Finally, Moomoom has some thoughts about land ownership: "Perhaps the most important area of misunderstanding between our culture and that of the Europeans was in our different understanding of what it means to own land. . . . We could no more sell land than we could sell the water or the air. . . . Kings and queens made people believe they own land. . . . It was [kings and queens] who often granted territory . . . without considering our aboriginal rights. . . ."

Well, the campfire is low, and it is time to bid Moomoom good-bye. I thank him for his thoughts and thank the folks who wrote the magnificent book *Maine Dirigo, I Lead.*

To the people of Mexican descent with Indian heritage, let me close out today's column with a question: Why don't you know more about your Indian ancestry? You need to know about it, and so do we gringos. If we did, we might have a better understanding of the family of man.

In peace, friendship, and respect. ★

THE MAGNA CHARTA

"Magna Charta Has Made Kings Bow to People,"
April 6, 1980

Johannes Dei Gratia rex Anglie dominus Hibernie dux Normannie et Aquitannie et comes Andegavie archiepiscopis, episcopis abbatibus comitibus baronibus justicariis, forestariis vicecomitibus prepositis, ministris et omnibus bellivis et fielibus sus salutem.

So begins the Magna Charta, originally written in Latin and translated: "John by the grace of God, king of England, lord of Ireland, duke of Normandy, and Aquitane, and count of Anjou, to the archbishops, bishops, abbots, earls, barons, justices, foresters, sheriffs, stewards, servants, and to all his bailiffs and liege subjects greetings. . . ."

Four original sealed copies of the Magna Charta are in existence. . . .

When it comes to liberty—we the people, we whites, blacks, browns, all races, all creeds—in serious degree owe our liberty to the Magna Charta.

In the beginning it was not a document for the ordinary people. The barons of Runnymede and members of the clergy wrested those words of liberty from King John for themselves, and only for themselves.

They were the rising classes, the new rich, the Johnnies-come-lately who were moving into power. Actually, the Magna Charta was not generally known by the plain people until 1750, when Blackstone printed it in his book *The Great Charter and the Charter of the Forest*. But liberty is contagious, and little by little from 1215 on the scholars, researchers, monks, dissenters, and other "strange people" became acquainted with the revolutionary idea that a king must answer to the people.

Centuries later it gave people like Patrick Henry ideas. Consider these words of Will and Ariel Durant in their book, *Rosseau and Revolution*, Simon & Schuster, 1967: "England decided to tax the colonies. In March 1765, Greenville proposed to Parliament that all colonial legal documents, all bills, diplomas, playing cards, bonds, deeds, mortgages, insurance policies, and newspapers be required to bear a stamp for which a fee would have to be paid to the British government."

Patrick Henry in Virginia and Samuel Adams in Massachusetts advised rejection of the tax on the ground that by tradition Englishmen could justly be taxed only with their consent or the consent of their authorized representatives. How, then, could English colonials be taxed by a parliament in which they had no representation? The barons asked that question for themselves in 1215.

Years ago my father wrote a book on constitutional liberty called *In Blood and Ink*, Starling Press, 1939.

His analysis of the Magna Charta was considered controversial at the time, 1939, and is here quoted in part: "In our high school and college history books we see pictures of King John properly robed in brilliant colors, surrounded by a brilliant assemblage of the nobility, dejectedly, yet magnificently, signing the Magna Charta. . . . But the facts are he did not sign it, that he was a plain-looking drably dressed fellow, and that the barons who forced him to agree were a lot of selfish men who, on their way to Runnymede, had stopped in London long enough to slaughter and pillage the Jews. . . . It was at the time a reactionary instrument, a sort of private treaty between the king and the nobles and the higher clergy. Most of the modern authorities on Magna Charta do not regard it as having had any constitutional worth at the time it was written. But Professor William McKechnie of Glasgow, in his great work, *Magna Charta*, says: 'The greatness of Magna Charta lies not so much in what it was to the framers of 1215, as in what it afterward became to the political leaders, judges, and lawyers, and to the entire mass of men of England in later ages.' After all, the charter did represent the will of more people than did the decrees of one selfish king; in that sense it was an extension of economic and political liberty. Thus Magna Charta gradually grew in the minds of the people as the Great Charter of Liberty. It has proved through our history a sort of spiritual shield of liberty, the original protector of habeas corpus, trial by jury, due protection by the court of the individual, and all those other rights that make for human decency, dignity, self-respect, and free government. Magna Charta—in 1215—was not a people's charter. It changed their miserable lot not one iota. But it did set forth for English-speaking people certain rights and liberties that all men desire and that many have since won. It is the first of a series of documents marking the people's long uphill battle for their freedom."

Actually some words in the Great Charter are quite inspiring. For example, Section 39: "No freeman shall be taken or imprisoned or disseised [dispossessed] or exiled, or in any way destroyed nor will we go upon him, except by the lawful judgment of his peers, or by the law of the land."

Of course, the barons and the clergymen meant that they were the ones to whom those rights should be afforded. But liberty, as I said, is contagious, and little by little, century after century, the plain people found out about Magna Charta and said: "We want this liberty, too."

Magna Charta gave people ideas. It helped John Locke to formulate the concept that man is born with certain natural rights. The late Robert Hutchins used to talk about the people of one time and era talking to people of another time and era.

In this sense, the barons of Runnymede talked to Locke, who talked to Blackstone, who talked to Jefferson, who talks to you and to me. As we fight our way past "the cross, the stake, and the hangman's noose," to use a phrase of Hugo Black's, the Magna Charta remains an incredibly important milestone. Maybe the most important.

The dreadful thing about all this is that we contemporary folks run out on our documents of liberty. Just as King John tried to repudiate the Magna Charta, and as the newly powerful of 1215 insisted it was only for themselves, we Americans ran out on the concept of the Bill of Rights when we tolerated the passage of the Alien and Sedition Laws [of the 1790s].

We ran out on the Fourteenth Amendment when it came to the blacks. Free speech is okay as long as you are not Red or a Ku Kluxer. State judges have totally ignored the Bill of Rights of the Texas Constitution, almost as if it had never been written.

During the Joe McCarthy days I was a member of the Texas House of Representatives and got a taste of all this. Attempts were made to intimidate schoolteachers, effort after effort was made to censor books, an Un-American Activities Committee was recommended to the legislature by the American Legion. In the middle of one such hot, unfriendly, and intemperate debate, I quietly read the following statement to the entire

House: "All political power is inherent in the people, and all free governments are founded on their authority, and instituted for their benefit. The faith of the people of Texas stands pledged to the preservation of a republican form of government, and subject to this limitation only, they have at all times the inalienable right to alter, reform, or abolish their government in such manner as they think expedient."

As soon as I left the podium, one legislator demanded of the speaker he be permitted to address the House on personal privilege. That is supposed to be a moment of great honor, great outrage, and when a member says those powerful words "personal privilege" a great hush ordinarily comes over the legislative body. So it was after I had spoken the above words. It was a scary and spooky moment.

My colleague told the House I had spoken "seditious words" and that I owed the members "an apology."

"Where did the gentleman from Bexar get that language?" it was asked. I finally told my brother legislators: "I got it from the present Constitution of the state of Texas." Word for word, and it was language at least distantly rooted in the Magna Charta. . . . ★

THE FIFTH AMENDMENT

"Don't Let the FBI Take Away the Precious
Rights of Dissent,"
January 11, 1987

If the good Lord said to me, "Maury, you can name the thousand persons you want for your island of liberty," I would begin with Eleanor Roosevelt, and then the two Toms, Jefferson and Paine.

I. F. Stone, one of the greatest intellectuals and brave journalists in the history of our country, would get an invitation because of the courage he demonstrated in standing up to the mean-spirited reactionaries of the Joe McCarthy era and for the courage he showed in crying out against the hydrogen bomb race.

The first blacks on my island of liberty would be Malcolm X and Martin Luther King, Jr., in the belief that there never would have been the latter without the former. . . .

G. J. Sutton, the first black state representative from San Antonio in modern times, would be on board the way he was as a young man teaching us blue eyes about the quest of black people for simple dignity.

I'd have Gus García there, the San Antonio lawyer who, with Carlos Cadena, invited me, the only dirty-dog gringo lawyer in America, to be associated with their case resulting in Mexican-Americans having the right to sit on juries in Texas. Gus and Carlos did all the work. I got a free ride, but I am proud of that free ride. . . .

On my island of liberty, I would have at least one living Yale-, Princeton-, or Harvard-educated patrician Republican with money in the bank. That person for me would be Erwin N. Griswold, [author of *The Fifth Amendment Today*, 1955, and later] solicitor general of the United States for President Richard Nixon.

Griswold, you see, is the hero of this column. Now, let me tell you why.

[In my] first session as a member of the Texas House of Representatives, a bill was introduced to fire any state employee who invoked the Fifth Amendment if asked if he or she was a communist. On its face it was blatantly unconstitutional.

At the time I read an Associated Press story that Griswold, then the dean of Harvard Law School, was making talks around the country in defense of the Fifth Amendment. One night, very late after a committee hearing, I personally typed and mailed a letter to Griswold asking help.

I was filled with despair and fright over the cruelty of those Joe McCarthy days. The beginning smell of a Hitler fascism was in the air.

Within a week a letter came back from Griswold. It was full of hope, courage, history and good cheer.

The person carrying the bill on the Fifth Amendment that so upset me was state Representative Bob Mullen of Alice. At the first reading of the legislation, he and I had a floor debate. . . .

Bob Mullen couldn't be all bad, so I went to him with a copy of Griswold's letter. We talked at length, and Mullen agreed not to push his bill. The truth is that he could have given me a good whipping because at that time he was with the majority. Because of Mullen's inherent sense of decency, he did not run with his nightmare legislation. Mullen saved the day.

All these years Mullen and I have added to our friendship. Today, on weekends, he attends Unitarian Church of San Antonio. Unitarians, delightful people, consumed with their anguished debates over how many angels can dance at the end of a needle while Rome burns, probably won't do it, but they ought to put up a statue of Mullen in the courtyard of their church. A graduate of Texas Military Institute, Mullen went on to have some gut-ripping combat experiences during World War II, this friend of mine of Irish whimsy.

But back to Dean Griswold.

In his lectures about the country, Griswold pointed out: "Historians can trace the origin of the Fifth Amendment back to the twelfth century." It began when the bishops in their "spiritual courts" began to examine and try people on matters that had nothing to do with religion and that were none of their business. At the same time, here mentioned as an aside, the idea of separation of church and state began to take hold. (Thank God for

91

you Baptists who urged it during the late eighteenth century.)

By the sixteenth century a bird came along by the name of Sir Edward Coke who, like Mullen, started out as a mossback but ended up a hero. Indeed, Coke got such a bellyful of those rotten bishops that he had a hand in the emergence of the maxim, *Nemo tenetur seipsum.* "No one should be required to betray himself."

The privilege against self-incrimination on American shores was included in the Virginia Bill of Rights as drafted by George Mason and then later included in our American Bill of Rights significantly at the urging of . . . James Madison. . . .

To conclude, I want to thank that hotsy-totsy Harvard Republican swell, Erwin Griswold, for standing up for the Bill of Rights and helping me when I was a kid legislator frightened out of my wits.

[Griswold] demonstrated how a brave teacher can inspire others. He had a hand in keeping me from running in battle. Not having the courage of John Wayne, God knows, I wanted to run. ★

THE FIRST AMENDMENT

"Don't Let the FBI Take Away the Precious Rights of Dissent,"
May 24, 1987

> *"**M**r. Wilkinson, are you now a member of the Communist Party?"*
>
> –Question posed to Frank Wilkinson by the House Un-American Activities Committee.

> *"I challenge in the most fundamental sense the legality of the House Committee on Un-American Activities. It is my opinion that this committee stands in direct violation of the First Amendment to the U. S. Constitution. . . . The Congress cannot investigate into an area where it cannot legislate [which includes] free speech."*
>
> Reply of Frank Wilkinson, July 30, 1958.

The House Un-American Activities Committee was conducting its business in a U. S. district courtroom in Atlanta while in the jury box sat twelve yellow-dog lawyers when Frank Wilkinson was asked: "Are you a member of the Communist Party?" [A "yellow dog" can be a person who, although very qualified and capable to perform a service, will not help others in need of that service.]

Frank Wilkinson, seventy-three years of age, ex-convict for invoking the First Amendment, was in San Antonio in 1987 for a meeting of the local chapter of the American Civil Liberties Union.

In his college days, the son of a wealthy Beverly Hills medical doctor, Frank headed up the Young Republicans for Herbert Hoover on the campus of the University of California at Los Angeles. Not only that, he led the fight against the on-campus communist students. This in the time of the Great Depression.

Because his father was one of the top lay leaders in the Methodist Church, Frank was destined to be a Methodist preacher. But first he would go on a tour of the Holy Land before entering the seminary. There for the first time in his life, he saw extreme poverty. No more Methodist preacher for him, and so when he returned to the United States he hooked on to the idea of social protest by working through the Catholic Church among the residents, many of them black, of the various federal housing projects in the Los Angeles area.

One day at a routine condemnation hearing where Frank was testifying on land values, he was asked if he belonged to the Communist Party. Refusing to answer the question, he was fired. Today he has an FBI file of more than 132,000 pages, although no one, I am told, has intimated he ever broke the law.

Don't laugh, for you may have an FBI file yourself. During the recent Vietnam War, when I was working with the San Antonio Women for Peace, the FBI began to keep files on those women who were about as seditious as a marshmallow. Ask the FBI for your file to see if you have been watched like a common criminal for expressing your viewpoint, liberal or conservative, under the First Amendment.

My father and I have a file kept by the FBI titled "Father and Son–Maverick." It is only twelve hundred pages long, or was until I started writing this column. It is largely devoted to the history of the liberal movement in San Antonio during the Joe McCarthy days. Dozens of blank pages demonstrate there were informers all over San Antonio. The local Unitarian church had one, maybe two, informers constantly reporting on its activities. My file seemed to always lump me with Catholic priests for working in areas that would give black people a measure of dignity. Ain't that seditious?

Now let me tell you about the "yellow-dog lawyers" and how Frank Wilkinson received a one-year penitentiary sentence. The ACLU in New York was looking all over the country for a person who, if asked about communism, would invoke the First Amendment, not the Fifth Amendment against self-incrimination.

Don't get me wrong, there's nothing improper with invoking the Fifth Amendment.

To rely on the First Amendment and not the Fifth is a terribly courageous thing to do. What you are saying to the government is: "Go to h---. My politics, left or right, under the Bill of Rights is none of your business."

I doubt if over half a dozen people stuck only to the First Amendment in the McCarthy days. One was an old labor organizer and book writer out of Seattle by the name of Harvey O'Connor, now nearly ninety, who is married to one of my Maverick cousins. I guess the worst sin Harvey ever committed was to write a book showing the hunky-dory relationship between Wall Street and Nazi cartels, which later had more than a little to do with the Holocaust.

Anyway, Wilkinson said he would rely entirely on the First Amendment before the House Un-American Activities Committee in Atlanta, and so the ACLU in New York gave him the names of twelve Atlanta lawyers. Frank went to each of these Atlanta lawyers seeking legal counsel for his appearance before the committee. Not a one would touch his case, although all twelve showed up at the hearing and sat in the jury box watching Frank, the poor guy, being bullied around without a lawyer. Hence, "yellow-dog lawyers."

The legal profession's record during this period of American history is a scandal beyond words. There are some brave lawyers, but not an excess of them. Money is the name of the game. Law schools train the kids to be reactionaries.

Wilkinson's case went all the way to the Supreme Court, where he lost on a 5-4 basis. The majority held that an investigation of "communism" was a legitimate function of the Congress, but Justices Black, Warren, Douglas, and Brennan said the decision was an outrage.

Consider these words by Hugo Black in his dissent: "Criticism of government finds sanctuary in several portions of the First Amendment. It is a part of the right of free speech. It embraces freedom of press. Can editors be summoned before the [Un-American Activities] committee and be made to account for their editorials denouncing the committee, its tactics, its practice? If petitioner [Frank Wilkinson] can be questioned concerning his opposition to the committee, then I see no reason why editors are immune."

Is this practice of the FBI keeping files on Americans for their political beliefs a thing of the past? It was over with, Wilkinson said at the ACLU meeting, "but beginning in 1981 under Ronald Reagan the FBI went back in the business of keeping track of people and churches because of political opinions."

This is increasingly so about the American "peace bishops" of the Catholic Church, which must be hard on the FBI agents because so many of them are Irish Catholics who went to Fordham University. . . .

Is there any confirmation of Wilkinson's claim about current activities? Consider these words from a letter to the editor by Margaret Ratner and Michael Ratner of the Center for Constitutional Rights in the May 16 issue of *The Nation*: "The Center for Constitutional Rights has been collecting information on harassment and surveillance of groups and individuals opposing U. S. policies in Central America for more than three years. The evidence shows that the FBI is watching dissenters closely and that such surveillance is a high priority for the administration."

A word of caution from this old one-time ACLU lawyer to young people starting out in life and who attend [political] meetings. . . . Always assume there is an informer in your midst. Don't make kidding remarks because they will be reported as serious remarks in your FBI file. But be brave, have your meetings, and stand up for peace and the ghost of Thomas Jefferson. ★

TEXTBOOK CENSORSHIP

"A Report on *Our Widening World*," Report to Speaker Byron Tunnell and members of the Texas House of Representatives of the Fifty-eighth Legislature by the House Textbook Investigating Committee of the Fifty-seventh Legislature April 2 and 3, 1963

My name is Maury Maverick, Jr. I am an attorney-at-law in this community. I am also a teacher on occasion at St. Mary's University, a member of the Texas State Teachers Association, and, in my heart, I am loyal to the schoolteachers and to San Antonians. . . . I am a committeeman of the Democratic Party. A man was slammed here yesterday at length; I rise for Franklin D. Roosevelt, to whose memory I am loyal. I also rise for a great man who is our president, John F. Kennedy. . . . I rise also as an ex-colleague of yours. I have a high regard for the Texas House of Representatives. I served in it for six years. The next man I want to rise for on the basis of integrity and decency of Americanism is John Alaniz, who is a fine citizen, as are all people on this committee. I have a high regard for the Americanism of all the people on this committee, and when one of you is attacked, it would seem that all of you would defend one another. Now, I want to say something further in testimony. I present testimony before you in behalf of the book, *Our Widening World* by Dr. Ethel Ewing. The publisher is Rand McNally & Company. What is the book about?

At page 377 it is stated, "the application of Marxist principles has resulted in poverty, forced labor, and widespread human misery." Doesn't sound very communistic to me. At page 689 efforts of the UN to stop communist aggression are described this way: "The warfare in Korea in 1950, with an army under the UN flag opposing the advance of the communist frontier, marked a strong stand by the United Nations."

But what is the book really about? For one thing, it is not about any one nation or its heroes and wasn't intended to be. To put it in a nutshell–this book is about the family of man–something that we Americans should appreciate most of all with our melting-pot culture. You see, gentlemen, we have a great nation not for the reason we are all alike, but because we are trying to live together in friendship despite our differences and diversities. Justice William O. Douglas, a man who loves the soil, put it this way: "There is room in this great and good American family for all the diversities the Creator has produced in man. Our

Constitution and Bill of Rights were, indeed, written to accommodate each and every minority, regardless of color, nationality, or creed—out of that diversity can come a unity the world has never witnessed."

The book, *Our Widening World*, then tells about the ancestral lands of the United States, about the Far Eastern society, about India, and Southeast Asia, the Middle East, and Moslem society—Slavic, European, Anglo-American, and Latin-American society. You will remember that Franklin Roosevelt once told the Daughters of the American Revolution that we Americans are all descendants of revolutionaries and immigrants.

The book I am testifying for is also about the United Nations and its dream for human dignity and the search for peace everywhere in the world. The "town hall of the world" some call it, and certainly young people ought to know about it.

Although I oppose the original petitioners who asked you to come here, though I think they mean well and will do harm, I also want to very carefully rise in their behalf, for if I would protect my own right to freedom of speech, I must also protect theirs. In the final analysis, then, I must rely on the democratic processes that mean, to a great extent, we citizens must depend on you committeemen to do the right thing after you have heard all the evidence. In short, we must rely on your love of liberty, your common sense, and your faith in academic freedom.

San Antonio is an appropriate place to talk about our widening world, to talk about freedom and liberty, and I hope you will let me, an ex-member of your body, tell you briefly about my hometown, a community made up of people from so many different races of our widening world. From both a historical and contemporary standpoint it isn't all good here in San Antonio. We have always had one of the highest death rates from infant diarrhea and tuberculosis. Our wage scale suffers badly by comparison with Houston or Dallas. But, St. Anthony's town is a dramatic place for the right kind of things, too; a town that can demonstrate the truth of and need for a book like *Our Widening World*. We have been at it a long time, here in San Antonio–we know something about our widening world. Evidence indicates that Domingo DeTran, the first governor of Texas, viewed this area in 1691. Here the Franciscans came and built their missions. Here to what was then called the "New Philippines" came the Canary Islanders–and before them the Apaches and Comanches watered their horses at San Pedro Springs, not far from here. Most anthropologists contend, by the way, that the American Indian is the descendant of Mongoloid groups, his ancestors having crossed the Bering Strait more than thirty thousand years ago.

To San Antonio the Anglo-Saxon began to migrate–pushing his way through East Texas not so very long after George Washington left the office of president. Here a young West Point graduate, Lieutenant A. W. Magee, joined together with Bernardo Gutierrez in a joint Anglo-Mexican effort against the Spanish crown. Gutierrez was one of Father Hidalgo's men, and on the streets and plazas of San Antonio men talked about liberty and died for it. Here Teddy Roosevelt, a New Yorker, organized his Rough Riders, and Black Jack Pershing strutted up and down Peacock Alley, of the St. Anthony Hotel, before going to the trenches of France after first thanking the French people for their contribution to the American Revolution. As a matter of fact, if you look hard enough here in San Antonio you might even see some of Pershing's old Chinese cooks who soldiered with him in his chase after Pancho Villa in Mexico. From our widening world, San Antonio has in retirement a soldier's soldier, Walter Krueger, immigrant. Go to our Irish flats while you are here in San Antonio, and you will know a people who came to San Antonio suffering from economic poverty. Go down to what we call, with some humor and much affection, Sauerkraut Bend, and you will learn something about people with names like Herff,

Steves, Oppenheimer, and Altgelt, who fled a despotic Germany in search of liberty. And while you are weighing the evidence presented at this hearing–go by the Alamo, Texas' greatest shrine, and understand that to a substantial degree the Alamo was defended by foreigners from our widening world. The Alamo is important because it belongs to the family of man everywhere. In its time– considering the lack of communications and transportation facilities–the Alamo was a sort of pre-United Nations effort of its own. Where did the defenders come from? Let me call the roll: fifteen men from England; ten from Ireland; four from Scotland; two from Wales; one man from Denmark, his name was Zanco; two from Prussia; eight were native born Texans with names like Guerrero and Fuentes, and I might also add, like John Alaniz; thirty-two were from Tennessee, and the rest from the other American states, although some of these defenders also emigrated from Europe.

Let me conclude with a final thought about Bowie, Fannin, Crockett, old one-eyed Guerrero, and all the other defenders of the Alamo, who gave their lives defending the Alamo. You see San Antonio is an aggressive type of provincial city. We didn't come from anywhere; we came from everywhere. This is a great melting-pot country that we have here. And a final thought about the defenders of the Alamo. A man named Ramsey Yelvington wrote a play about the Alamo that is produced each summer here. A brave man can see that play and weep. At the end of the play the dead defenders of the Alamo assemble on the stage. Satan walks out and mocks the dead defenders and asks them why they died. This is their reply:

> "We died there;
> And from our dust the mammoth thing freedom
> Received a forward thrust
> The reverberations we continued

Are something to which man may respond
Or not respond at pleasure."

Every man who has ever served in the Texas House of Representatives, as I did and as you are now serving, is an old colleague, and so on that friendly basis, I put the question to you as if I were standing at what you and I call the "Snorting Pole":

How do you committee members respond?
Will you give freedom a forward thrust?
Do you believe in academic freedom?
Don't you generally agree that the State of Texas
    already has an adequate screening process for the
    selection of books?
Don't you agree that we cannot adopt the censorship
    tactics of a fascist Spain or a communist Russia?
Don't you agree that he who would intelligently
    cope with any totalitarianism must first love
    democracy most of all?

Gentlemen, let me finally conclude with a Texas saying which my old professor, [folklorist] Pancho Dobie, J. Frank Dobie, taught me. It describes a man who won't run out on you or on an ideal. It goes like this: "He'll do to ride the river with." I know you committee members will do to ride the river with. Ride it for liberty, ride it for academic freedom, ride it for good schoolteachers to keep them from being bullied around, ride the river from the glory of Texas and these United States of America. I thank you. ★

THE ACLU

"ACLU Fighting for Ollie North,"
September 4, 1988

. . .I am a member of the National Advisory Committee
of the ACLU and was for years its vice chairman for the entire
country. In his prissy way of talking, George Bush [during the
1988 presidential campaign] called Michael Dukakis a card-
carrying member of the ACLU. I hope the charge is true; certainly it is true about me. . . .

The ACLU includes in its membership profoundly decent
and enlightened Republicans, even graduates of Yale University,
who know that it has spoken not just for the left, but for the right
as well . . . the ACLU's recent filing of a friend-of-the-court brief
for Oliver North, John Poindexter, and Albert Hakim as regards
the Iran-Contra scandal.

In making an appeal for North the ACLU has pointed out
in its brief that the idea of making a person testify against himself
is offensive to Anglo-Saxon law. In this regard two cases cited in
the brief are especially exciting and need to be considered in
memory of your distant ancestor about four hundred years ago
who had an eye gouged out or his nose slit to make him testify
against himself. It is something Hugo Black had in mind when he
wrote that mankind has to fight its way past the cross, the stake
and the hangman's noose.

The first of the two cases concerns a man named Boyd.
There the U.S. Supreme Court, more than one hundred years
ago, denounced the idea of making a person testify against himself with this language: "It is abhorrent to the instincts of an
American. It may suit the purposes of despotic power, but it cannot abide the pure atmosphere of political liberty and freedom."

The second case is *Miranda v. Arizona.* Chief Justice Earl
Warren, a Republican, notes that the principle underlying the

privilege of the Fifth Amendment has not diminished over the years. Here is Warren's language: "To respect the inviolability of the human personality, our accusatory system of criminal justice demands that the government seeking to punish an individual produce the evidence against him by its own independent labors, rather than by the cruel, simple expedient of compelling it from his own mouth."

When society protects the constitutional rights of the least of its members, it also protects the swells. . . .

"Using Public Money for Pope's Visit
Contrary to Constitution,"
August 16, 1987

Even after I left the House and took the *Stanford v. Texas* case to the U.S. Supreme Court, this equation remained true. The Stanford case involved the Communist Control Law, which I had voted against. . . .

The day before I argued the Stanford case, the ACLU had me go through a dry run in New York City. I went before three lawyers who acted like they were Supreme Court justices. They had names like "Goldstein," but were not modern-looking like Gerry Goldstein, the San Antonio criminal lawyer. In fact, they had beards and looked like Moses and were just as smart. What's more, they read *The Nation* magazine, a good sign.

God Almighty but those Jewish lawyers kicked me around getting me ready for the High Court, but I'll tell you this–by the time I got to the Supreme Court and Chief Justice Earl Warren called the Stanford case it was like stealing candy from children.

I won a unanimous decision, one that was written by a middle-of-the-road Republican, an old Yale boy, Potter Stewart.

The decision set forth that blunderbuss search warrants are illegal under the Constitution, an idea that began to take place when the English king kicked Boston businessmen around. . . .

John Stanford in his case did not appreciate the unconstitutional search warrant issued against him. Conservative businessmen who today are confronted with the same issue ride in Stanford's stirrups. So, too, might greedy yuppie bankers under indictment with more indictments to come.

There is a procedure wherein a federal judge can grant immunity to a witness who then can be compelled to testify against himself, but with the proviso that such testimony cannot be used in a subsequent trial. But such is an impossibility as regards North, Poindexter, and Hakim, who were on television night and day. The ACLU explains it this way: "Their immunized testimony was widely—indeed pervasively—broadcast to the public and has been used extensively by witnesses who testified before the grand jury and who will testify against petitioners at trial. . . . Robert McFarlane, who appears on the independent counsel's list of proposed witnesses, is likely to be a key government witness and testified before and after the immunized testimony of defendant North. He requested a second appearance specifically to respond to North's testimony . . . at which time he **revised** his prior testimony based on his review of North's testimony. . . ." (Emphasis supplied to demonstrate how North's own testimony is being used against him.)

The irony of all this is that Bush evidently knew what was going on in the Iran-Contra scandal. The strong evidence suggests that he sat there like a ninny and made no moral protest.

Now, at least indirectly, Bush is being protected by the very ACLU he mocks from the stump. Such mockery is a cheap shot and demonstrates to me that Bush needs some lessons in intellectual honesty. Indeed, the Bill of Rights needs a better ally than Bush as president of the United States.

Although I dislike North and think him a dangerous person, he is entitled to the protection of the Bill of Rights as much as any citizen. . . .

104

"ACLU Fights for Bill of Rights,"
September 11, 1988

I have never thought of the ACLU as being "liberal."

What is liberal about standing up for the Bill of Rights? Is it liberal to give some suffering person a blood transfusion?

Why do so many of you conservatives use the word "liberal" to describe the ACLU? Is a love of constitutional liberty a monopoly of liberals? Are we not, all of us, the heirs and beneficiaries of Alexander Hamilton and Thomas Jefferson?

Wasn't William Jennings Bryan right when he said that a liberal is like an old mule pulling ahead, and that a conservative is like a plow holding back, and that between the two of them they break the soil? Why can't we look at constitutional liberty that way and make it the province of all Americans? Why insult one another over the Bill of Rights?

The poor old ACLU gets in so much trouble. For about five years it ran off its best contributors, American Jews, when it supported the right of Nazis to walk along the streets of Skokie, Illinois.

And do you want to know something that will knock you for a loop? The executive director of the ACLU at that time was Areyeh Neier, a Jew who had been brought to this country from Nazi Germany as a child. Otherwise, he would have died in a gas chamber, as did his relatives.

How do you think he felt? He hated the Skokie Nazis, but he loved the Bill of Rights more. One of the legends of the ACLU is that members of the Jewish Defense League spat in Neier's face.

Many of the people we have helped have been members of racial minorities. This has been particularly so with blacks and somewhat so with Hispanics, but the strange thing is that we have had relatively few black and Hispanic members. . . .

We Anglos who care about constitutional liberty need the

help of blacks and Hispanics. They need us. All of us with any sense of history ought to understand that. . . .

I particularly urge lawyers of conservative leanings to help out the ACLU with both contributions and free legal services. On so-called "radical" cases that I handled as a young lawyer and that involved questions of free speech and due process, I often had the help of famous Wall Street law firms that represented the most wealthy and powerful corporations in the country. ★

SEPARATION OF CHURCH AND STATE

"State Approved Religion Just Will Not Work,"
May 16, 1982

One, Two, Three, Four, Who Are We For? Jesus!

Maury Maverick, Jr.

Congress shall make no law respecting an establishment of religion. . ."

First Amendment, U.S. Constitution.

You Presbyterians, Lutherans, Quakers, Methodists, and Baptists deserve a pat on the back. It was your religious predecessors who saved our country one time long ago from having a state religion. Now the living must again save the country, but this time from the crazies of the Moral Majority who would have a football coach tell your kid how to pray.

Presbyterians, Lutherans, Quakers, Methodists and Baptists flocked behind the banner of Thomas Jefferson and James Madison and were responsible for the enactment of the famous Virginia Bill for Religious Liberty. From that great document came the First Amendment of the Bill of Rights. . . .

The idea of having a government-sponsored period for

prayer finds its roots in the *Book of Common Prayer* of the Anglican Church. That religious body persuaded Parliament to pass acts in 1548 and 1549 making the Anglican way of prayer the official and proper way to pray. Because of this, England was disrupted, and it became worse and worse as each new king or queen struggled to impress his or her viewpoint upon the government on how to pray.

Minorities in England, outraged by the Anglicans, came to these shores and, becoming the majority in certain areas, began periods of religious tyranny of their own.

Justice Hugo Black, in the [1962] landmark case of *Engel v. Vitale*, the decision that people of limited vision are now trying to overturn, caught the spirit of religious liberty by writing: "By the time of the adoption of the Constitution, our history shows that there was a widespread awareness among many Americans of the dangers of a union of church and state. These people knew, some of them from bitter personal experience, that one of the greatest dangers to the freedom of the individual to worship in his own way lay in the government's placing its official stamp of approval upon one particular kind of prayer. . . . They knew the anguish, the hardship, and the bitter strife when zealous religious groups struggled with one another to obtain the government's stamp of approval from each king, queen or protector. . . ."

"But, Maverick," I can hear the innocents say who do not know their history, "all we want is a neutral prayer."

A *neutral prayer*? Man alive, we already tried that and it didn't work!

In *Engel v. Vitale* the state of New York caused the following "neutral prayer" to be read aloud: "Almighty God, we acknowledge our dependence upon Thee, and we beg Thy blessings upon us, our parents, our teachers, and our country."

Of this state-devised "neutral prayer" the Supreme Court declared "it is no part of the business of government to compose official prayers for any group of Americans to recite as a part of a religious program carried on by government." In other cases of the Supreme Court in situations where children ostensibly could refuse to participate, the result was to demean and intimidate those refusing.

Whenever in this world there is state-approved, regimented and official religion, there is trouble. . . . In our own century it has been the Jewish students who have, generation after generation, suffered at schools by being forced to participate in the Christian exercise of religion. How would you like a Jewish principal of a public school telling your Christian kid to pray a Jewish prayer?

Priests, preachers, rabbis, and mullahs can be tyrants just like anyone else. When our Texas ancestors signed the Declaration of Independence of the Republic of Texas, they understood how abusive clergymen can be and specifically described them in that great document as the "eternal enemies of civil liberty, and the usual instruments of tyrants." There ain't nothing mushmouth about that language.

But our brave forefathers didn't stop with the declaration. They wrote into the Constitution of the Republic of Texas: "Ministers of the gospel, being by their profession dedicated to God and the care of souls, ought not to be diverted from the great duties of their functions: therefore no minister of the gospel, or priest of any denomination whatever, shall be eligible to the office of the executive of the republic, nor to a seat to either branch of the Congress of the same."

Our present Texas Constitution reads: "No money shall be appropriated or drawn from the treasury for the benefit of any sect or religious society; nor shall property belonging to the state be appropriated for any such purpose." The latter phrase means you don't turn a government-funded public school over to the pope or a football coach for the purpose of student praying. . . .

"Keep State Out of Church Business,"
January 9, 1994

As a Jefferson deist four days a week and a Thoreau pantheist the remaining three, I go to church nearly every morning. My church is a secret live oak in Brackenridge Park. That tree and I have had some fine conversations. Let me, as an outsider, ask you Christians, Jews, and Muslims some questions. Each Sunday, television evangelists proclaim that Jesus can do or stop anything. Why then the Nazi Holocaust? Why the slaughter by Christians in Bosnia?

Why be Jewish in Israel, where status is determined not by citizenship but by a single religion? Isn't that ultimately a formula for national suicide?

Just what do Muslims have in mind regarding the following provision in the Koran: "They who believe not shall have garments of fire fitted unto them; boiling water shall be poured on their heads; their bowels shall be dissolved thereby and also their skins, and they shall be beaten with maces of iron."

Do not those questions lend credence to Robert Ingersoll's contention that "to hate man and worship God seems to be the sum of all creeds"?

. . . . Julio Noboa, an educational anthropologist, wrote: "Fundamentalist Protestants are foremost among those in the religious right who have made a career of attacking values in government schools." (It may even be worse than Noboa has said, because the *National Catholic Reporter* recently had a disturbing article contending that the right wing of the Roman Catholic Church is considering an alliance with the fundamentalist Protestants.)

Then Noboa states: "Deists, who were prominent in the early [American] revolutionary movement, are accused, by the fundamentalists, of having an unbiblical view of God." Well let's talk about those revolutionary deists.

Tom Paine, the most ardent of the American revolutionaries, wrote in *The Age of Reason*: "I do not believe in the creed professed by the Jewish church, by the Roman church, by the Greek church, by the Turkish church, by the Protestant church, nor by any church that I know of. My own mind is my own church."

About the Bible, Paine tore his britches with the Puritans when he wrote the following boob-shocker: "Whenever we read the obscene stories, the voluptuous debaucheries, the unrelenting vindictiveness with which more than half the Bible is filled, it would be more consistent that we call it the word of a demon than the word of God. It is a history of wickedness that has served to corrupt and brutalize mankind."

Thomas Jefferson was first offended with Christianity through his headmaster and Episcopal priest, the Reverend James Maury, my fairly close cousin. Jefferson, like Paine, not only denounced the Bible, but also wrote his own Bible, leaving out the nonsense and cruelty. . . .

"Guard Against Evils of Religious Faith,"
June 5, 1994

Writing to John Adams in 1815, my hero Thomas Jefferson stated: "I never told my religion, nor scrutinized that of another. I never attempted to make a convert, nor wished to change another's creed. I have ever judged of others' religion by their lives . . . for it is from our lives and not from our words, that religion must be read. . . . The question before the human race is whether the God or nature shall govern the world by His own laws, or whether priests and kings shall rule it by fictitious miracles."

Seven words Jefferson spoke went around the world like a shot in the night. They got him into trouble then, and they still do with the fundamentalists: "This loathsome combination of church and state."

Benjamin Franklin . . . in *Poor Richard's Almanac* . . . would write: "Lighthouses are more helpful than churches."

If in fact there is a hereafter, then surely the ghost of [the late folk humorist and civil rights activist] John Henry Faulk is entertaining the ghost of James Madison. Johnny loved him and quoted these words of Madison to me, "During almost fifteen centuries, the legal establishment of Christianity has been on trial. What have been its faults? More or less, in all places, pride and indolence in the clergy; ignorance and servility in the laity; in both, superstition, bigotry, and persecution."

Baptist leader Roger Williams, founder of Rhode Island, hit a homer when he wrote: "There goes many a ship to sea with many hundred souls in one ship. . . . I affirmed that all liberty of conscience . . . turns upon these two hinges–that none of the papists [Roman Catholics], Protestants, Jews, or Turks [Moslems] be forced to the ship's prayer or worship nor compelled from their own particular prayer or worship, if they practice any."

Cut the deck by reading that provision of the Bill of Rights providing for separation of church and state. Protect the public schools and protect your own integrity.

Separation of church and state came to us from Jefferson, Madison, Franklin, Paine, Roger Williams and is kept alive by the living John Henry Faulks. They knew a secret–that mankind has had to fight its way past the cross, the stake, and the hangman's noose. . . .

"State Approved Religion Just Will Not Work"
May 16, 1982

Don't you see the danger in the proposed constitutional prayer amendment urged by the lunatics and [endorsed] by Presidents Ronald Reagan and George Bush? What the goofy crowd wants to do is to take away the right of the federal judiciary to protect you or me if the state does violate religious liberty.

Years ago I wrote to a famous jurist and asked him to inscribe on the flyleaf of a book those words about liberty that he had written and that he considered his best comment on the subject.

The judge was a deeply religious man, but he knew the state ought to keep its nose out of prayer and the courts should be available to prevent state abuse of religion. From a chamber of the U. S. Supreme Court, the jurist took pen in hand and wrote these words back to me, words that can make your spine tingle, and even weep: "Under our constitutional systems, courts stand against any winds that blow as havens of refuge for those who might otherwise suffer because they are helpless, weak, outnumbered, or because they are nonconforming victims of prejudice and public excitement. . . ." [He] concluded with a personal note: "In love of freedom and country. Washington, D.C. 1962. Sincerely, Hugo Black."

"Thank God for Liberal Baptists,"
April 12, 1987

[Then, there is the] Georgia lawsuit of a young high school student [named Doug Jagar] of professed agnostic leanings seeking to force his high school teachers and administrators in Douglas County, about fifty-five miles from Atlanta, to desist from having state-orchestrated prayers over the public-address system before a football game.

Young Jagar was assisted by attorneys for the American Civil Liberties Union. . . .

The prayers over the school public address system were exclusively Protestant and most likely Baptist, Methodist, Church of Christ, and evangelical.

Presbyterian and Episcopalian prayers were harder to come by than hen's teeth.

Worse still, one of the Georgia ACLU lawyers told me: "In the last thirty years only one Catholic priest lived in Douglas County, and another time, it is true, a rabbi drove through the county at seventy-five miles an hour, never stopping until he got to Atlanta."

As an aside, that remark by the Georgia ACLU lawyer reminds me of a story that black civil rights activists used to tell.

An elderly black man in a Harlem church asked God if he would go with him on a visit to Mississippi where he was born. "My son," said God, "I will go with you as far as Atlanta."

So maybe the rabbi driving seventy-five miles an hour through Douglas County knew what he was doing.

The U.S. district judge's ruling in the Jagar case was a mixed bag that offended all sides.

No longer could Protestant ministers pray over the public address system, but in their place there could be "equal access," which the judge described this way: "All clubs and organizations at the school can designate members of their clubs to give invocations. Also, any student, parent or school staff member can submit his or her name. The student government will then select the invocation speaker at random. No ministers will be involved. . . ."

At a football game after the ruling, a man in the stadium suddenly began reciting the Lord's Prayer in a loud voice and about a third of the spectators joined in.

One pretty high school girl had the word "pray" painted in large letters on her cheek. She told the press she loved Jesus.

The cheer for Jesus that I have . . . never happened, but it is not much more undignified than what has already occurred in Douglas County.

Better to invoke the name of Jesus in churches on Sunday in the hope that football will be outlawed so that young men will not be killed, paralyzed or otherwise injured.

The increasing brutality of football, contributing to a Rambo-America mentality and the mounting money dishonesty of college football, is no place for Jesus. . . .

The trial judge in the Jagar case had doubts himself about

the practical application of his own ruling. He was worried how school officials would enforce his order.

To illustrate this dilemma, the judge told in court of a young boy who frightened his mule and ruined half an acre of cotton. When the boy's father was asked about this, he said, "Well, he's a good boy. He minds real well. The only thing is that I just can't think of enough things to tell him not to do. . . ."

Most folks around my age, who went to the University of Texas at Austin before Pearl Harbor, will remember John "Dub" Singleton, then a big man on campus, a mixer of good drinks at the Delta Tau Delta house and today a crackerjack good chief U. S. district judge in Houston.

Old Dub done quit preaching and went to meddling when he ruled as unconstitutional this orchestrated Houston school prayer: "Dear God, please bless our school and all it stands for. Help keep us free from sin. . . . In Jesus' name we pray, amen." You say that doesn't offend you? Suppose the prayer had ended, "In Moses' name we pray, amen"?

There is much controversy about public prayer in Baptist circles, but before the Baptists fall out with me I hasten to inform that my eighty-five-year-old mother was born and reared in Groesbeck, fifty miles east of Waco, as a Baptist.

The truth of the matter is that my mother's father was the head Baptist deacon, or whatever Baptists have, who at forty-two married my eighteen-year-old grandmother, a member of the choir. . . .

I don't quite know what to do with Baptists, and they know even less what to do with one another. Just when you are about to give up on those folks, one of them will save the Bill of Rights on separation of church and state.

In that regard, I leave you on this Sunday, praise the Lord, with portions of a Sunday sermon by Dr. Peter Rhea Jones of the First Baptist Church of Decatur, Georgia, which is an enlightened response to this business of having the state tell us how to pray. Watch.

"What we need to remember is that Baptists in particular . . . are the ones who fostered the First Amendment to the American Constitution. . . . We needed a system like the Puritans in New England or the Episcopalians in Virginia [to teach us about the abuses of state prayer]. There was no provision in the Constitution specifically for religious freedom. . . . Thomas Jefferson was attracted to a certain Baptist preacher by the name of John Leland [who] was a strong advocate of religious freedom. The Virginia Baptists turned to John Leland who, by the way, was also against slavery. They requested him to write George Washington and obtain some kind of amendment to the Constitution. "And so he wrote to President Washington asking that there might be a provision for religious liberty and freedom. The president wrote back and agreed to such an amendment. With the sponsoring by James Madison [as pushed by the Baptists], it came into being–the First Amendment to the Constitution. Any Baptist who ever reads the Constitution ought to be proud. . . . Keep on being a Baptist championing religious liberty."

And so, as the child of a Groesbeck Baptist, I hope you will always have a strong resentment in your heart against state-orchestrated prayer. . . .

"Keep State Out of Church business,"
January 9, 1994

Violating separation of church and state "just a little bit" is like saying a single girl is pregnant "just a little bit." One thing leads to another. . . .

There are good individuals in all religions. Father Bill Davis, the San Antonio Catholic priest, is a fine fellow. I hope he gets a pope who believes in artificial birth control.

When I was co-chair of the National Advisory Committee of the ACLU, rabbis in New York, the liberal kind, were an inspiration for the cause of liberty.

Because of McCarthyism when I was a young legislator, a lone-wolf Methodist bishop, G. Bromley Oxnam, helped me against the terror of those days. Edmond Browning, the presiding bishop of the Episcopal Church, knows more about the world than you can shake a stick at. . . .

Finally, they don't come a dime a dozen, but to the extent they exist, thank God for liberal Baptists. ★

ORGANIZED RELIGION

"Ingersoll and Organized Religion,"
November 5, 1989

I had just fallen asleep when Robert Green Ingersoll, [self-educated lawyer, Civil War Union soldier, Illinois attorney general, and] the "Great Agnostic" who turned America upside down in the last century, appeared to me in my dreams. This after I had done my evening pantheist devotions of reading a poem by Rosemary Catacalos, who has abandoned me for Stanford University, and then one by Naomi Nye, who has abandoned me for her chickens.

Dead ninety years, Ingersoll said to me: "Let us have a discussion about organized religion. You ask me questions and the answers I give will be precisely the ones I gave while on earth." So this is what happened.

Q. Mr. Ingersoll, as a conservative Republican called "Royal Bob" by President James Garfield, what do you have to say about the Bible?

A. Somebody ought to tell the truth about the Bible. The preachers dare not because they would be driven from their pulpits. . . . They forget its ignorance and savagery, its religious persecution; they remember heaven, but they forget the dungeons of eternal pain. Liberty is my religion. "Liberty" is a word hated by kings–loathed by popes. It is a word that shatters thrones and altars. Ministers wonder how I can be wicked enough to attack the Bible. I will tell them: This book, the Bible, has persecuted, even unto death, the wisest and the best. This book stayed and stopped the onward movement of the human race. This book is the enslaver of women.

Q. Mr. Ingersoll, I have had enough. How dare you say the Bible is the "enslaver of women"? After all, you are the son of a Presbyterian minister!

A. Maverick, what do you think about the following from the Bible? "They (women) are commanded to be under obedience. . . . And if they will learn anything, let them ask their husbands. . ." (1 *Corinthians* 15:34-35). "Wives, submit yourself to your husbands. . . . For the husband is the head of the wife even as Christ is the head of the Church" (*Ephesians* 5:22-24). "Ye wives be in subjection to your own husbands" (1 *Peter* 3:1).

Q. Mr. Ingersoll, when you were on earth, you spoke of the "real Bible." What did you mean by that?

A. All the poems, crystals from the brain, flowers from the heart, all the songs of love and joy, of smiles and tears, the great dramas of imagination's world, the wondrous paintings, miracles of form and color of light. All the wisdom that lengthens and ennobles life, the victories of heart and brain, the histories of noble deeds. These are the treasures of heart and brain. These are the sacred scriptures of the human race.

Q. What do you say about a generation of free women?

A. I said there will never be a generation of great men until there has been a generation of free women and of free mothers.

Q. What was that shocking statement you made about Baptists, Presbyterians, and Methodists?

A. Is it possible that an infinite God created this world simply

117

to be the dwelling place of slaves and serfs? Simply for the purpose of raising orthodox Christians? That he did a few miracles to astonish them? That he is finally going to turn heaven into a kind of religious museum filled with Baptist barnacles, petrified Presbyterians, and Methodist mummies?

Q. What did you say is the sum of all organized religious creeds?

A. To hate man and worship God seems to be the sum of all creeds.

Q. What would you have the pope and other men of the cloth do?

A. I would have the pope throw away his tiara, take off his sacred vestments, and admit that he is not acting for God, is not infallible, but is just an ordinary Italian. I would have all the cardinals, archbishops, bishops, priests, and clergymen admit that they know nothing about theology, nothing about hell or heaven, nothing about the destiny of the human race.

Q. Should God be mentioned in the Constitution of the United States?

A. What God is proposed to be mentioned in the Constitution? Is it the God of the Old Testament who was a believer in slavery? If slavery was right then it is right now. Is it the God who commanded the husband to stone his wife to death because she differed with him on the subject of religion? Are we to have a God who will reenact the Mosaic code and punish hundreds of offenders with death?

Q. Do you distinguish between individual Christians and churches?

A. There is a distinction to be made between churches and individual members. There have been millions of Christians who have been believers in liberty, millions who have fought for the rights of man, but churches as organizations have been on the other side.

Q. What is the noblest work of man?

A. An honest God.

Q. In your book, *The Ghosts,* what did you say to preachers?

A. You have no right to erect your tollgate upon the highways of thought.

Q. What is the difference between a believer and a free thinker?

A. A believer is a bird in a cage. A free thinker is an eagle parting the clouds with tireless wing.

Q. What did you say about Abraham Lincoln?

A. Let us hold fast to the sublime declaration of Lincoln. Let us insist that the republic is "government of the people, by the people, and for the people."

Q. Mr. Ingersoll, we pantheists are generally more interested in hoot owls than in organized religions, but I sure wish you had lived on this earth long enough to have known the popular church. And I wish you had known Penny Lernoux, a future Catholic saint, who died the other day.

A. Who was Penny Lernoux?

Q. She was an inspiring journalist of the Christian left. Because of her and people like her you see the advertisement in *The Nation* that reads: "Don't fall out with the religious Left. It is the only Left today in the United States."

How about a compromise, Mr. Ingersoll? Do away with the meanness, the claims of superiority, the degradation of women by all organized religions and settle instead for the simple statement of St. John, "God is love"?

Just then Samantha, my hound, nudged me. It was time for our morning walk. I didn't hear Ingersoll's reply.

We pantheists have the darnedest dreams. ★

FLAG BURNING AND THE PLEDGE OF ALLEGIANCE

"George Bush is a Scoundrel,"
October 9, 1988

> . . . . *it was not until 1892 that the Pledge of Allegiance was writ-*
> *ten by an editor of* Youth's Companion *as a voluntary affirmative for*
> *little kids. . . . The compulsory pledge (for adults) is exactly the sort of*
> *thing to which totalitarian states resort—precisely because they lack confi-*
> *dence in the loyalty of their citizens. . . . What has happened to our sense*
> *of humor about ourselves?*
>
> Arthur Schlesinger, Jr., The Wall Street Journal,
September 20, 1988.

When George Bush first began reciting the Pledge of Allegiance in his acceptance speech at the Republican National Convention in 1988, I thought he was simply indulging in some good-natured, permissible political puffery. When it is nothing more than a shot of Tabasco sauce in the stew of American politics, it can be fun.

But what Bush did that night was not innocent fun. This has become clear since then by his repeated references to [then-Massachusetts Governor Michael Dukakis vetoes of legislation] requiring the recitation of the Pledge of Allegiance by school-children.

The governor had followed a decision by the Massachusetts Supreme Court wherein three of the five judges in the majority were Republicans.

Dukakis first asked the [state] high court for what lawyers call a declaratory judgment. In other words, he asked the Supreme Court justices of his state to tell him if the law passed by the legislature requiring the pledge was constitutional or not. A majority of the judges said the law was unconstitutional.

The judges explained in their decision [that the law

decreed] that "each teacher at the commencement of the first class of each day in all grades in public schools shall lead the class in a group recitation of the Pledge of Allegiance to the flag. A flag shall be displayed in each classroom in each such schoolhouse. Failure (to so comply) . . . shall be punished (for every such failure to so pledge) by a fine of not more than $5 (against the teacher)."

Further, the Massachusetts Supreme Court went on to say: "*In West Virginia Board of Education v. Barnette,* the [United States] Supreme Court on June 14, 1943, Flag Day, held that a requirement that a student recite the Pledge of Allegiance to the flag and salute the flag, under the threat of expulsion for failure to comply, unconstitutionally violated the rights of a student who objected to the requirement on religious grounds. . . . Although most citizens find affirmation of the patriotic sentiments contained in the Pledge of Allegiance unobjectionable," the court pointed out to Dukakis, "the teaching of the *Barnette* decision is clear. Any attempt by a governmental authority to induce belief in an ideological conviction by forcing an individual to identify himself intimately with that conviction through compelled expression of it is prohibited by the First Amendment."

Not only was Dukakis told that the law was unconstitutional by his highest state court, but also he was given a written opinion by Francis A. Belotti, the attorney general of Massachusetts, who concluded that opinion with this sentence: "It is my opinion that (the bill) insofar as it categorically requires teacher participation in it, is inconsistent with the First Amendment of the Constitution of the United States and may not be enforced. . . ."

Dukakis did indeed veto the bill. In his veto message he said: "My oath of office . . . requires me to uphold the Constitution of the United States. I cannot sign any bill that violates the Constitution as this bill has been declared to do. . . ."

The Massachusetts legislature overrode the governor's

veto, but the law has never been enforced, which means that both Republican and Democratic district and county attorneys know that it is unconstitutional.

The controlling case that the Supreme Court of Massachusetts relied on . . . [concerned] the Jehovah's Witnesses refusal to take the pledge and salute the flag because they took literally *Exodus* 20:4-5, which says: "Thou shall not make unto thee any graven image, or any likeness of anything that is in heaven above, or that is in the earth beneath, or that is in the water under the earth; thou shall not bow down thyself to them, nor serve them."

Here, the majority of the [U.S.] Supreme Court pointed out: "They consider that the flag is an 'image' within this command. For this reason they refuse to salute it."

With Justice Felix Frankfurter dissenting, the majority of the court stood with the Jehovah's Witnesses, pointing out: "The very purpose of a Bill of Rights was to withdraw certain subjects from the vicissitudes of political controversy, to place them beyond the reach of majorities and officials and to establish them as legal principles to be applied by the courts. One's right to life, liberty, and property, to free speech, a free press, freedom of worship and assembly, and other fundamental rights may not be submitted to vote; they depend on the outcome of no elections. . . ."

I have some social friends, all Republicans, who are social friends of George Bush. They describe him as an enlightened conservative without any mean-spirited qualities. "Maury, he comes from such a good family, and he graduated from Yale."

So Bush is no unknowing redneck. He knows he is in the gutter and deliberately went there, which makes him all the more evil for reflecting on Dukakis' love of country.

Tell me, Mr. Bush, now that you support a forced Pledge of Allegiance, declared unconstitutional, when will you come out for state-directed prayers in public schools? . . .

122

Bush is not merely some poor little lamb who has lost his way, as they sing at Yale. More to the truth and in the language of Samuel Johnson, Bush is a scoundrel for making the Pledge of Allegiance a campaign issue. He knows better. . . .

"Leave First Amendment Alone,"
July 16, 1989

It seems to me that it would be well to carefully think out the flag-burning issue and then give it what a Republican jurist, the late Learned Hand, called "the sober second thought of the community."

Do you really want to tinker with a constitutional safeguard that has stood the test of time since 1791? Are you ready for other exceptions to the First Amendment that will surely follow?

Two years before the adoption of the First Amendment, James Madison, outraged that our Constitution had no Bill of Rights, declared that specific rights should be set out to "provide those securities for liberty . . . and expressly declare the rights of mankind. . . ."

Madison, Jefferson, George Mason and others explained that the purpose of the Bill of Rights was to limit and qualify power, guard against legislative and executive abuses, and protect the minority against the majority.

All three men, not by burning a flag but by ways far more expansively destructive, had desecrated England's flag, the Union Jack.

Their courage in this regard is what Mark Twain had in mind when he said: "The country is the real thing . . . to be loyal to rags . . . belongs to monarchy, let monarchy keep it. . . ."

But you say you still insist on supporting Bush's efforts to amend the First Amendment of the U.S. Bill of Rights, which will have the effect of opening the door in future years to a Pandora's box of crazies who will want other expectations?

Okay, pals, let's assume you the people will open that door with Bush's incredibly dangerous flag-burning prohibition. But having turned loose the crazies, what will the second amendment be? The third? The fourth?

Ladies and gentlemen, look at your handiwork. I give you the First Amendment of the year 2100: "Congress shall make no law respecting an establishment of religion (*but the Christian religion shall be the preferred religion*), or prohibiting the free exercise thereof (*except that prohibitions may be made against Jews and Catholics*); or abridging the freedom of speech (*but conservatives shall have less free speech than liberals*) or of the press (*but no newspaper may editorially oppose the right of abortion*); or the right of people peaceably to assemble (*but not blacks or Mexican-Americans*), and to petition the government for a redress of grievances (*but this right shall not be given to Baptists being such a quarrelsome bunch*). . . ."

The greater desecration of the flag is not the burning of it at a political rally, but rather when a president would diminish free speech, which the flag symbolizes. . . .

Supreme Court Justice Louis Brandeis wrote in 1927: "Those who won our independence by revolution were not cowards. . . . They did not exalt order at the expense of liberty. . . . Recognizing the occasional tyranny of governing majorities, they amended the Constitution [by adopting the Bill of Rights] so that free speech and assembly should be guaranteed."

If we pass the constitutional amendment making it a crime to desecrate the American flag, perhaps the first person to be prosecuted ought to be Bush who, as Sam Donaldson of ABC-TV noted, was being tacky when he gave the Chinese leader, Deng, cowboy boots with the American flag on [them].

It seems to me that we ought to stand by the Bill of Rights and give it as Judge Learned Hand advised, "the sober second thought of the community." Then, just as Yankee Doodle did, I would advise you to stick a feather in your cap and call it macaroni. . . . ★

124

THE DEATH PENALTY

"Overture Sounds for Death Drama,"
November 18, 1979

Every human being that believes in capital punishment loves killing, and the only reason they believe in capital punishment is because they get a kick out of it.

Clarence Darrow.

Peanuts! Popcorn! Hot dogs! Get your program! The state of Texas is about to kill a person on Death Row.

Get your program! Get your program!

What follows is the precise procedure to be used in executing a person at Huntsville by painless injection:

Step one: Inmate sentenced to death will be kept on Death Row at the Ellis Unit, some sixteen miles northeast of Huntsville.

Step two: When time for killing the inmate arrives, the condemned will be transferred from the Ellis Unit to the Huntsville Unit not less than twenty-four hours nor more than seventy-two hours before the scheduled time of execution.

Step three: The condemned will be constantly observed. Up until 6 p.m. on the day immediately prior to the execution, the condemned may be visited by ministers, Department of Correction chaplains, attorneys, family members, and friends.

Chaplains may visit after the 6 p.m. deadline. No media visits at Huntsville Unit.

Step four: Between 6:30 and 7 p.m. the last meal will be served.

Step five: Between 8 and 8:30 p.m., the condemned will shower and dress in clothes specially ordered for the execution.

Step six: At 11:45 p.m. witnesses shall be escorted to the Death House. They shall include: one Texas bureau representative designated by the Associated Press and one Texas bureau

125

representative designated by the United Press International. These two must act as pool reporters. No recording device, audio or video. Under Texas Code of Criminal Procedure the condemned may have up to five friends or relatives present.

Step seven: By midnight all arrangements necessary to kill the condemned will have been made. At that time, midnight, the inmate will be taken out of his death cell and the door between the death cell and the Death House will be opened.

Step eight: The condemned will be secured to a hospital gurney (a hospital litter on wheels) and rolled into the Death House. A medically trained individual (not to be identified) shall immediately insert an intravenous catheter into the condemned person's arm.

Step nine: The warden will ask the condemned man if he has any last statement. Upon completion of the statement the warden shall say the precise words: "We are ready."

Step ten: At this moment, the designee(s) of the director of the prison system shall begin the flow of a neutral solution, and, subsequently, introduce by syringe thiopental sodium necessary to cause death. Individual(s) producing death shall be visually separated from the execution chamber by a wall and, locked door and also shall not be identified. A physician shall pronounce the inmate dead, but shall have no other function.

Peanuts! Popcorn! Hot dogs!

Get your program! Get your program! . . .

"The Death Penalty is Not Equally Applied,"
November 25, 1979

I detest crimes of violence and people who commit them. So why am I against killing an accused at Huntsville? Mostly, I suppose, for the following three reasons:

First, I agree with Justice William O. Douglas, who ruled against the death penalty not so much because it is "cruel" but because it is not equally applied. . . .

Douglas went on to quote the late Warden Lewis E. Lawes of Sing Sing, who once was for capital punishment but changed his mind after witnessing more executions than any man in modern times. This is what Warden Lawes had to say: "Not only does capital punishment fail in its justification, but no punishment could be invented with so many inherent defects. It is an unequal punishment in the way it is applied to the rich and the poor. The defendant of wealth and position never goes to the electric chair or to the gallows. . . ."

Second, I agree with Clarence Darrow, who said in debate: "We are told, 'Oh, the killer does it: Why shouldn't the state?' I would hate to live in a state that I didn't think was better than a murderer. . . . The thing that keeps one from killing is the emotion they have against it; and the greater the sanctity the state pays to life, the greater feeling of sanctity the individual has for life."

Third, I believe in the doctrine of earned redemption to be passed upon by a no-nonsense parole board. That's not a successful argument, I suppose, because it has a religious basis to it. Religious arguments are more effective for the rich than for the poor, but they ought to be made anyway.

The Quakers say there is something of God in every person, even the most evil. Do we kill that spiritual dimension, too, by state execution when there is time for other solutions, including the possibility of redemption? Tell me, is God on death row?

I feel a personal anguish in writing this column because I do so detest people who kill other people. A round of cheers for a district attorney who takes a killer off the streets. But why do we ordinarily execute only the minorities: the blacks, the browns, the poor whites?

In the final analysis, I guess old Clarence Darrow rang the bell for me. Let me quote him again: "The greater the sanctity the state pays to life, the greater the feeling of sanctity the individual has for life."

Good for you, Mr. Darrow. Good for you. ★

CONTRACEPTION AND ABORTION

"The Baby Bomb,"
March 29, 1981

The Roman Catholics who write for *National Catholic Reporter* cover a multitude of controversial subjects and in the process shake up their more conservative brothers and sisters with their truly astonishing publication. On the subject of birth control, for example, they especially know a secret: Pope John Paul II is a stick in the mud regarding artificial contraception.

The waters are lapping at the pope's feet. Consider these statistics supplied by the Population Institute of Washington, D.C.:

Item. Today, the earth can support its population of 4.6 billion only because much of that population lives in poverty. If every person on earth had the living standard of an average European, the earth's resources could support only half its present population.

Item. Every five days one million more people are added to the earth's population.

Item. Though the growth rates have slowed in the wealthy countries, there has been little change in the developing countries, where 90 percent of the world's population increase is projected for the next twenty years. . . .

Tick-tock! Indeed, in the few seconds it takes you to read this short paragraph, thousands of children will be born, constituting an invitation to global famine, wars, pollution, erosion, water shortage, and the death of the oceans. Why can't John Paul II hear the ticking of the biological clock?. . .

"Pope's Contraceptive Stance Suicidal,"
September 18, 1983

Liberal Catholic friends of mine ask me: "Why raise the point? No one in the United States pays any attention to the pope about birth control." Population studies at Princeton University show that 80 percent to 90 percent of young Catholic couples do indeed use artificial contraception, but the question still has to be raised once you get south of the Rio Grande. . . .

According to Professor John Noonan, Notre Dame Law School, in his book, *Contraception*, Harvard University Press, 1965, women virtually forever have sought the right of artificial contraception. Egyptian women two thousand years before Christ "used pulverized crocodile dung in fermented mucilage," the precise details of which I will spare you in this lovely family newspaper.

The Jews of ancient times were practitioners of birth control, as *Genesis* 38:8-10 and the books of the *Talmud* will confirm.

In the Greco-Roman era, Pliny the Elder suggested that a woman should wear an amulet with two worms in it placed around her neck before sunrise, a compromise solution that John Paul II would surely accept as modern thinking. In an aside, let me say the following as I do not want to put out bad medical advice in this column: Girls, the amulet won't work.

The argument is made that in centuries past people died at an early age and so there was no need for birth control. But today an anti-birth control attitude is global suicide, especially in Latin America. . . .

Some 127 nations in 1979 had to import grain to feed their people. Brazil's imports of food rose from 1,266,000 to 5,977,000 metric tons. In Mexico, 246 children are born every ten minutes. In the middle of all this, to give only one example, the world's fish catch declined 11 percent between 1970 and 1973. Why doesn't the pope wake up and smell the coffee?

Lester Brown of Worldwatch Institute insists that: "Human population growth is closely tied to earth's energy resources and has depended heavily on the earth's basic biological system–fisheries, forests, grasslands, and croplands," all of which are disappearing.

John Paul II in telling the American bishops "they must strongly reaffirm [the] church [stand] against contraception" has indulged in an appalling act of nonsense. We Americans will find that out as desperate and starving people by the thousands upon thousands begin to cross the Rio Grande in a way that will make everything in the past look like a trickle. . . .

"Abortion Must Have Sensible Limits,"
December 10, 1989

Since the *Roe v. Wade* decision in 1972, there recently was rendered the 1989 Missouri case of *Webster v. Reproductive Health Services*, which does not reverse *Roe v. Wade* but does seriously cripple it.

Webster says facilities and medical doctors paid for by the state can be denied a woman seeking an abortion no matter when a child is conceived.

In short, *Webster* virtually means that if you are a poor woman and cannot afford a doctor and a private hospital, you give birth to the child no matter what the circumstances are. Otherwise, you go to a back alley and have an abortion with a coat hanger. If you have money, *Webster* doesn't apply.

Justice [Harry] Blackmun, who wrote the majority opinion in *Roe v. Wade*, said in his dissent in the *Webster* opinion: "this court implicitly invites every state legislature to enact more and more restrictive abortion regulations. . . . I fear for the future. I fear for the liberty and equality of millions of women who have lived and come of age in the sixteen years since *Roe* was decided. I fear for the integrity and public esteem for this court. . . ."

Why is the fetus of a rich woman less sacrosanct than the fetus of a poor woman? Or asking the opposite question, how can a poor woman be denied an abortion while it is perfectly legal for a rich woman to have one?

Before Blackmun wrote his 1972 *Roe v. Wade* decision, he spent the entire summer in Rochester, Minnesota, at Mayo Brothers Clinic talking with doctors, nurses, and ethicists. Pretty much middle of the road in his politics, the Republican justice's opinion is neither all white nor all black. It is a common-sense, nonextremist opinion that, I suspect, infuriated the purists on both sides of the question. But the country has to move on, and Blackmun in that opinion was a well-meaning judge who loved the country and tried to hold it together over an impossible issue. . . .

I am put off by the antiabortion crowd who say life begins at conception. But I am also put off by the "emancipated woman" who claims absolute control over her body even to the extent of willy-nilly aborting an unborn child who can live outside her and ignoring the third trimester limits of *Roe v. Wade*. Why not have reasonable limits? Why not at that point give serious thought to adoption? Why don't more of the prochoice women say: "We believe in *Roe v. Wade* limits"?

U. S. Representative Barney Frank recently pointed out that he has been hit with a double whammy in life because he is a "nice Jewish boy who is gay." But he is also one of the most brave and civilized members of the U.S. House of Representatives. Of the extreme antiabortionists he claims they believe: "Life begins at conception and ends at birth." What irony!

What Frank means is that once the child is born many (not all) members of the extreme antiabortionists couldn't care less about the future of the child. They do not fight for day-care centers, better schools, racial justice, or virtually anything else. They are only one-issue people.

Of course, there are folks within the ranks of the antiabortionists who generally care about many issues, and I respect them to the extent I have moved from the liberal position to the middle of the road, which I deem to be the one taken by Justice Blackmun. . . . ★

MAVERICK WRITES ABOUT WAR AND PEACE

Maverick has long held conflicting views about war. He would like to become a Quaker or pacifist but cannot seem to abide by such a philosophy when applied to all wars.

He fought as a U. S. Marine in World War II, spending thirty-eight months in the South Pacific. He cheered when he first learned of the atomic bombing of Hiroshima and Nagasaki. He approved the bombing even more when a few months afterward he received word that one of his cousins, a prisoner of the Japanese for four years, had died of starvation only three days before the armistice with Japan. Later, however, Maverick changed his mind about America's use of atom bombs against Japan. He gave two main reasons. First, Japan was more than ready to accept unconditional surrender, thus making atomic bombing unnecessary. Second, destruction of Hiroshima and Nagasaki was a U. S. effort to intimidate Joseph Stalin and the Soviet Union—which led only to a nuclear arms race.

His thinking about war took another turn during the domestic turmoil created by U. S. involvement in Vietnam during the 1950s–1970s. Maverick came to know and as a lawyer to represent many conscientious objectors wishing to avoid serving in that war. As a result, he gradually assumed an antiwar stance. In the process he again applied his lawyer's skills to win another case that went to the U. S. Supreme Court, thereby helping to add another precedent in American constitutional history.

When asked what he recalled about the Vietnam episode and all the young men he represented in court, Maverick replied: "Vietnam was a revolutionary war affair. People were trying to throw off the yoke of the Europeans' dominating their country. World War II was simply Hitler trying to destroy the Jewish people and other peoples about the world. It wasn't a revolutionary war, and so, I guess that's the principal difference. When I first started representing

133

young conscientious objectors, I didn't do it for philosophical reasons of one war versus the other war. I did it because they couldn't get any lawyers at that time. I did it first because I said to myself those kids are entitled to a lawyer, but then after about two years of working with young people—young enough to be my children—that turned me around philosophically, and I then began to distinguish between a revolutionary war and a World War II. Those kids really educated me as much as I educated them."[1]

Maverick never accumulated any sizable income from defending conscientious objectors during the Vietnam War. Indeed, the effort reduced his checking account drastically. When asked about this, he said: "Well, I never have made a lot of money in the law, but I made less then than I ever did in my life, and at the end of my seven to eight years representing conscientious objectors one of my labor union clients [whose fees] I paid my rent with came to me, and they were working people—the kind of people who were killed in Vietnam—and he said we don't want a lawyer who represents 'yellow bellies.' I lost that account, and I think the first year after the Vietnam War I made $9,300. It didn't help me a great deal financially. I didn't do it for that purpose. The bad thing about it is that those kids had no money, and their fathers were all my age. They had been in World War II, and they wouldn't help their sons, quite frequently, because they thought the Vietnam War was another World War II. So the kids were paying me out of their own pockets, and, of course, that didn't amount to very much."[2]

When asked if it was worth it, Maverick answered: "Oh, sure, I have young friends now all over the United States of America, and it kept me alive and kept my interest up. A very interesting thing happened. After the Vietnam War was over, I called Mel Wolf, who was then the legal director of the American Civil Liberties Union. I began to complain about being broke and talked about three or four minutes to him. And he said: 'What the hell are you calling me for? Most lawyers can spend their lives representing corporations and writing deeds and writing mortgages, and, when the time comes to die, they then might suspect that they've never lived at all. And you've had an exciting life in the law, and you've had a lot of fun, and you've met many interesting people. So, what the hell are you really calling me for?' He got me to laughing, and so I don't recommend my type of life, but being a lawyer can be a hell of a bore. It is most of the time. But it never was a bore doing conscientious-objector work. It was tough, it was exciting, and I met a lot of young people."[3]

Maverick once represented as many as fifteen of those young conscientious objectors at one time, and one of them was Daniel E. Pitcher. His case led to the U. S. Supreme Court decision of *Pitcher v. Laird* in 1970, Maverick's most dramatic conscientious-objector case. In it he defended Pitcher, who had been refused a request for discharge from the U. S. Army because of his religious beliefs, which opposed U. S. involvement in the Vietnam conflict. Maverick got a stay from U. S. Supreme Court Justice Hugo Black just as the army was about to place Pitcher on an airplane for Vietnam. Soon after, the Fifth U. S. Circuit Court of Appeals decided the army could not deny Pitcher his discharge request if, in sincerity, he based his plea primarily on his religion. Maverick recalled: "I've always suspected that the army would have gotten this kid in Vietnam and would have sent him down a combat trail and then the Viet Cong would kill the boy for them. This is a harsh thing for me to say, and I can't prove it, but I suspected it, and it filled me with apprehension, for I felt that I wouldn't merely be losing a lawsuit; if I lost the case, the boy was really getting a death penalty."[4]

The *Pitcher* case helped Maverick when some conscientious objectors he represented talked of becoming violent if judges ruled against them. He recalled: "I was telling them to give the courts a chance. For about two years I was losing all my cases. The young people were telling me they were going to burn the military barracks down around the country. I said, 'Don't do it. Give the system a chance.' That's the great danger today. If you just have judges with high IQs and no hearts, there's a very good chance we'll go back to wild riots and 'burn, baby, burn.'"[5]

On a related topic Maverick has long argued: "The yuppie mentality runs me wild and almost puts me in the hospital when I think about it. The New Deal created an upper middle class in this society, and they get pretty selfish. They worship money. And they were the

135

same ones who let the poor and minorities go to war in Vietnam while they systematically avoided it. I'm one of the few liberals in America who supports the draft, provided it's 100 percent honest. If your number comes up, you go, or stand up and protest. We've become such a money-oriented society that when I see some person who loves justice more than money—whether it's a poor uneducated black or a Ph.D. who's the head of a college—it gives me strength. I need them. They help me out."[6]

Maverick has also been quick to acknowledge valuable help he received from Julia, his wife, during the troubling times he worked with young men objecting to being drafted and sent to Vietnam. He often tells that during "the Vietnam War when, as a lawyer, I was representing privates and corporals applying for conscientious-objector status at Fort Sam Houston, I was bringing home only about $600 a month. It was my wife's money that made the difference in keeping us going. She is simultaneously the most hot-tempered and funniest woman in the history of the world. About once a week she calls me things that would make a Marine Corps drill instructor blush. I am still in love with her. She has expanded my life. I will go to my grave a contented person if Julia most of all, then my two dogs, and my purple martins don't quit me."[7]

The Vietnam experience, the *Pitcher* case, and similar ones led Maverick to devote over fifty of his *Express-News* columns to the subjects of war and peace. As illustrated in the following, he wants readers to think about questions of how one should view the warrior, what could justify going to war, to what extent one should wage war, what could cause one to oppose war, and how wars might be avoided. ★

THE ALAMO

"Critics Can't Dim Alamo Symbolism,"
April 22, 1979

*"You d- - - gringos can have the Alamo. We Mexicans
want Kelly Field."*

Gus Garcia to Maury Maverick, Jr., Gunter Hotel, 1947,
when both had had too much to drink.

. . . . In the summer of 1960 I received a letter from . . . Jack
Fischer, then the editor of *Harper's* magazine, asking that [histori-
an and journalist] Walter Lord be shown around because he was
coming to Texas to do a book on the Alamo.

Fischer grew up on a farm across which, he claimed, the
boundary lines of Texas and Oklahoma ran. Successor to
Bernard De Voto in writing a historically famous column, "The
Easy Chair," Jack was a one-time working newspaper reporter.
[He was] an immensely decent editor who loved our country in
a way no yahoo could understand, [and] I was glad to accommodate him.

Walter Lord turned out to be a delight. Bright, friendly, and
the first to laugh at himself, he quickly won the approval of the
good sisters at the Alamo library. . . .

We left for Goliad on a fact-finding expedition. A hundred
and twenty some odd years earlier, Travis had asked [James]
Fannin to join him in San Antonio. What was the extent of com-
munication between the two? We discovered a thing or two about
that, but as an interesting sidelight we came upon a nugget of history, the original journal of Dr. Joseph H. Barnard, the surgeon
who was spared at the Goliad massacre.

In the journal there was this remedy by the doctor for cur-
ing colds: "Tincture of Cannabis India, three ounces; extract of
Calabria Livorice, half pound; salts of tartar, one-tenth pound;

warm water, one gallon." Lord would later write: "Under such ministrations it took a deep love of liberty indeed to march to the rescue of Texas."

When his book, *A Time to Stand*, Harper, 1961, was finally published, Walter raised some questions about the Alamo. Did Travis really draw the line? (There is no concrete proof that he did.) Did Travis wear the fancy uniform artists put him in? (No.) Did David Crockett surrender? ("It's just possible that he did.") How many Mexican casualties? ("Best estimate seems about six hundred killed and wounded.") What flag did the Texans fly? ("Probably the azure flag of the New Orleans Greys"). . . .

What's the truth generally about the Alamo? Were there any warts? Yes.

The battle was fought in direct violation of General Sam Houston's orders to abandon the place. Like a wildcat strike, it was a wildcat battle.

While the defenders spoke of liberty for themselves, they were perpetuating the institution of slavery. After the battle was over, the black slaves in the Alamo were spared by Santa Anna. One slave named John chose to fight alongside the Texans; he was put to death. History does not even do John the dignity of giving him a last name.

G. J. Sutton, the late black legislator, used to rawhide me about the Alamo and slavery. In between denouncing my ancestors, he would call John the dumbest black in history for fighting with the Anglo-Texans. Even if they had won, John would have remained a slave, Sutton said, glaring at me all the time. . . .

"Remember the 'Real' Alamo,"
December 29, 1985

My old pal, Gus Garcia, may his soul rest in peace, invited me to be the only Anglo lawyer in the United States to be a co-counsel on the U. S. Supreme Court case that declared unconstitutional the exclusion of Mexican-Americans from the right to serve on juries.

That was when Gus stood before the High Court and referred to Sam Houston as "that wetback from Tennessee" and made the judges laugh. . . .

Gus Garcia was wrong in contending that Mexican-Americans should have no interest in the Alamo. Anglo historians are entitled to an even harder rap on the knuckles for they, along with Gus, have ignored the "Tejanos" or Mexicans who died at the Alamo [and that included Gregorio Esparza]. . . .

The cat, therefore, is about to slip out of the bag about the "Tejanos"–the Texas-Mexicans at the Alamo who had strong ideas about liberty, completely distinct from the likes of the hated Santa Anna to the south and the encroaching Anglos from the north, one of whom was my great-grandfather, Sam Maverick, who was elected by the defenders of the Alamo to sign the Declaration of Independence of the Republic of Texas. (It was the luckiest election any Maverick ever won in San Antonio.)

[But all this] is not about the Tejano Alamo. That will come a bit later. Rather, this is mostly about the Alamo as seen by the Anglo and by Hollywood.

I'm also reviewing the excellent article, "Remembering the Alamo: The Story of the Texas Revolution in Popular Culture," by Don Graham, professor of English, University of Texas at Austin. You can find it in the July 1985, issue of the *Southwestern Historical Quarterly.* . . .

The late Frank Norris, the radical right-wing Baptist preacher who hated Baylor University, the Catholic Church, blacks, Mexican-Americans, and especially Al Smith, wrote: "And the Alamo! There is a trumpet-call in the word: And only the look of it on the printed page is a flash of fire." But Anglos, forgetting the Tejanos, have used the Alamo as a racist symbol.

John Wayne's movie, *The Alamo* (1960), had a then-record

$11 million budget, but the script had some of the worst mistakes in the history of Hollywood. The actors referred to the Rio Bravo (an old name for the lower part of the Rio Grande) as the river running near the Alamo. In one scene Colonel Travis explains to his fellow defenders that the Alamo is north of the Sabine, which is strange because the Sabine is the boundary between Texas and Louisiana. In another scene, Fannin is said to be marching south to San Antonio from Goliad. Every time I have ever gone to Goliad it has been the other way around. . . .

Professor Don Graham gives all Texans, Anglo and Mexican-American, some good advice with these words: "What the Alamo story needs more than anything else is the application of critical intelligence to its tradition, legends, and stock images. And that, of course, is what it has least often had. Confronted directly, the Alamo story seems to make the eyes glaze. The heroes take on the smooth patina of public statuary seen from a distance. In fiction or film such pageant-like figures are deadly. . . ."

There is a play about the Alamo by the late Ramsey Yelvington called *A Cloud of Witnesses.* In technique it draws from the Greek theater, the morality play of the Middle Ages, the Japanese, and from the ballad singer.

At the conclusion Satan suddenly appears in a puff of smoke, the fires of hell swirling about him. He mocks the dead defenders, who by then are standing at the front of the stage with the women of Gonzales humming their song of death in the background. A dialogue develops with the Devil. The Alamo defenders, Abamillo, Badillo, Espalier, Esparza, Fuentes, Guerrero, Losoya, and Nava, have their say along with the rest.

Then in one voice the slain Texans, Anglo and Mexican, speak their final words, "Only this we know: We died there, and from our dust the mammoth thing freedom received a forward thrust. The reverberations we continued are something to which man may respond or not respond, at pleasure."

Well, there is an excess of nonsense written about the Alamo. How can anyone write with total objectivity on such an explosive subject? Worse still, too often the Alamo is presented in a way that makes it a jingoistic insult to present-day Mexican-Americans. . . .

Now and then I walk through the Alamo grounds. It's a good place to think about our country, for courage is courage whether it is a Cleto Rodriguez in World War II or blacks dying out of proportion to their numbers in Vietnam. Or, yes, the blue-eyed ones, who, legend has it, first listened in the dark of the night to the battle of John McGregor's bagpipe versus the fiddle of former Congressman Davy Crockett and then died hard.

The Alamo is a controversial, even sore, subject in this city, but even its critics have taught me some things–black people like G. J. Sutton and hell-raising Mexican-American intellectuals like the late Gus Garcia. And there have been old Anglo friends and relatives, poems, books, plays, Walter Lord, and wonderful librarians who have all combined to give me an expanded view. What we see with our mind's eye is more important than [what we see] with the physical eye.

In that sense, warts and all, I care deeply about the old Alamo. ★

MEXICAN AMERICANS IN WORLD WAR I
"Brave Mexican-Americans in WWI,"
June 24, 1990

Brave Mexican-Americans. Thanks to Dr. Donald Everett, history professor of Trinity University, I have a copy of a story in the January 14, 1919, San Antonio *Express* with the headline: "Maverick Boys Returning from Battle-Torn France." They were

Lieutenant Maury Maverick, my father, and his brother, Lieutenant George Maverick, both wounded. Also, Robert, Lewis, and another George Maverick.

Perhaps you will forgive me this outburst of family pride after you read Lieutenant Maury Maverick's comments about the Mexican-American soldiers he saw in combat with him in the battles of St. Mihiel and the Argonne Forest, where Maury, Sr., won the Silver Star and Purple Heart when part of his shoulder was blown away. Said the lieutenant: "While I was waiting to be carried in (by the medics to the army hospital) a Mexican boy— he was just a boy—said he was from El Paso. He had both his legs blown off and was lying near me. He was smiling and joking and reached into his pocket for some tobacco and rolled a cigarette. I never saw anything that impressed me more. 'I'm sorry, boys,' he said, 'that I can't fight with you anymore, but you be sure and get the Kaiser.' He did a whole lot to uphold the morale of the boys, all right, and he was typical of what the Mexicans did in this war, for I saw a whole lot of them, and although little has been said of them, I never saw a braver bunch of men. . . ." ★

NAZI MURDERERS

"Nazis Murdered Millions of Non-Jews,"
May 17, 1981

I was repelled by the conglomeration of races, repelled by this whole mixture of Czechs, Poles, Hungarians, Ukrainians, Serbs, and . . . Jews. . . .

Adolph Hitler, *Mein Kampf*

The conclusions here are totally my own, although I must thank Paula Kaufman, a member of San Antonio's Temple Beth El, for providing me with a hefty part of the research on which this particular column is based. I found her a cheerful working person.

I had gone to the synagogue for background information after reading the July 15, 1979, story by Michael Getler of the *Washington Post* entitled, "The Man Who Stalks Nazis." It was about Simon Weisenthal, who spent nearly five years in a Nazi concentration camp at Mauthausen, Austria, and who is more famous for his capture of Adolph Eichmann.

Getler quoted Weisenthal at length, but the remarks attributed to him that especially caught my attention were these: "I am not dividing the victims. This was one of the biggest mistakes made on the side of Jews. Since 1948, I have fought with Jewish leaders not to talk about six million Jewish dead but rather eleven million civilians, including six million Jews. This is our fault that in world opinion we reduced the problem to one between Nazis and Jews. Because of this we lost many friends who suffered with us, whose families share common graves. After the war, there was a possibility to make a brotherhood of victims and survivors against dictatorship. But the survivors were sometimes misrepresented after the war by people sitting in safe countries during the war. . . ."

Who were the non-Jews—some say as many as nine million—murdered by the Nazis? Who gives a hoot in hell in our country? For the most part, American Jews have been just about the only ones in America who have cared enough at least to do research on gentile civilians killed by Hitler. Virtually no one else has done this research and least of all have American gentiles done anything about it from a standpoint of scholarly research. Isn't this rather astonishing?

For two years I went from library to library trying to find out the truth. Through U.S. Senator John Tower's office I enlisted the help of the Library of Congress, one of the greatest libraries in the world. The research it sent back to Tower wasn't worth a bucket of warm spit. How in the name of God could four to nine million non-Jewish helpless human beings be systematically put to death and we know so little?

I suspect our own Jim Crow notions have something to do with the lack of concern. Most of the dead were Eastern European Roman Catholics. Others were Marxists, labor leaders, iconoclasts, and gypsies. More specifically they evidently were:

-One million Polish civilians, including seven Roman Catholic priests killed not too long after Poland was invaded.

-Two million Soviet prisoners of war. All unarmed.

-One million Soviet citizens and Slavs.

-Two hundred thousand gypsies, mostly the ones used for medical experiments by German medical doctors who didn't bat an eye, plus retarded people.

-Several hundred Spaniards hiding out in France—men who had fought Franco.

-One hundred seventy disarmed British soldiers near Dunkerque, and later seventy unarmed Canadian soldiers near Caen, France.

-Thirty-two thousand German civilians killed for "political crimes" including communists, writers, labor leaders, teachers, pacifists, and homosexuals.

The other night, I went to a memorial service at Temple Beth El for the Holocaust Jewish dead. It was a heart-wrenching experience watching twelve Jewish survivors walk down the middle aisle to the strains of a violin.

But there was something missing that evening. The words of Simon Weisenthal came back to me.

Why separate the family of man when it comes to helpless human beings murdered by the Nazis? Christians had been invited to attend, but only a few Roman Catholics and a Lutheran preacher plus half a dozen other gentiles were there. Why not next time have a cross section of the community present and all victims of the Holocaust be remembered? We good Christians did the killing, and most of all we are the ones who need to be there.

One way to remember what went on at those camps where Jews and non-Jews were murdered is to buy the phonograph record, "Songs from the Depths of Hell," by Alexander Kullsiewicz, a Folkways album. A young clockmaker from Bilgoraj, Poland, was forced to watch as his wife was taken into a crematorium at Treblinka. Then he saw his three-year-old son's brains bashed out. The father, a musician, that night wrote a song about it and actually sang it in some kind of a strange hope it might bring his child back to life. This song and others were sung to Kullsiewicz, also a concentration camp inmate, who gathered them together and made them into the album. They are, indeed, songs from the depths of hell.

Can it happen again? Maybe . . . [if we forget the statement attributed after World War II to] pastor Martin Niemoller: "First the Nazis came for the communists; and I didn't speak up because I was not a communist. Then they came for the Jews, and I didn't speak up because I wasn't a Jew. When they came for the trade unionists I didn't speak up because I wasn't a trade unionist. And when they came for the Catholics I didn't speak up because I was a Protestant. Then they came for me . . . and by that time there was no one left to speak up for me." ★

JEANNETTE RANKIN: ANTIWAR CRUSADER
"Jeannette Rankin Celebrated for Courage
of Convictions"
June 4, 1989

It was December 8, 1941, the day after Pearl Harbor, in the [U.S.] House of Representatives. John McCormack of Boston, trembling as he did it, moved to suspend the rules so that the resolution calling for a declaration of war could be taken up against Japan.

Speaker Sam Rayburn ordered that the clerk read the resolution, which stated in part: "Resolved, that the state of war between the United States and the imperial government of Japan . . . is hereby formally declared."

Rayburn then laid the resolution out for a vote. The moment he did, U. S. Representative Jeannette Rankin [of Montana] rose and said, "Mr. Speaker, I object."

There was a silence in the House that went to the bone. Rayburn, his face crimson red, cried out: "You're out of order." Old Sam rolled the resolution over Rankin like a freight train, but time after time she rose to address the chair, saying, "Mr. Speaker, I would like to be heard."

Hisses from the gallery. Members of the house began to shout, "Sit down, sister." But "sister" wouldn't sit down, and when her fellow legislators whispered to her: "They really did bomb Pearl Harbor," she replied, "Killing more people won't help matters."

Then when the speaker called her name in alphabetical order, Rankin rose and said: "As a woman I can't go to war, and I refuse to send anyone else." By then the gallery was booing her.

When she left the floor of the House [after being the only representative to vote against the resolution of war against Japan], the crowd was so hostile she had to take refuge in a telephone booth until the Capitol police escorted her back to her office, where she was forced to lock the door from the public.

The press universally came down on the lady from Montana like a ton of bricks; but one old newspaper editor, one of the most decent in the country, William Allen White, saluted her courage although disagreeing with her vote.

Here is part of White's editorial: "Probably one hundred men in Congress would have liked to do what she did. Not one of them had the courage to do it. The *Gazette* [White's newspaper] entirely disagrees with the wisdom of her position. But Lord it was a brave thing. . . . When in one hundred years from now, courage, sheer courage based on moral indignation, is celebrated in this country, the name of Jeannette Rankin, who stood firm in folly for her faith, will be written in monumental bronze not for what she did, but for the way she did it."

A year later, on December 8, 1942, the anniversary date, in a farewell speech to the house, she said that although the United States would probably win the war, it would not win the peace. This prediction was confirmed, Rankin said some years later, by the Korean and Vietnam wars. Further, she predicted that revolution was coming to Asia, that the white man in general and the English in particular had to cease colonial domination.

The first and all-consuming political fight in Rankin's life was her effort to make it so that women would have the right to vote. In 1910, she was the first woman to address the Montana legislature. Her subject was women's suffrage.

In 1917 Rankin went to the U. S. House of Representatives as the first woman in the history of our country to do so. Christopher Morley, a famous writer of the time, wrote the following poem making fun of her and the idea of a woman in Congress:

> *Her maiden speeches will be known*
> *For charm and grace of manner*
> *But who on earth will chaperone*
> *The member from Montana?*

In 1918, while on the floor of the House fighting for the right of women to vote, she said: "They have stood back of men. . . . The women have done all that they were allowed to do, all that the men have planned for them to do. . . ."

147

On another occasion she declared on the floor of the House: "The boys at the front [in World War I] know something of democracy for which they are fighting. Those courageous lads, paying with their lives, testified to the sincerity of their fight when they sent home their ballots in the New York election and voted two-to-one in favor of woman suffrage at home."

Rankin was particularly offended by southern congressmen who led the fight against women voting for fear that might give blacks the idea that they also should have the right to vote.

When she was about to take her stand against World War I, the speaker, Uncle Joe Cannon, gave her a "listen, woman" lecture, but when the clerk called her name she rose to her feet and said: "I want to stand by my country, but I cannot vote for war. I vote no."

World War I was not as popular as World War II, and so on that day of voting there was a flurry of applause for her in the gallery.

But then the Montana papers went after her. The *Helena Independent* said that she was "a dagger in the hands of the German propagandists, a dupe of the Kaiser, a member of the Hun army in the United States, and a crying schoolgirl."

The preachers of Montana thundered that she was a disgrace to womanhood and that her behavior proved how inadequate women were for the demands of political office.

Jeannette Rankin died in her sleep a few weeks short of her ninety-third birthday at Carmel, California. At the very last of her life, still fighting for justice, she was working on a project with Ralph Nader.

In 1941, when her patriotism was attacked, she placed her "creed" in the *Congressional Record*. Watch. "I believe in national defense against racial antagonisms. . . . I believe in national defense against the persecutions of minorities. . . . I believe in national defense against state coercion of the individual's conscience. I believe in national defense against those who use patriotism as a cloak in order to reap profits. I believe in national defense against an economic system which lacks sufficient opportunity for the young. I believe in national defense against demagogues. . . . I believe in national defense against the futile faith that a strong army and navy is all that is needed to preserve and perpetuate freedom. I believe in a national defense against any 'ism' harmful to human personality which, under God, is sacred. . . ."

Because of my wife, Julia, and because of the women journalists I have come to know at the *Express-News* (my two immediate bosses are women young enough to be my children), I have become, more than ever, an ardent backer of the rights of women in all walks of life. They are treated unfairly and it is a disgrace.

I would urge the women of South Texas who believe in equal rights for women to dust off the name of Jeanette Rankin and to place her in their pantheon of heroes. ★

JAPANESE-TEXANS

"Memory and Mending Fences,"
December 1, 1985

Eighteen thousand individual decorations for valor including one Congressional Medal of Honor, fifty-two Distinguished Service Crosses, one Distinguished Service medal, 560 Silver Stars and twenty-eight Oak Leaf Clusters, twenty-two Legions of Merit, fifteen Soldiers' Medals, four thousand Bronze Stars and twelve hundred Oak Leaf Clusters, twelve French Croix Guerre, two Italian Medals of Valor, 9,500 Purple Hearts and Oak Leaf Clusters. As a unit: forty-three Division Commendations, two Meritorious Service Unit

Plaques, and seven Presidential Distinguished Unit Citations.

Awards of the men and of the 442nd (Japanese-American) Combat Team,
the most highly decorated military unit of its size of all U.S. combat outfits
in World War II; from the book *Nisei: The Quiet Americans*,
Morrow, 1969, by Bill Hosokawa.

*The truth was that not one living person of Japanese
ancestry living in the United States or Territories of Alaska and
Hawaii was ever charged with, or convicted of, espionage or
sabotage.*

From the booklet, *The Japanese-American Incarceration*,
published by the Japanese American Citizen League.

"Japanese Camps were America's Worst Move," October 24, 1982

Have you ever driven down a highway with a fellow native-born American who was in an American concentration camp? Well, I did a few days ago with [Japanese-American] Alan Y. Taniguchi, former dean of the School of Architecture, University of Texas, and . . . a highly regarded Austin architect in private practice. We were on our way to Crystal City, where Alan's father, Isamu, mother, Sadayo, and brother, Izumi, had been interned [during World War II]. Alan, an adult at the time and separated from his family, was in an Arizona camp. "The first one in our family to be picked up," Alan began telling me, "was my father in January of 1942. I was studying architecture at the University of California at Berkeley when I got a call to come home immediately. We had a farm near Brentwood in northern California. My mother had set the table for lunch in the Japanese style with chopsticks. A sheriff, his deputy, and an FBI agent were there. The deputy said he had come to America from Ireland when he was six, but upon observing the chopsticks remarked, 'You people never will be Americans.' I said back to him, 'Do you still eat Irish potatoes?' He pulled a pistol from his belt and pointed it at me. The FBI agent knocked the pistol out of the deputy's hand and told him to be courteous. To this day I appreciate the decency of that FBI agent. Then they carried my father away, and I was not to see him for around three years."

In the back of our car as we drove to Crystal City was a model of the monument that Taniguchi has designed and that is going to be located over the foundation of one of the homes where the Japanese were interned.

"Alan," I asked him, "are you still bitter?"

There was a pause. "I don't know. My wife, Leslie, says I am because I won't stop talking about the concentration camps. . . . Suppose we went to war with Mexico. What would happen to Mexican-Americans in San Antonio?" Taniguchi asked.

"Well," I answered, "San Antonio has a huge Mexican-American population."

Once we made it to Crystal City, we were met by various local officials and citizens who could not have been more courteous at the official ceremony when the model was presented. One speaker said the concentration camp site was a place of sorrow not only for the Taniguchis but for others as well. Before the Japanese were there, it had been a temporary home during the New Deal for migratory workers. They rested there before following the crops north under sorry conditions.

After the Japanese left, it became a segregated Jim Crow school for Mexican-Americans.

On the way back to San Antonio, Taniguchi handed me the book, *Years of Infamy*, Morrow, 1976, written by his cousin, Michi Weglyn. He asked me to read the introduction by James Michener. Husband to a woman of Japanese descent, Michener wrote: "[W]hen Tom Clark resigned from the Supreme Court in 1966 he did purge his conscience, confessing that while attorney general of the United States he shared the national guilt regarding the Japanese-American internments. 'I have made a lot of mistakes in my life. . . . One is my part in the evacuation of the

Japanese from California. . . . Although I argued the case, I am amazed the Supreme Court ever approved it.'"

But Michener had more to write. "And the stoic heroism with which the impounded Japanese-Americans behaved after their lives had been torn asunder and their property stolen from them must always remain a miracle of American history. The majesty of character they displayed then and the freedom from malice they exhibit now should make us all humble."

"Maury," Taniguchi suddenly asked me as we got near San Antonio, "do you know how I got the first name of Alan?"

"No."

"My first name at birth was Yamamoto. Well, it was decided I wasn't a security risk and that I could get out of the camp while the war was still going on. At that time the Japanese battleship Yamamoto was prowling the seas, and so my buddies in the camp said: 'You need a new first name.' That's how I got the name Alan."

Alan Yamamoto Taniguchi is an easy fellow to be around, laughing at himself, smiling often, and full of hope for a better America. He could not, as an aside, be more proud of his father who designed the incredibly beautiful Zilker Gardens in Austin, just beyond Barton Springs.

My friendship with this Japanese-American has forced me to study and understand for the first time some unhappy history: the real drive against people of Japanese descent in our civilian government at the time came from liberals–liberals who ran out on their principles. The single most important legislative voice supporting procedural due process for the "Japs" came from a staunch Republican conservative: U.S. Senator Robert Taft.

But everything has to come to an end. By then Taniguchi had driven me to my home. "Thank you for going with me to Crystal City. Don't ever forget those concentration camps," he said. We waved good-bye, and I watched him drive away, a good fellow, and a fine American. . . .

"Memory and Mending Fences,"
December 1, 1985

[Later], Alan Taniguchi . . . was on the telephone asking me: "Will you give the dedication speech for the concentration camp marker at Crystal City?"

Of course, I would make the speech. After all, the much-respected Jingu family, who used to live at the Japanese Gardens of San Antonio, had taught me over half a century ago about the decency, patriotism, and hard-working qualities of Japanese-Americans. . . .

Grandpa Taniguchi, five feet two inches tall and weighing less than a hundred pounds, died in 1992, but he was everybody's pal in Austin. Not only that, he was the No. 1 hero of the Men's Garden Club with his Japanese vegetables, bonsai trees, and Japanese cherry trees, which he planted all over Austin after grafting Japanese cuttings to the roots of a wild Texas plum.

I enthusiastically point out that the words "concentration camp" are engraved on the historical marker at the site rather than some sweetie-pie euphemism like "evacuation center." A rose is a rose, and a concentration camp by any other name is still a concentration camp.

One person's hero is another person's villain. My hero, Franklin Roosevelt, is a villain to many Japanese-Americans because on February 19, 1942, he signed Executive Order 9066 resulting in the incarceration of the [U.S.] mainland Japanese.

Roosevelt did this at the urging of the professional military but against the advice of his then-attorney general, Francis Biddle, who considered it an immoral act.

Here's a good question: If the people of Japanese ancestry were so "disloyal," why were the Japanese on the Hawaiian Islands, in the very heart of U. S. military operations for the

Pacific, permitted to go free?

But one of my heroes is a hero to the Japanese-Americans: Eleanor Roosevelt. I asked Alan Taniguchi if he had any memory of her. "Oh, yes," he replied, "because she came to my concentration camp and walked among us without guards, inquiring as to our well-being. Eleanor Roosevelt is a saint to the people of Japanese ancestry. . . ."

The dedication ceremony would not have been a reality without the help of the people of Crystal City. Former County Judge Angel Gutierrez first proposed the concentration camp marker. Rudy Espinosa, the superintendent of schools, is the person who most consistently worked for the memorial. County Judge Ronald Carr has been a friend, as have various city officials.

Crystal City has had its own local racial tensions but as to the honoring of Japanese-Americans, all groups in that community joined together to do the kind and thoughtful thing. Maybe the marker will be a symbolic flower working its way past economic despair and occasional racial bitterness. A round of cheers for the good folks down there!

There was a table in front of the marker we dedicated, on which was placed a plate of biscuits. After the ceremony was over, the people of Japanese ancestry walked among those present, inviting one and all to break the bread as a symbol of brotherhood and sisterhood. It could not have been a more touching moment.

But the more dignified those Japanese-Americans were at the ceremony, the more I thought about how we Caucasians had done them.

Even the "New Deal" U.S. Supreme Court ran out on the people of Japanese ancestry. In *Hirabayasi v. U.S.*, the court decided that one group of citizens could be singled out, expelled from their homes and imprisoned for years without a trial, again based solely on race. Justice Robert Jackson stated in a dissent: "The Court for all time has violated the principle of racial discrimination in criminal procedure."

Justices Hugo Black and William O. Douglas were among those who ran out on the Constitution, but Black's words about a black who had been beaten to a pulp by Alabama police officials might be appropriate here: "Mankind has had to fight its way past the cross, the stake, and the hangman's noose, and those who have suffered the most have been the helpless, the weak, and the unpopular."

Standing there the other day at Crystal City, as a cold wind blew against the concentration camp marker, and observing the people of Japanese ancestry (the "quiet Americans"), it was obvious that all of us assembled that morning had walked spiritually, in microcosm, past the cross, the stake and the hangman's noose. . . .

"Japanese Camps Were America's Worst Move,"
October 24, 1982

Epilogue. The Nazi war criminals at Nuremberg "justified" their concentration camps by pointing out that the United States had established concentration camps for Japanese-Americans. These Nazi war criminals actually invoked U.S. Supreme Court decisions, the worst decision by the great liberal Hugo Black, legalizing the camps in obvious disregard of the Bill of Rights and thus bringing to mind Adolph Hitler's remark: "Those who now oppose our methods will ultimately adopt them."

Such Supreme Court decisions sit there like time bombs waiting to be used again, if there is a next time. Who will it be then? You? Me? What say you, gentle reader? ★

CHESTER NIMITZ COUNTRY

"Think Kind Thoughts for Our War Heroes,"
September 5, 1982

Late at night when the moon is high above the Golden
Gate Cemetery near San Francisco, reflections flicker on the
tombstone of an old towheaded boy from Texas: Chester Nimitz.
Next to Nimitz is Admiral Raymond Spruance, and next to him
is Admiral Kelly Turner. Their wives are with them. It is a cemetery arrangement laid out by Nimitz for sailors who fought the
good fight in life; now they are together in death.

In the wee hours, a cold fog rolls in from the Pacific as huge
ships growl their way through treacherous harbor waters to the
Orient while smaller craft go "hoot, hoot hoot." Buoys moan a
lament to seagoing men. It is an evening symphony that Nimitz
wanted to wash over his grave.

What memories those three graves have!

At the Battle of Midway, June 3-6, 1942, Spruance's force
sank four Japanese carriers. On August 7, 1942, Kelly Turner put
General Alexander Vandergrift's First Marine Division ashore on
the lower Solomons.

And Nimitz, what about him? During World War I he was
chief of staff to the commander of the submarine division,
Atlantic Fleet. In World War II, with subordinates Halsey,
Mitscher, Spruance, Kincaid and Turner, he moved up from
Guadalcanal and across the Pacific. Then on September 2, 1945,
aboard his flagship, the *Missouri*, the old man of the Pacific was
one of the few who took the surrender of Japan for our country.

Born February 24, 1885, in Fredericksburg, reared in
Kerrville where he attended Tivy High School, Nimitz was
appointed to Annapolis in 1901. That was a minor scandal in San
Antonio at the time, for the "Germans" were still suspected of
having opposed slavery and remaining loyal to the Union during

the Civil War. A Henke on his mother's side, Nimitz was a "German" coming and going.

How would you like to celebrate the memory of Chester Nimitz and have fun doing it? Well, I have a country drive for you to Fredericksburg's Nimitz Steamboat Hotel . . . where a U. S. Navy exhibit occupies three floors . . . one of the fine navy museums in the country.

Here comes the super surprise; walk outside and see the Peace Garden. But first a side story. Nimitz greatly admired Admiral Togo–not to be confused with General Tojo–who defeated czarist Russia in a magnificent naval battle in 1905. After World War II, Nimitz found Togo's flagship, the *Miska*, falling to pieces. As a kind of nation-to-nation healing gesture, Nimitz contributed his own money and called on the people of Japan to restore the ship. They did, and Nimitz became a hero to the Japanese.

As a result, a move started in Japan to contribute funds to the building of a Japanese garden, dedicated to peace, at the rear of the Nimitz Hotel. Some seven Japanese botanists and crafts-men came to Fredericksburg. For about six months you could hear a babble of four different languages–English, German, Spanish, and Japanese–as folks worked shoulder to shoulder to create the garden, today an absolute gem.

You make your way to the garden by walking along an outer wall that has dignified-looking plaques dedicated to those who gave their lives in the Pacific: "Aaron and Allen Roeder, twin brothers, of Stonewall, Texas"; "Seventeen graduates of U.S. Naval Academy of 1925, all killed in action"; "In memory of the officers and men of the USS *Houston* who went down with their ship"; "Sergeant William J. Bordelon, USMC, San Antonio, killed while assaulting machine gun position, Tarawa." Those plaques go straight to the heart; they are heavy medicine. . . .

As you leave the Peace Garden, follow a white line and do

the history walk past a Japanese Zero, a coast watcher's hut, the conning tower of the submarine USS *Pintado*, and other memorabilia of World War II. Do you have a memento to contribute to the history walk or the museum? . . .

[Go] home by taking U.S. Highway 87 to Comfort where you ought to take a look at the Union monument in front of the Lutheran church dedicated to the [thirty-four] pro-Union Texans murdered by the Texas Confederates at the Nueces [and Rio Grande] during the Civil War. The German names on that monument are good ones: Steves, Schriener, Stieler, Felsing, Rubsamin, and Pablo Diaz, among others.

Pablo Diaz? Yes, sir. Pablo, oh, Pablo, why did you end up a victim in that killing? What is your secret?

. . . The road back from Comfort to San Antonio is our old friend I-10. As you drive along, think some kind thoughts for Admiral Chester Nimitz, who hit some pretty good licks for the country. ★

LELAND "LOU" DIAMOND
"A Real Diamond in the Rough,"
December 4, 1988

The late Colonel Clyde Metcalf, USMC, in his 1939 book, *A History of the United States Marine Corps*, wrote: "The first recruiting of the Continental Marines appears to have been at Tun Tavern in Philadelphia, 1775. The proprietor of the tavern, Robert Mullan, was made captain of a company of marines. . . . The method of recruiting was largely by 'drumming up' in the technique of the Salvation Army. . . . The recruit was lured by promise of ample grog. . . ."

Brothers and sisters, come sit with me in a make-believe contemporary Tun Tavern with ample grog, of course, and I'll tell you a sea story about a [fifty-three-year-old marine and gunnery sergeant] named [Leland "Lou"] Diamond. The mere mention of Gunny Diamond is enough to make the eyes light up of any World War II leatherneck from private to four-star general.

Listen, pals, don't you know that marines tell each other that the Diamond named Lou put a mortar shell down the smokestack of a Japanese destroyer some fifty yards off Guadalcanal?

Would you believe me if I told you that during the worst of a shelling by the Japanese, Gunny Diamond ran up and down the lines crying out: "Steady as she goes, boys, it's only Eleanor Roosevelt coming in to trade with the natives"?

Be a good sport and do not press me for ironclad proof of everything I now tell you or I'll have Lou fire off a mortar round from up there with the ghost riders in the sky . . . where he went on September 20, 1951, from the Great Lakes Naval Training Center Hospital.

Aren't you supposed to lie a little bit about a grand old sergeant? Gimme a break!

In an old issue of *Leatherneck* magazine, Master Sergeant Steven Marcus wrote these thoughts about Diamond: "In twenty-six years of Marine Corps service he had become a legend–the unconquerable, indomitable master gunnery sergeant of the old school. Paunchy and goateed with a profound respect only for perfection, Lou Diamond stood as the epitome of the professional marine. . . . He was a top-notch NCO, a chain cigarette smoker and an extraordinary trainer of men. He was without equal at the beer garden table. Dungarees were practically his uniform of the day, and nothing he touched bordered on mediocrity. The first offensive American blow of World War II at Guadalcanal brought with it a host of correspondents, hungry for news. The fifty-three-year-old animated roar that hit the 'Canal on August 7, 1942, provided them with all they needed and more. Stories of World War I feats at Chateau-Thierry,

Belleau Wood, and the Meuse-Argonne provided vivid backgrounds for the stories of the 'fabulous marine' that began to filter into stateside papers and magazines. The Diamond experiences in the Sino-Japanese conflict splashed additional color on tales of the epic struggle in the lush jungles of Guadalcanal. His incredible voice and qualities of leadership, coupled with the hundreds of sea stories, made Lou Diamond an irresistible and inexhaustible source of news copy. The 'Lou Diamond legend' was firmly established for all time."

In 1949, Diamond's exploits were recounted on a radio show named "The Cavalcade of America" and then again a few years later on the television program, "The Marine Who Lived 200 Years." Actor Ward Bond played Diamond.

The television production opens in an aid station on Guadalcanal. Diamond is suffering three broken ribs, malaria and feet so swollen he can't put on his shoes. The Japanese are moving in on the marines.

To the aid station comes a Captain Collins, who asks Diamond: "We need a gunnery sergeant to direct a mortar mission on the Japs. Do you know one?"

"Captain," roars the old sergeant, "I was getting to like you and you were shaping up Okay. But I knew you when you were a lousy PFC. So don't start being cute with me. Is there a better gunny in the Fifth Regiment than Lou Diamond?"

Too crippled to walk, Diamond is hauled by ammo cart to the mortars, where he saves the day, but only after a dreadful mishap. A mortar shell does not fire.

Diamond turns the barrel upside down and then talks to the shell: "Come on . . . come on . . . don't play hard to get with old Lou." As the shell slides into his hands, Diamond defuses it.

Over his protest Diamond is then sent to a U. S. Navy hospital in New Zealand. A young woman nurse, a lieutenant, orders the gunny to shave off his goatee. He tells her: "Lady, most of the time I don't even talk to lieutenants."

(Paul Yoes, a retired chief pharmacist's mate from the U. S. Navy, was assigned to the marines and knew Diamond. Paul told me that Diamond had special permission to wear a goatee because his face had been burned in combat. Yoes also said that when he made "chief," Lou Diamond celebrated the occasion by urinating in the chief's new cap. Today Yoes is an officer in the court of [Texas State] District Judge Susan Reed.)

But back to the television movie.

Diamond, without orders, leaves the hospital in New Zealand, bumming rides to his outfit, the Fifth Marines, which he finds in Australia after first searching New Caledonia and Guadalcanal.

General A. A. Vandergrift gives Diamond a letter of commendation that reads: "Your matchless loyalty and love of the Marine Corps and all it stands for are known to hundreds of officers and men of this division and will serve as an inspiration to them on all the battlefields on which this division in the future will serve."

When Vandergrift passed out the medals, the orders were for the troops to wear the more formal "greens," but Lou Diamond, the only one to do so, showed up in his fatigues.

He told the general: "I won my medal in these fatigues and now I'm taking my medal in these fatigues."

On June 15, 1945, Diamond was transferred to Camp Lejeune, North Carolina, his last post. In November of the same year, "Old Lou" retired to Toledo, and in 1951 when he died he received full military honors.

You army, navy, air force and coast guard guys have kind thoughts for Gunny Diamond; for if you ever gaze on heaven's scenes, you just might find "Old Lou" waiting for you, guarding the streets just as the Marine Corps hymn says it will be.

Semper fidelis. . . . ★

ARMED FORCES NURSES

"Nurses Unsung Heroes of WWII,"
May 1, 1988

The idea for this column came to me from Father Bill Davis of St. Mary's Catholic Church, who called to say May 6 is National Nurses Appreciation Week and that more than one hundred flying nurses [of World War II's Army Air Force Evacuation Service] will gather at San Antonio's St. Anthony Inter-Continental Hotel to reminisce and celebrate a war heroes' reunion.

At the reunion will be some of the most decorated women of World War II. A few are from the first graduating class that sent twenty-five nurses to the South Pacific and twenty-five to North Africa. Throughout World War II flight nurses received the same air medals awarded to pilots, bombardiers, navigators, and gunners.

They landed, gathered the wounded and took off into dangerous skies amid ack-ack and enemy planes. They consoled the shell-shocked, cauterized wounds, and administered drugs to more than a million servicemen while in the air.

"Maury," said Father Bill, "I hope you will call my aunt Helena. She's Harold Tynan's wife and was the first American woman to set foot on Emirau of the Admiralty Islands in the Pacific, and before it was over with handled over 1,193 patients with over 298 hours flying in combat zones. She won't brag on herself, but I will. Helena has a suggestion for a story which involved another nurse and the country of Albania. It's a story that has never before been told to the press."

Helena Tynan, who was born on the island of Krk, Yugoslavia, would not talk about herself, but after talking about the heroism of other women, she particularly suggested I contact seventy-six-year-old Ann Maness, retired to San Antonio after twenty-five years as a nurse and twenty years as a medical librarian.

In the month of November 1943, Maness, with twelve other nurses, thirteen medical corpsmen, and the men flying their C-47, left Sicily for Bari, Italy, where they expected to care for wounded American soldiers from the fighting lines north of Naples.

As they began their flight it was a cloudy day that got worse by the minute. After a while the pilot saw a hole in the clouds and began to ease down through it, where they were met with German antiaircraft fire.

Then they flew south to where they landed on a lake bed with the C-47 tipping over on its nose. From the surrounding hills, men with rifles gathered around them announcing: "You are in Albania, and we are occupied by the Germans."

The men were friendly and even cheered because of the American markings on the airplane.

With that introduction, let's have Maness tell her own story. Listen.

"We were taken to the city of Berat and were hidden in various homes. The next morning twenty-seven of our group went off to meet an American OSS officer whose name was Smith. Three of us, of which I was one, remained hidden in a home in Berat.

"The Albanians told us to keep wearing our uniforms, to act natural, and that if the Germans found us to immediately admit to being American nurses. In two days we saw Germans out of the windows.

"Some Hungarian soldiers, forced to fight for Germany, did find us. When they found out that we were nurses and Americans they shook our hands, and upon leaving told the Albanian hiding us: 'Take care of the girls.'

"Around April 18 we were told to make dresses so that we would look like Albanian women. Our hostess taught us how to make them in the style of an Albanian dress. When not making dresses, we played three-handed bridge.

"Then one night after we had been in the home some four months we three nurses began driving with two Albanian men who told us we would come to a German roadblock. When we got there we were to keep our eyes lowered in the manner of Albanian women. I was sitting in the front seat when we reached the roadblock. The German soldier walked around the car, and all the time we kept our eyes to the floor. They let us pass.

"That night we camped in hills that looked a little bit like the Texas Hill Country, and in the morning were met by the OSS officer Smith, the same man who had earlier met with the rest of our group.

"We got plenty of help from the British, who seemed to be well liked. The Albanians who helped us wore red caps and were called 'partisans.' The talk was that they were backed by the Russians. Even an Albanian administrator who was working for the Germans helped us. The OSS man was paying money, but they all took risks that money would not alone buy.

"Late one night we were put on a boat on the southern coast of Albania and were ordered below deck. It was a rough ride in the Adriatic Sea, and all night long there was the risk of the Germans finding us.

"The next morning we put into a southern harbor of Italy called Brindisi. If you look at a map of Italy, Brindisi is precisely at the top of the heel. It was under Allied control and from there we were taken to Bari, Italy.

"The army gave us orders to keep our mouths shut, I suppose because of the OSS. To this day I have never talked with the press, but at long last, though, I would like to let the people know some of the things women went through for our country. I am simply telling you history.

"From Bari we went to Sicily, and from there I returned to the United States, landing in Dallas on April 14. After some leave in the little country town I grew up in near Paris, Texas, I became an instructor at the School of Air Evacuation, which was then located at Randolph Air Force Base.

"I cannot tell you how thrilled I am to know that in a few days I will be meeting with nurses who served in the Pacific, Europe and North Africa. Many of those women had hours and hours of flying under combat conditions. And I am told that the OSS officer who led us out of Albania will be at the reunion."

. . . I hope this old military town will open its heart to the visiting nurses who will be here from all over America. Not only are they patriots, but they have been in the vanguard of demonstrating that women, if given equal opportunity in employment and in the professions, are capable of the best. ★

RACHMONES

"Jerusalem as 'Corpus Seperatum'?"
October 17, 1993

> *[There is]* one emotion that has been crucial to Jewish ethics *and communal life for centuries. I mean the feeling that in Hebrew is called* rachmones, *meaning pity, mercy, sympathy, empathy, compassion for people who are worse off than oneself.*
> Marshall Berman, *The Nation*,
> September 21, 1985.

I [once] quoted a source estimating that the Israelis had killed some twenty-five thousand civilians with the invasion of Lebanon. [Then] on February 19, 1989, I wrote to the embassy of Israel asking for confirmation or denial of the statistics I had found. The following is part of that letter: "I am writing a newspaper column on the 1982 Israeli invasion of Lebanon. From the *Journal of Palestinian Studies*, Vol. XIII, No. 2, Winter 1984, Mark Garfield writes: 'The 1982 invasion of Lebanon resulted in the deaths of nineteen thousand Lebanese, Palestinians and Syrians. Possibly as many as thirty-five hundred Lebanese were slaughtered in the Israeli-sponsored Sabre-Shatila massacre, thirty thousand were wounded in the war; thousands are still listed as missing. The vast majority of the victims have been Lebanese and Palestinian civilians.'"

Then I posed directly to the Israelis: "Do you question the above statistics? If your answer is yes, tell me specifically how they are wrong, and what instead do you say are the true statistics? . . ."

One source that Mark Garfield . . . relied on was [an article in] the Spring 1983 issue of a magazine called *Race and Class*. . . . The article is titled "The 1982 Invasion of Lebanon: The Casualties."

There reference is made to *An Nahar*, described as "an independent Beirut newspaper." *An Nahar* estimates that "19,085 were killed, most of whom were civilians, and that 30,302 were wounded." According to *Race and Class* these are "conservative figures." [Yasser] Arafat [head of the Palestinian Liberation Organization] is quoted as claiming forty thousand Palestinians and Lebanese civilians killed, fifty-three hundred fighters killed and wounded, and six thousand missing. . . .

The Palestinians want their independence; they are on a roll, and the world knows it. This is something not to ignore because World War III may hang in the balance.

Indeed, if World War III does come about because of Israel's treatment of the Palestinians, the reaction against Jews from one end of the earth to the other could be savagery. "The time to stop a revolution is at the beginning, not the end," Adlai Stevenson said.

Justice is the hope for peace, not bombs. Justice is the hope for independence of Palestine and for the survival of Israel.

In December 1988, Professor Walid Khalidi of Harvard gave the annual distinguished lecture in Arab studies at Georgetown University. That address can be found in the book, *At a Critical Juncture,* published by Georgetown University Press. Here's a paragraph from that lecture:

> Twenty-six "injuries and usurpations" were listed in the American Declaration of Independence to justify the revolution against the king of England. Here are twenty-six not-incomparable Israeli 'injuries and usurpations' in the occupied territories that would be cited by Palestinians: seizing our land, stealing our water, deporting our citizens, maiming our mayors, smashing our bones, killing our teenagers, blowing up our houses, threatening our expulsion, closing our schools and universities, imposing armed settlers on us, giving them free rein arresting us in thousands, denying us election, detaining us without formal charges or trial, closing our newspapers, harassing and physically abusing our detainees, discriminating against us in court, imposing endless curfews, maligning our nation, restricting our travel, assassinating our leaders, curtailing trade, refusing us political organizations, opposing the return of our compatriots, claiming our patrimony and threatening our holy places. . . .

"Palestinians Are New Jews,"
April 16, 1989

We can do more. Americans can emulate "The Women in Black" of Israel who regularly picket the Likud. They are brave Jewish women who stand up to the reactionary crowd that now runs Israel. . . .

I was told by a reliable Washington, D.C., source that "The

Women in Black" organization is now being formed in the United States and will include both gentile and Jewish American women. . . .

Let these American women, as John LeCarre urged in *The Little Drummer Girl*, Hodder and Stouston, 1983, be an example for the rest of us to have "the simple courage to tell out loud the cruelest joke in history: that the thirty years of Israel have turned the Palestinians into the new Jews of the earth. . . ."

"Columnist's Israeli Information
Comes from Jewish Americans,"
February 21, 1988

All roads this morning lead to the Hebrew word *rachmones*, a word of such exquisite meaning that it is virtually impossible to translate into English with all the original nuances.

If I cannot escape my track record, good or bad, neither can Jews escape the word *rachmones* because their track record of pity, mercy, sympathy, compassion [for] people worse off than themselves is historically superior to those of us with a Christian heritage. That is a big reason why the contemporary situation in Israel is so painful.

One of the experiences I had in life that helped me to understand *rachmones* was when I was representing young medical doctor conscientious-objector applicants to the Vietnam War. A significantly high percentage of those doctors were Jewish.

When a lawyer prepares a person for a conscientious objector hearing, he must work his way past that person's heart, guts and, if we have such a thing, the soul. After turning those doctors inside and out, which involved much talking about Jewish history, some of it especially moving, the word *rachmones* takes on new dimensions.

When our "good Christian" businessmen ancestors brought chained black slaves to this country, there was not much compassion in that. Nor was there when Anglo-Texans, at the urging of [then-Republic of Texas President] Mirabeau Lamar and over the objection of Sam Houston, repeatedly broke treaty commitments with the Indians.

When America turned a ship of Jewish refugees away from Florida and sent the passengers back to Europe to face Hitler's ovens, there was no *rachmones* in that.

And so now, what about Israel and the Palestinians? In the beginning the idea to write about that subject did not come to me on my own. It did not come to me from Palestinians because I hardly knew who they were. . . .

The people who initially educated me on abuses against the Palestinians were Jewish—residents of San Antonio, across Texas, and in New York City, where I have extensive contacts in the areas of civil liberties and civil rights. That information, being fed to me by Jewish sources, continues to this very day.

After that beginning education, I came to know Muslims and Palestinians who write to me from all over the country. Before then, in the days of my ignorance, I would not have adequately understood Tony Clifton's book, *God Cried*, which swept like a brush fire over England. Here is some of what Clifton wrote, and now I do adequately understand it: "If I were a Palestinian I would have to be a Buddhist. I would not be able to put up with all that misery unless I thought the wheel was turning and that in the next incarnation I would be better off. . . . The Palestinians are frequently compared with the Jews. . . . The Palestinians now, like the Jews once were, are a people without a country."

Here are two reasons why I will continue to write about Israel and the Palestinians.

First. Perhaps this is a bit selfish (patriotic?), but the first reason concerns the survival of our country. In a world of well over 750 million Muslims, increasingly offended by our

169

American blank check to Israel, we face a rising Islamic hostility, even hatred.

Those Muslims, particularly the ones in the Middle East, are like chickens coming home to roost. (Ask the 220 dead marines killed in Beirut about the fury of Islam.)

Second. The other reason centers around *rachmones.* There is no escape from that word. Always and always it will bubble up. . . .

"Jerusalem as 'Corpus Separatum'?"
October 17, 1993

[Now that Israel and the Palestinian Liberation Organization have agreed in principle to allow some Palestinian self-rule in the West Bank and Gaza Strip, why also] not strive for a Jerusalem equally fair to and controlled by Jews, Muslims, and Christians? . . . After all, Harry Truman, the best gentile friend Israel ever had, said Jerusalem should be a *corpus separatum* [a divided Jerusalem].

When Jordan took Jerusalem, it was . . . more oppressive to Jews than what presently exists. But having said that, would you as a Christian or Muslim enjoy going to your Jerusalem church or mosque "guarded" by Israeli soldiers with automatic rifles hanging from their shoulders?

Jerusalem is not a happy place. It cannot be a happy place as long as it is dominated by only one of the three great religions. There will never be peace until that question is resolved. All parties must be more courteous. . . .

[Israeli Prime Minister] Yitzhak Rabin and Yasser Arafat shook hands. It is time for the people in Jerusalem to shake hands and to treat each other in the spirit of the Hebrew word *rachmones.* . . . ★

VIETNAM AND THE WAILING WALL

"You Plan the Wars, We Will Point the Gun,"
July 19, 1981

There was no declaration of war by the Congress at any time during the Vietnam War.

Even presidents of the United States ought to follow the law. For example, the Constitution places the power to declare war solely in the hands of the Congress. The highest and most precious document of our land makes it crystal clear the president does not have the power or moral right to make war without a formal declaration by the Congress.

When John Kennedy, backed by the "beautiful people" of Camelot, sent troops to Vietnam and engaged in a sustained war without a formal congressional declaration, he violated the law. So did Lyndon Johnson when he expanded the war in Vietnam, and so did Richard Nixon when he invaded Cambodia.

Time after time the defense of "no declaration of war" was raised by defendant after defendant in draft cases, but every U. S. district judge in the country faced with such a defense ran like a cottontail rabbit. Surely a U. S. district judge knows how to read and write. . . . Is there anything vague about the words: "The Congress shall have the power . . . to declare war"? After ten thousand American combat men are killed? After thirty thousand? After fifty thousand?

Appellate courts all over the country were likewise asked to rule on the question. The result? Not a single one of those courts did the brave thing. Why didn't the intermediate appellate judges have the judicial spine to follow language plain enough to be understood by a little girl in the fifth grade?

The U. S. Supreme Court then turned its back to the law. How do we know this is so about the High Court? Well, William

171

O. Douglas in his last book, *The Court Years 1939-1975*, Random House, 1980, let the cat out of the bag. Consider what he wrote:

> There were many challenges during the Vietnam War. At least cases were filed with the court, in no one of which the court granted *certiorari* (right of review). I noted my dissent in each case. . . . Article I, Section 8 of the constitution says: "The Congress shall have the power . . . to declare war." The presidential war that we experienced in Vietnam has no sanction in the constitution. There had been no declaration of war on Korea . . . when Truman seized the steel mills during labor trouble to keep production under way. As we have seen, the Court in a 6-3 decision held the seizure unconstitutional because Congress had not acted by declaring war. If it is "justifiable" when the executive seizes property, why not when he seizes persons and forces them to go overseas to fight an undeclared "war"? Life and liberty are supposed to be as important as property under our constitutional system. . . .

"America's Wailing Wall,"
March 25, 1984

Paul B. Blunt, Jr.
Born: Oct. 3, 1946
Died: Jan 3, 1970
Panel 15W, Line 124

Vietnam Veterans War Memorial,
Washington, D. C.

. . . . we mortals hear only the news, and know nothing at all.

Homer, the I*liad*.

Around 1940 Paul Blunt, Sr., and I were college roommates

at the University of Texas when he was courting his high school sweetheart, Ann Nibbi. Their son, Paul, Jr., born six years later, used to bounce on my knee.

While in Washington, D.C., recently, I visited the Vietnam Veterans War Memorial and ran my finger across Paul, Jr.'s name engraved on a panel of black granite. . . .

Even on the bitterly cold day I was there, some 150 people were standing along the wall while a Vietnam veteran in a wheelchair made his way past the fifty-eight thousand names of the American dead.

"There's Johnny's name," said one weeping grandmother standing next to me. No pretense of stoicism is evident as total strangers huddle together, touch hands, and comfort one another. . . .

[The two walls of the memorial have] seventy separate panels. The largest panel has 137 lines of names; the shortest has one line. The names of the first casualties (July 1959) appear in the first line of Panel 1 on the [left] all below the date "1959." The listing continues on panels to the right until the last casualties of 1975. It will take your breath away to walk those panels.

The Vietnam War, fought by soldiers without protection of a constitutional declaration of war, ran longer than any war in the history of our country—from July 8, 1959, when two "advisers" were killed, to May 15, 1975, when the last casualties were suffered in connection with the Mayaguez incident. Around 2.7 million Americans served in the war zone: three hundred thousand were wounded and approximately seventy-five thousand were permanently disabled. Hundreds more remain missing and unaccounted for.

Three presidents had their places in history destroyed or seriously tarnished: John Kennedy, egged on to fight by Harvard intellectuals whose own sons never heard a shot fired in anger; Lyndon Johnson, who equated Vietnam with a yahoo understanding of what happened at the Alamo; and Richard Nixon, who forgot everything the Quakers taught him. . . .

After I left Washington, I went to Boston, where the inequity of the Vietnam War hit me like a ton of bricks while standing in Harvard University's Memorial Chapel.

For World Wars I and II, when there were honest drafts, hundreds of Harvard men gave their lives. All are listed on the walls of the chapel. For the Vietnam War, only twenty-one Harvard names are listed. The Harvard swells didn't have to die because Mexican-Americans, blacks, poor whites, and Roman Catholics died for them. Ironically, this scandal of gargantuan dimensions was imposed upon our country more by Democrats than by Republicans.

I am told by old friends (and new enemies) that I have too frequently mentioned the dishonest draft of Vietnam days. "For God's sake, get on another subject," the advice goes. But the unfairness continues to this very moment by virtue of a "volunteer" military that is even more intellectually dishonest than the Vietnam draft.

The truth is that we Episcopalians, Presbyterians, Unitarians, and Jews, we residents of the more affluent Alamo Heights, Terrell Hills, and Olmos Park will send you brown, black, poor whites and less affluent "South Siders" of America off to die. . . .

The Vietnam Veterans War Memorial is America's Wailing Wall. ★

DRAFT THE "SWELLS"

"Objectors Face Hard Questions,"
June 3, 1979

Save [this] for your son or grandson if he is or will be of draft age. . . .

It was late in the month of June 1968, when the young soldier came to see me. "My name is Fred Slimp II," he said, and I remembered going to summer Y Camp on the Guadalupe River with his cousins around 1929.

He wanted out of the army as a conscientious objector and was willing to do alternative civilian service. A handsome nineteen-year-old, he looked like an escapee from a boys' choir, but as I was to find out, that baby face had more steel in it than all of the John Wayne movies about phony courage put together.

There was and is something unique about Slimp. Of the hundreds and hundreds of young people I talked to for the Quakers from one end of the Old South to the other, he was the only young person from the "upper classes" I ever came across who voluntarily gave up his student deferment at a time when he was making all As, a few Bs, and had another year to go at college.

He wrote his draft board: "I hereby renounce my present [student deferment] classification and ask that [my draft board] reclassify me [as a conscientious objector]. . . ." For such rare integrity, Slimp was immediately drafted. During all this, Reverend Buckner Fanning of San Antonio's Trinity Baptist Church stood by Slimp and gave him a supporting letter as to his sincerity. Slimp won his case.

Today Fred is a first-rate, highly regarded librarian on the West Coast and has sense enough to expertly run any library in the country. We never talked about politics. I don't know if he is Republican or Democratic, conservative or liberal, and I don't care.

A conscientious-objector applicant seeking alternative civilian service must answer questions presented in a slick way. One is: "Are you against all wars?" No picking and choosing is allowed.

"Surely you are for the war of the American Revolution when we became a country?" A "yes" answer to that and the applicant was out of business.

American Jews were repeatedly hit with questions about Israel. Catholics were asked: "Would you fight in a war where the Vatican was being defended?"

Kids from the South would get tricked by questions on the Civil War.

One medical doctor I knew was either dumb or cute. He said he would fight in a war where they only fought with bows and arrows. Because he wasn't against all wars, the court turned him down.

Another question asked was: "Will you serve the military in any capacity?"

The question had booby traps all over it, and a significant number of the military chaplains, the most command-dominated bunch I ever saw, laid the traps.

"Surely, son," the man of God asked, "you would work as a chaplain's assistant and do the Lord's bidding?" An affirmative answer instantly put the kid out of business with reference to doing alternative civilian service because the young man had admitted he would do one job in the military.

I know there were some fine military chaplains during the Vietnam War, even heroic ones, but for the most part I would rather have stuck my hand into a basket full of coral snakes than deal with a large percentage of the military preachers. Give me a rough, tough, straight-talking, mustang colonel any time of the day. But these sugar-coated chaplains? Look out, kids.

Among the enlisted men, I worked with more Roman Catholics than with any other group. They were among my favorites.

Funny, smart, half-mean, and irreverent, the mackerel-snappers knew they were getting called up out of proportion to their numbers while Episcopalians and Presbyterians remained home.

The Catholic chaplains were, for the most part, captives of their "he-man" image. If too many Protestant chaplains were oily-nice, and they were, too many of the Catholic chaplains thought they had to play Jimmy Cagney in that old, old movie when Cagney was the macho boy walking the last mile to the electric chair. . . .

During the Vietnam War the psychiatrists always fascinated me. As a general rule the regular military shrinks would tell soldiers they were crazy if they didn't approve of that insane war, but now and then a reserve military shrink would advise the colonels and generals that they were the ones who were nuts, not the kids.

I saw one little skinny psychiatrist backed up against the wall with what the army thought was one question the doctor couldn't answer.

"Wouldn't you at least be willing to treat soldiers with a drug problem?" he was asked. This was his reply: "I learned that there were forty thousand GI heroin addicts in Vietnam. I think of those addicts I have seen in withdrawal; they lie there, weeping like babies, shivering, their noses running. They come from places of desperation. I can only reason that drugs help our men from their own desperation and guilt from killing and destroying, from violating their own consciences, from desecrating life. And can I help them, when telling them the truth would only deepen their desperation?"

The all-volunteer army without the citizen-soldier lacks necessary elements of political morality. My psychiatrist friend, and hundreds of others like him, taught me that. Do we really want a volunteer army in place of a draft army?

"Draft Citizens of Every Class,"
June 10, 1979

[Yet, one] time a black sergeant taught me the lesson of my life at Fort Sam Houston. The sergeant was harassing white conscientious-objector applicants.

177

Of all the people to kick around, he was intimidating whites most likely to treat him like a decent human being in civilian life.

I complained to the sergeant about his being such a horse's behind and asked him: "Why don't you go back to civilian life where you came from?" He didn't hesitate with a reply, "I come from Mississippi, and if I go back there, I will have to pick cotton. You go to Mississippi, Mr. Maverick, and pick cotton."

What we have done to minorities is to give them more democracy in the least democratic of institutions, the military, and deny it to them more in civilian life. They become our hired guns, a status rooted in Jim Crow.

People of color, they go about the world killing other people of color while we upper-class whites stay at home and fight with brave words. . . .

I am for a draft that cuts across all classes. No volunteer army for me. No exceptions from the draft. No deals. No fix on the draft board if you are a swell. If you have an army like that, the middle and upper classes will not let their children be needlessly killed in a Vietnam. . . .

"Draft the Swells and There Won't Be a Way,"
February 17, 1980

I resent all those Ivy League intellectuals who egged on the Vietnam War. They had endless ideas on how to fight, but they never did any of the fighting themselves. I'd see them now and then when I'd go to Washington. Bright, witty, urbane, and not within five thousand miles of combat.

Do you remember how we went to war over Vietnam? The experts said we had to go to war. They used fancy slogans. Slogans make you quit thinking.

There is a story maybe more legend than fact, but who cares? It is a great story of how Lyndon Johnson came back from his first cabinet meeting. All the Kennedy experts had been there. Lyndon is supposed to have told House Speaker Sam Rayburn how smart they were. They had gone to Ivy League schools. "Well," Mr. Sam is supposed to have said, "that's mighty fine, Lyndon, but I wish one of those fellows had at least faced the people and run for sheriff."

There's something I don't trust about experts on war. They may know the best way to kill, but they don't understand the politics of war. . . .

So let's have a draft [if needed].

But no exemptions. Not for college, medical school, or seminary. No exemptions for women. No exemptions for minor medical reasons. The fine sons and daughters of suburbia will have an equal chance to die alongside blacks, browns and poor whites. Uncle Sam will be an equal opportunity employer.

And do you know what will happen? The swells will stop the war as they finally stopped the Vietnam War. Three cheers for the swells, but they have to be involved. They have to be threatened.

A low point for me during the Vietnam War was one day in front of the Alamo [when] I heard some wealthy, high society-oriented male students from Trinity University give patriotic addresses in support of the war while all the time they were holding onto their student deferments. Late that same afternoon I went to South Main Avenue outside the Selective Service headquarters. As usual the buses were filled with kids about to be taken away. I walked the length of the convoy: black and brown faces, white faces, but obviously poor white faces. Country boys. Plenty of Roman Catholics, but darn few Episcopalians, Presbyterians, Unitarians, or Jews. That ain't right, brothers and sisters. That ain't right. ★

QUAKERS, PEACE, AND WAR

"The Quakers Seek Preparedness for Peace,"
March 30, 1980

We should then, like the Quakers, live without an order of priests, moralize for ourselves, follow the oracle of conscience, and say nothing about what no man can understand, nor therefore believe.

Thomas Jefferson in a letter to John Adams, 1803.

The Quakers, the Society of Friends, small in numbers but big in moral clout, have established a meeting in San Antonio at restored St. Paul's Square in the middle of what was once a thriving red-light district.

Each Sunday at 10:30 a.m. they meet for thirty minutes of discussion, then for an hour of what could very well be sixty minutes of total silence.

There isn't a nicer bunch of people, and in this city where the chamber of commerce, newspapers, unions, and many churches cheer on federal appropriations for the making of war—and a better San Antonio economy?—it is good to have folks like the Quakers around who are so tenaciously devoted to the cause of peace. First and last they are extraordinarily polite people, which makes it all the more difficult to intimidate them. They shame you with good manners and good cheer.

If you mention Richard Nixon, a Quaker, to them, they roll their eyes into the back of their heads and begin to emit low moans. But other than that they seem to rise to any occasion.

Persecution is nothing new to the Quakers. Almost immediately after the first of their group began to arrive in colonial Massachusetts, they were flogged, imprisoned, branded, banished, and lynched as they were considered "scandalous in life," not being "orthodox Christians."

[Following the thinking of] George Fox in England, they stressed and continue to stress "inner light," separation of church and state, and opposition to oaths and all wars. When they refused to participate in the violence of the American Revolution, the hatred against the Quakers reached a white-hot frenzy.

Quakers opposed the slaughter of the Indians, helped set up the Underground Railroad for blacks escaping from the South around the time of the Civil War, opposed discrimination [against] Irish immigrants, went to prison for opposing World Wars I and II, and have consistently made "nuisances" out of themselves by objecting to such abuses as child labor and the incarceration of Japanese-Americans during World War II.

If they think the so-called liberal viewpoint is wrong, they will be quick to tell you about it.

I got a taste of this as a young man when, with Mexican-American labor leaders, we would make speeches against Mexicans coming to this country to work. I remember a Quaker asking me: "Do you think people south of the Rio Grande are any less human than people north of the Rio Grande? Don't you understand they get hungry and need work? Where is your sense of charity?"

My deep involvement with the Quakers started when I finally began to realize that the Vietnam War was an outrage. If I figured that out before some people, it was because the kids kicked me in the pants, and some of those kids were your children, gentle readers.

The Quakers sponsored what is known as the American Friends Service Committee (AFSC). It is not a formal part of the Society of Friends any more than the Knights of Columbus is the Roman Catholic Church. Quakers are quick to point this out; sometimes they are too quick to make the distinctions. Quakers without their AFSC would be like the Catholics without the renaissance provided within that church by [Pope] John XXIII.

The AFSC has projects virtually everywhere in the world and seems to be widely respected because of its absolute, never-relenting neutrality. In Northern Ireland, the "Quaker cars," which dart back and forth between the Protestants and the Catholics, are not bombed. Quaker types in Vietnam were tolerated by all sides. Whenever they help, they do not say "you must first accept my religion."

Overwhelmingly, the folks who work for the Quakers in AFSC do not belong to the Society of Friends. For example, my choice for the top authority in the country on conscientious-objector law during the Vietnam War was an AFSC worker named Mike Whittels, the grandson of a rabbi, who wasn't even a lawyer, but a sculptor who, while in prison as a war protestor, made himself into an expert on the law. Many churches contribute to the AFSC because that's where you find Baptists, Methodists, Catholics, Jews, and Episcopalians who, sensing a void in their own religions, turn to the Quaker [way] not as a formal religion but as a way to help mankind. Indeed, in the seven years I worked with AFSC I never once saw the Quakers try to religiously convert people. "Go back to your own churches and be better people," they seemed to say. . . .

[The Quakers'] hour of silence may make you want to run outside afterward and shake, rattle, and roll with the Baptists or run to the nearest swinging Roman Catholic mariachi mass, but it is stimulating, nevertheless, to sit with the Quakers, be quiet, and think about things. Dr. Homer Rainey, an ordained minister and former president of the University of Texas, used to say: "I can go anywhere in America and preach Christianity without the slightest bit of trouble until I use the word 'now.'" The Quakers say "now." ★

CHRISTMAS, WAR, AND PEACE

"No Santa Claus, No War Games for Kids,"
January 25, 1981

Or consider Christmas—could Satan in his most malignant mood have devised a worse combination of graft plus buncombe than the system whereby several hundred million people get a billion or so gifts for which they have no use, and some thousands of shop clerks die of exhaustion while selling them and every other child in the western world is made ill from overeating—all in the name of the lowly Jesus.

Upton Sinclair.

When I made the telephone call, it was the night before Christmas and all through the house not a person was stirring, not even Ronnie Dugger, publisher of the *Texas Observer* and one-time enfant terrible of Brackenridge High School in San Antonio.

"Merry Christmas, Ronnie," I said in a tone of joy for which I am deservedly known throughout all of Bexar County.

Silence. Then a stream of words hit me, the kind I dare not repeat in this column.

"What's the matter with you, Dugger?"

"Christmas is what's the matter with me. I can't play the game any longer. To hell with Christmas."

"Ronnie, that's no way for a former altar boy to talk."

"Maverick, do you like Christmas?"

"I hate Christmas."

"Then don't give me that ho, ho, ho stuff."

I had made the right call. If there is a bigger sorehead in town than I am about Christmas, it is Ronnie Dugger. Except for children, whom we corrupt with commercialism and teach nothing about the radicalism of Christ, we are all prisoners of

183

Christmas, a "religious" event that has turned into an exhausting, money-grubbing, privacy-invading outrage.

I'm glad I called Ronnie. I needed a soulmate. Gentle reader, are you my secret soulmate?

I can always tell when Christmas is upon us. There's a store that sets up on [San Antonio's] Houston Street a moth-eaten, electrical Santa Claus around the last day of October when the sweat is still running down your face from our dreadful Texas summers. Santa spastically jerks his body left and right; he sighs, burps, groans, and breaks wind. I won't go near that part of Houston Street until after the first of the year.

I can think of only two times in my adult life when Christmas made a favorable impact on me.

One was on the island of Guadalcanal, British Solomon Islands, after it had been secured by the United States during World War II. Almost every night a single Japanese airplane would fly over, drop a bomb, and go away. We called the pilot "Washer Machine Charlie."

On Christmas Eve we were out in the coconut trees watching the movie where Bing Crosby sings "White Christmas." Since then the song has became a commercial pain in the neck to me, but on that night it was the sweetest music I had ever heard. I guess we were all homesick.

Anyway, Bing began singing, and at the most moving moment who should show up but Washer Machine Charlie? On came the air raid warning; off we ran to our foxholes. At the sound of all clear we returned to the coconut trees and Bing finished his song.

The other time Christmas grabbed me in a moving kind of way was more than thirty years ago when D. B. Hardeman, my former legislator colleague, and I were riding around Mexico. I think it was the town of Matehuala, late at night around December 24, when we were mellow from Mexican brandy. A religious procession came by and headed for the local church. To my astonishment I saw that the Indians were carrying Indian gods in a position of equal importance with the Christian god.

D. B. and I, the only Anglos, got in among the Indians, who were polite to us. We paraded all over town and had a big time. The Mexicans are not as big a bunch of fools about Christmas as we Americans are; they keep it far less commercial. . . .

"Jesus' Ministry Was to the Poor,"
December 24, 1995

I know less about the Bible than a hog does about a sidesaddle, but retired Episcopal minister the Reverend Paul Osborne insists that in the Bible you can determine that Jesus identified with the poor. Surely he was not invited to join the Jerusalem Chamber of Commerce.

For example, read *Luke* 4:16-20 which says, in part: "He [Jesus] came to Nazareth . . . [and] He went into the synagogue. Then He did preach the gospel to the poor . . . and recovering of sight to the blind and set at liberty them that are bruised."

Emerging New Testament scholars are not concerned with the concept of the virgin birth or related beliefs. Instead, as Russell Walker points out in the April 4, 1994, *Newsweek*, Jesus was "a spellbinder, itinerant preacher, a social revolutionary who presented a peaceful, but brazen challenge to both Roman rule and the Jewish elite. . . . He wanted people to experience God directly, unimpeded by hierarchy of temple or state. . . ."

Look what happens when the hierarchy gets in the way. The December 9, 1995, *National Catholic Reporter* lets the cat out of the bag that [Roman Catholic] Cardinal Joseph Ratzinger, director of the Congregation for the Doctrine of Faith, has proclaimed that Pope John Paul II's decision that women, half the population of the world, cannot be priests was done on an infallible basis, which means "women cannot now be Catholic

185

priests; nor can they be in ten thousand years, or in ten million years."

With that the publication turns to Jesus for help and gives the editorial the headline, "Before Infallibility There Was Jesus."

. . . . I'll also always remember what happened one Christmas at a Maverick family reunion. An in-law, Cousin Elizabeth, not her real name, began giving the Jews hell and saying how much she loved Jesus.

My father finally turned on her and said: "What the hell is the matter with you? Don't you know Jesus was a Jew?"

Cousin Elizabeth, bosom and hands trembling, answered: "It's the first I ever heard of it."

Poor Jesus. We make so many dumb claims about him. There was a woman opposing bilingual education before the State of Texas Textbook Committee. She didn't want any school-books in Spanish. "If English was good enough for Jesus," the lady claimed, "it ought to be good enough for Mexicans."

Buckner Fanning, the Baptist preacher at San Antonio's Trinity Baptist Church, is one of the few television preachers who doesn't offend me. Many of those television preachers are either fools or plain dangerous, as Mark Twain would surely contend. They lend credence to something George Santayana once said which I heard quoted for the first time by a college kid at a Quaker meeting in Austin: "My atheism, like that of Spinoza, is true piety towards the universe and denies only gods fashioned by men in their own image, to be servants of their human inter-est; and even in this denial, I am no rude iconoclast, but full of secret sympathy with the impulse of idolaters."

Those rotten college kids can shake you up, can't they?

.. . . . Why do Americans give their children war games, especially at a time of the year when the man of peace is cele-brated? Poor, suffering Jesus. ★

FLEAS AND WAR

"Scratching Won't Kill the Flea,"
October 21, 1990

The White House, February 2, 1967

> *Dear Mr. Maverick:*
> *The president [Lyndon Johnson] asked me to thank you for*
> *your kindness in arranging for him to receive a copy of Robert*
> *Tarbor's book,* The War of the Flea: A Study of Guerrilla Warfare,
> *Carol Publishing Group, 1970. He is glad to have this particular*
> *study brought to his attention and is pleased that it bears your per*
> *sonal inscription.*
>
> Juanita Roberts, personal secretary to the president.

> *To President Lyndon Johnson, my father's old friend, with*
> *affectionate regards for the past and high hopes for the future.*
>
> Maury Maverick, Jr., as inscribed to
President Johnson on *The War of the Flea.*

Since I was seventy in January 1991, there's no fool like an
old fool, and especially when he goes to repeating himself. This,
you see, is the third time in the nearly fifteen years I have been
doing this column that I have mentioned Robert Tarbor's out-of-
print book, *The War of the Flea.*

I was reminded of *The Flea* when Dr. Mike Gillette of the
Lyndon Baines Johnson Library sent me the above proof that I
had mailed President Johnson a copy of the book during the
worst of the Vietnam War.

If Lyndon had read *The Flea*, all about guerrilla warfare,
and especially had he paid attention to the following quote, he
would have ended up a hero: "Analogically, the guerrilla fights

187

the war of the flea, and his military enemy suffers the dog's disadvantages: too much to defend, too small, ubiquitous, and agile an enemy to come to grips with. If the war continues long enough–this is the theory–the dog succumbs to exhaustion and anemia without ever having found anything on which to close his jaws or to rake with his claws. . . . The flea [multiplies] to a veritable plague of fleas through a long series of small victories, each drawing its drop of blood. . . . Time works for the guerrilla both in the field–where it costs the enemy a daily fortune to pursue him–and in the politico-economic area. . . ."

Global underdogs, as symbolized by the flea, suffer their defeats in such places as Nicaragua, El Salvador, and devastatingly so in Guatemala, where the United States has systematically participated in the murder of at least thirty thousand Indians. . . .

The flea is down but not out unless we kill him all over the world, as Hitler tried to do with the Jews in Europe. What's more, the flea, by getting that drop of blood here and there, has brought upon us Americans near economic ruin through our own excessive military appropriations.

Michael Klare in the October 15, 1990, issue of *The Nation* says that the flea is causing this nation to ponder two questions.

First: Is the decline of the Soviet Union without danger to the United States? Second: What kind of a country do we want America to be in dealing with Third World revolutions? In other words, how shall we cope with the flea?

As for the first question, U.S. Senator David Boren, D-Okla., has stated: "I don't think that we fully understand [that] the decline of the Soviet Union might lead to our decline as well. . . . As long as there was an external Soviet threat, as long as there was a threat from the Warsaw Pact, as long as we were providing the shield of military protection from [Germany and Japan], [those in the Third World] needed the United States."

But they do not need the United States, and with the German and the Japanese constitutions providing they cannot make war and thus not bankrupt themselves with military appropriations, they are eating our breakfast on matters of economics.

The question of how well we shall cope with the flea is answered by Klare, who contends that the solution is "a scaled-back U.S. military establishment and a greater U. S. investment in science, technology, education, and trade development. If we are to compete successfully in world markets we must become like Germany and Japan, that is, we must spend less on military forces and more on domestic industrial revitalization."

And now for the politicians who are pretty much a reflection of the electorate and often are better.

They have about as much character as the voters have and having said that, why did you, the people, vote out of office the senators who told the truth about Vietnam?

Little wonder that the present members of the Senate are not loaded with courage. . . .

You know what? This will offend some of my left-wing pals, but because of his integrity and courage I'd rather have the late Republican Senator Robert Taft in the Senate than most of the mushball liberals there today.

If we stand by brave politicians and not abandon them . . . the United States can be an inspiration for peace, justice, and world trade. . . .

If we keep on being bullies, our nation will enter an age of darkness. ★

Over half of Maverick's columns for the *Express-News* deal with biographical sketches and interviews with a multitude of individualists—human interest stories about soldiers, poets, medical doctors, sculptors, photographers, singers, artists, teachers, architects, historians, political scientists, politicians, chefs, preachers, folklorists, civil rights activists, bankers, judges, coaches, and athletes, as well as conservatives and liberals, male and female, of all races.

His use of this technique stressed by Leon Eel in *Telling Lives: The Biographer's Art* illustrates that biography "is the art of human portrayal in words" and also biographer David McCullough's observation that "there's nothing more interesting in the world than our fellow human beings, and the fact that these human beings lived in a different time from us doesn't mean that we should be cut off from them." Historian Barbara Tuchman went further to argue that biography illustrates what is truly representative about human nature with all of its comedies and tragedies—a study of the universal in the particular. Perhaps even more so, Gertrude Himmelfarb in *The New History and the Old* claims biography allows us to see those solitary mavericks who dared to experiment or speak out on their own.

The lives and thoughts of individualists featured by Maverick in his Sunday columns also signify something else. They reflect much of what Maverick himself seems to value—his heroes and heroines are people whose actions encompass themes stressed by Maverick in the preceding columns.

Samples of those lives follow, beginning with Michael Muldoon, Hendrick Arnold, and Sam Houston, all among Maverick's most admired characters in Texas history. ★

MICHAEL MULDOON: UNUSUAL ROMAN CATHOLIC PRIEST

"Many Early Texans Were Muldoon Catholics,"
April 13, 1980

A Roman Catholic priest, his name was Muldoon—Michael Muldoon, in fact, the son of an Irish father and of a Spanish mother—a big, good-natured man, and he was a bit of a whiskey priest. Not a bad fellow about it, you know, but he did tend to have a deep affection for the spirits, the drinking kind, and he had been drinking that day in 1832 at San Felipe when some of the colonists of Stephen F. Austin had assembled in front of him.

They were Methodists, Baptists, and Presbyterians who had come to Texas under a promise to convert to the Catholic Church.

"With papal authority invested in me I proclaim you to be Roman Catholics," said the priest as he gave the sign of the cross."

Time and time again he so declared Anglo-Protestant immigrants to be his fellow Catholics after about thirty seconds of "instruction." Thus came to be known the term "Muldoon Catholic" in Texas history, and I'll tell you something else—he was a grand fellow and a friend to one and all.

Who was Father Muldoon? How did he happen to come to this continent? Was he deeply involved in Texas politics? Was he both Santa Anna's confessor and Stephen F. Austin's protector? Yes, he was both. Astonishing, you say. He was that, indeed. And so, neighbor, lend me your ear. You and I need to meet Michael Muldoon. For starters let's get him born. Through a mixture of fact and legend we know—or think we know—that the Muldoon family lived in the parish of Moybolge in the northern part of County Meath, Ireland. There is an ancient tombstone standing today in the cemetery of St. Patrick's Movbola that tells of Father Muldoon's ancestors. [When] he was eight his family moved to the town of Killacunny near the river Backwater. Relatives of the padre, according to the historian Phillip O'Connell, "live today in Lurgan Parish, County of Cavan, Diocese of Kilmore."

[When Muldoon declared] that he wanted to be a priest, the records suggests, his parents sent him to what was then a popular Irish college in Seville. Spanish became his second language. Another story is that his father killed an English soldier and fled to Spain, where he married a Spanish woman, the mother of Muldoon.

Some historians claim that the priest came to Mexico in 1821 and in time became the "almost inseparable companion of Santa Anna," and before that chaplain of Juan O'Donoju, the last viceroy of Mexico.

He was first in Texas around 1829 at the Irish colony of San Patricio de Hibernia, founded on the north bank of the Nueces River of present-day Nueces County.

In the early part of 1831 Stephen F. Austin and Father Muldoon met in the city of Saltillo. They became close friends, and Austin was so delighted with the priest he wrote to Samuel M. Williams, his secretary at San Felipe:

"I have had the pleasure of a visit from el Cura de Austin y Vocario gra'de Texas, Doctor Miguel Muldoon . . . I am greatly pleased with him. He is a very intelligent and gentlemanly man, and quite liberal in his ideas.

"I must believe that if the general government wished to harass us, they would not have sent a man who is so liberal and so enlightened on religious subjects. . . . He has been accustomed to the best society in Mexico and Europe, the society of the nobility and the gentry, and I fear he will think us a rather rough set in Texas."

Austin's colony had been in existence a few years before

Muldoon arrived. When he did arrive it must have been a rare sight. He probably came by boat up the Brazos River. The committee appointed to welcome him was made up of three members, one of whom was R. M. Williamson, who in time became a famous figure in Texas under the name of "Three-Legged Willie."

Because of an illness, Williamson's right leg was drawn back at the knee. To walk he used a wooden leg, hence "Three Legged Willie." In time he became a much-respected judge and fought so hard for the annexation of Texas by the United States that he named one of his sons "Annexus."

It was in the spring of 1831 when the good padre first met the colonists. Dressed in a cossack, white hair, and probably around fifty-five years of age, he walked the main street of San Felipe, and at first was eyed with much suspicion by people who never before had seen a Roman Catholic priest.

To own land in Texas, one had to be a "Muldoon Catholic."

[That] was not much of a Catholic at all, but still the colonist was forced to make that small gesture. David G. Burnett, the first president of Texas, a Presbyterian of the old school, refused to become a Catholic, refused to remarry in the Catholic church, and refused to let his children be baptized by Muldoon. For this Burnett was not declared "a good Catholic colonist" and remained a poor man.

Sam Houston had other ideas. By that time he had been a Protestant and a follower of an Indian religion. When in Rome do as the Romans do, and so, around the latter part of 1833, Houston became a "Muldoon Catholic." Stephen F. Austin did the same thing, but that didn't keep him from secretly participating in a Masonic lodge at San Felipe.

Father Muldoon's fees were $2 for each person baptized, and $25 for each marriage; payment, more often than not, was in the form of cows and calves. Actually, "the Friar Tuck of Texas," as Frank Tolbert used to call him, often collected nothing at all.

This was especially so when he insisted that the black slaves had the right of baptism and a religious marriage. San Felipe had a newspaper of sorts, and from time to time it would publish the poetry of the friendly priest. Here's how he described a barbecue and festivity after a baptism:

The fiddle plays, all dancing go!
Upon the light fantastic toe.
Vermillion cheeks, and many faces,
Seemed angels dancing with the graces.
And the old boy would give a toast or two
*   after a few nips:*
May all religious discord fall
And friendship be the creed of all.
With tolerance your pastor views,
All sects of Christians, Turks, and Jews.

During the actual fighting of the Texas Revolution, Muldoon was seen everywhere and nowhere, sometimes with the Texans, sometimes with the Mexicans. He would visit and help Texans who were prisoners of war and then do the same thing for Mexicans who became prisoners.

In 1839, as a passenger on a ship from New Orleans to Veracruz, he left Texas for the last time. On board with him was Barnard E. Bee, a diplomatic agent seeking peace with Mexico.

Upon arrival the priest was thrown in jail, accused of being too friendly with the Texans. Then, as one historian put it, "he walked off the stage of history."

Was Muldoon murdered? Where did he meet his death? Mexico? Spain? Ireland? Where is he buried? No one knows.

Anson Jones, secretary of state under Houston and the first president of the Republic of Texas, wrote Muldoon just before he left Texas that last time, "the people of Texas will not cease to have an abiding recollection of the great friendship you evinced."

On October 13, 1946, near the town of La Grange, not far from the village of Muldoon, a historical marker was unveiled to Michael Muldoon. The speaker that day said: "If Stephen F. Austin was the father of Texas, then certainly Father Muldoon was the godfather of Texas, a good Irishman, a good Texan, a good Mexican."

They called him that day "the forgotten man of Texas." Maybe the folks in the Shamrock Society ought to correct that injustice.

Here's to Father Paddy Muldoon! ★

HENDRICK ARNOLD: PATRIOT

"Meet Hendrick Arnold, S. A.'s Black Hero,"
August 2, 1981

Who will follow old Ben Milam to San Antonio?

That was the question late in November 1835, an inquiry that traveled by word of mouth to the forks of the creek, along the Brazos, and to the Piney Woods. On and on it worked its way across Texas like a long narrow line of burning gunpowder.

It was "manifest destiny," the Anglo-Americans claimed; they were conquering a land, making a nation. Yes, who will follow old Ben Milam? Brothers and sisters, it's time to take a time capsule. Let's go meet those folks.

Around December 3, 1835, rebel Texans were camped somewhere near the vicinity of present-day Central Catholic High School [in San Antonio]. There would be a two-pronged attack with Ben Milam leading one contingent and Francis W. Johnson the other. General Martin Perfecto de Cos, later brother-in-law to Santa Anna, held San Antonio with about twelve hundred Mexican soldiers.

Wasn't it time to attack? "No, not yet," insisted some one hundred of the Texans. "Where is Hendrick Arnold? No Arnold, no attack," they demanded. The man was wanted as their guide to lead them into combat. Late that same day Arnold did arrive on the scene. It was time to make war.

With "Deaf" Smith, J. W. Smith, and Hendrick Arnold as guides, the assault began on the fifth day of December. Ben Milam was killed as he entered the courtyard of the Veramendi home as house-to-house fighting broke out. On December 9, General Cos hoisted a white flag. An armistice was signed. The Texans had San Antonio; Cos was permitted to return to the Rio Grande with his troops.

"Maverick, we are tired of your kooky history stories. What do you mean the siege of San Antonio was held up because of a bird named Hendrick Arnold?"

Gentle reader, you ain't heard nothing yet. Hendrick Arnold was black and was one of the significant heroes of the Texas Revolution. What's more, Arnold went on to San Jacinto and fought in "Deaf" Smith's spy company. Got cited for bravery at both places.

"Maverick, the schoolbooks we had as children never mentioned any black having a big hand in the capture of San Antonio. Are you sure about this?"

Yes, I'm sure. Arnold is recognized by the Institute of Texas Cultures—go look at the section set aside for black history. Besides, the man is in book after book of the more serious kind. You can find those books in the Alamo library, the best place in town to do serious research.

Who was Hendrick Arnold? What ever happened to him?

Well, for one thing he is buried on the ranch of Joe Straus some seven miles east of Castroville, just above the banks of the Medina River.

Apparently most of Arnold's relatives in Texas were white,

not black. His people were among the "Old 300," the original colonists Stephen F. Austin brought to Texas.

Because of his white relatives, Arnold was a "free Negro." Only a handful of blacks in Texas were free. The very thing the white community did not want was free blacks, and so it was set out in the Constitution of the republic that a slave owner could not free his slaves even if he wanted to do so. Here's some of the constitutional language: "No free person of African descent . . . shall be permitted to reside in the Republic without the consent of Congress. . . ." It took an act of congress to free a black, and those acts were about as prevalent as hen's teeth.

Although Arnold had rendered great service to Texas, the knowledge he was a black without full rights was sharply brought home to him when he sold his own daughter into slavery. He was free; she was not. Actually, this sale was a subterfuge; part of the agreement was that in five years she would be given her freedom. Under the circumstances, he was doing the best he could for his family.

For his services to Texas, Arnold received two land grants– one in Bexar County that today constitutes part of the Joe Straus ranch and the other in Bandera County. The land in Bandera County was a plot that, according to J. Marvin Hunter in the October 1937 issue of *Frontier Times*, "no white man would accept." Today the ground is premium land.

Hendrick Arnold died in the 1849 cholera epidemic that swept over Bexar County. By that time he had the start of a grist mill at what is today called Berg's Mill and that, a century ago or more, may have also been called Arnold's Mill. It is also believed he had a business on the San Antonio River near present-day Houston Street. At last he was married to a Mexican-American woman named Martina. . . .

The rank-and-file black slaves of Austin's "Old 300" deserve vastly more attention for their heroic contributions to early Texas. Their descendants by the hundreds walk the streets of San Antonio.

Remember that name—Hendrick Arnold—a forgotten black of the Texas Revolution, a man for whom a battle was held up a day. After all these years, isn't it time to give him the recognition he deserves? ★

SAM HOUSTON: TEXAS LEGEND

"Blacks Wrong on Sam Houston,"
July 22, 1990

Yes, Sam Houston owned slaves, some twelve at his death. He was not a John Brown abolitionist, but when in the U.S. Senate he voted against the extension of slavery to the new territories.

When Houston voted against the Kansas-Nebraska Act, an act that brought slavery to Kansas, he stated on the floor of the Senate: "If this bill passes there will be a tremendous shock; it will convulse the nation from Maine to the Rio Grande." Sam knew his political onions, or did not Kansas come to be known as "bleeding Kansas"?

The story I want to tell about Sam Houston may sound patronizing coming from me, a white, and so I will now give the floor to a former black slave named Jeff Hamilton.

At age ninety-five, Hamilton told the press this story: "I was just a little boy when I was brought to a slave auction in Huntsville. There was a crowd around me on the square, poking at me, making me cry. General Houston came along and he said: 'What's all the fuss about?' They told him it was 'just a little n————r.' The general said: 'You can't sell the child without his mother.'"

Houston bought the child, Jeff Hamilton, and his mother,

and in time the black man and white man became good friends.

Houston did not look on people of color as most whites did. Indeed, he lived with a succession of Indian women and at least one Indian wife. . . .

"Houston: Texas Lover and Fighter,"
June 17, 1979
Born March 2, 1793, in Rockbridge County, Virginia, Sam Houston moved with his widowed mother to Maryville, Tennessee, when he was fourteen years old. . . .

Before he died at Huntsville on July 26, 1863, Houston was twice wounded in combat, the first time in Alabama [fighting] against the Creek Indians, when his general, Andrew Jackson, gave him a field promotion to lieutenant, and years later at San Jacinto when the Republic of Texas was born.

He was district attorney for the Nashville area, a member of the U.S. House of Representatives from Tennessee, then governor of that state until he resigned and went back to the Cherokee.

In Texas he became commander-in-chief of the army, twice the president of the Republic of Texas, fourteen years a U.S. Senator after Texas joined the Union, and . . . governor of Texas only to be forced to resign after opposing Texas' becoming a part of the Confederacy.

Alcoholic, intellectual, iconoclast, soldier, lover, show-off, statesman, a late-in-life convert to the Baptist Church–Houston was all of those things and like Robert Penn Warren's Big Billy Potts:

> . . . his holler and shout
> made the bob-cat shiver
> And the black-jack leaves shake
> In the section between the rivers. . . .

"Sam Houston as Boy Lover,"
November 15, 1987

One historian pointed out that Sam, as a sixteen-year-old boy, was about six feet two inches tall, was "fair skinned with russet hair, [with] pale blue eyes and rather soft blurred features."

It was then that this handsome boy fled to Hiwassie Island where the waters of the Hiwassie River merge with the Tennessee.

The Cherokee Indian chief with whom Houston made friends had two names, one Indian, Oolooteka, meaning "He puts down the drum," and a white name, John Jolley.

The chief, discovering that Houston's natural father was dead, adopted Houston and gave him the name of "Colonel," meaning "the Raven."

The raven is a close cousin of the crow, but much larger. It is the largest songbird in North America, weighing as much as three pounds and as long as twenty-six inches, and to the Cherokees of those days was a sacred symbol of good fortune. . . .

M. K. Wisehart in his book, *Sam Houston: American Giant,* R. B. Luce Publishers, 1962, questions whether Houston at the age of sixteen indulged in sex because the "Cherokees had a high regard for the chastity of their young virgins."

But when Houston wrote about this period of his life, referring to himself in the third person, as was the Indian tradition, these words do not suggest celibacy. Watch: "It was the molding period of life, when the heart, just charmed into fevered hopes and dreams of youth, looks wistfully around on all things for light and beauty—when every idea of gratification fires the blood. . . . I passed months . . . wandering along the banks of the stream by the side of some Indian maiden." To these Indian girls he read the *Iliad* by Homer, and I suspect did more.

The *Iliad,* the oldest surviving Greek poem, written proba-

201

bly in the 700s B.C., describes the events in the final year of the Trojan War, which was fought between Greece and the city of Troy over Helen, the beautiful wife of King Menelaus of Sparta. To understand the *Iliad* better, Houston even studied the Greek language.

When Houston returned to "civilization" from his sojourn with the Cherokees, his brothers put him down and proclaimed him as the black sheep of the family. But Houston held on to Indian ways, even when he ran a school for small children: "I kept a country school. . . . I would go out into the woods and cut me a 'sourwood' stick, trim it carefully in spirals, and thrust one-half of it in the fire which would turn it blue, leaving the other half white. With this emblem of ornament dressed as I was in a hunting shirt of flowered calico, and a long queue down my back, I experienced a higher feeling of dignity and self-satisfaction than from any office or honor which I have since held."

Houston continued to teach for a few years, but in 1812, when President James Madison issued his call to arms against the British, Houston by then had had enough of the proper life.

In March of that year a U.S. Army recruiting team came to town. The fifes began to play with a roll of the drums. It was the custom then, if you wanted to be an enlisted man, for a recruit to pick up a silver dollar, which Houston did.

Houston's brothers and contemporaries were outraged that a member of the Houston family would join the ranks rather than getting a commission.

It was then that Houston is said to have made his first oration: "And what have you craven souls to say about the ranks? Go to with your stuff. I would sooner honor the ranks than disgrace an appointment. You don't know me now, but you shall hear of me. . . ."

"Houston: Texas Lover and Fighter,"
June 17, 1979

[People did indeed hear of him after he became a U. S. Representative and a governor of Tennessee. But his reputation suffered, as shown when] on April 16, 1829, Sheriff Willoughby Williams rode up on his horse to the Nashville Inn.

"Have you heard the news?" he was asked. "Sam Houston and his wife have separated. She's gone home to her family."

On the night of January 22, 1829, Governor Sam Houston of Tennessee had married Eliza Allen. In less than three months their marriage was over.

Why did Eliza leave Houston? His enemies said he was impotent, but he wasn't with his other wives and other lovers. Was she the delicate flower, and he the wild lover? Whatever the truth, it was devastating to Sam Houston; years later he told his Baptist preacher, Dr. Rufus Burleson, he was near suicide.

On April 16, 1829, Houston wrote the speaker of the Tennessee Senate: "It has become my duty to resign the office of chief magistrate of the State. . . ." It was then he went into what he called his exile. Houston boarded the steam packet *Red Rover* at Cairo, Illinois, a week after his resignation, going aboard smelling of whiskey and wearing an Indian blanket over his shoulder. The former heir apparent of Andrew Jackson to the presidency of the United States turned his thoughts back toward Chief Jolley.

Sam Houston was returning to his beloved Indians with whom he had lived as a boy. He needed to be with the running rivers, the trees, wild animals, and the Cherokee. Thoreau did the same thing, and his explanation would have satisfied Houston.

"I went to the woods," Thoreau wrote, "because I wished to live deliberately, to front only the essential facts of life, and to see if I could not learn what it had to teach, and not, when I came to die, discover that I had not lived."

As the *Red Rover* pulled away from the bank of the river, a man walked up and offered Houston a drink. He said his name was Jim Bowie.

From Little Rock, Arkansas, Houston went upriver to Fort Smith aboard the steamship *Felicity*. It was dark when he reached his destination, but Chief Jolley was there with his black slaves holding lighted torches. The Cherokee disliked the white man, but copied his ways with plantations and runaway slaves.

"I had heard that a dark cloud had fallen on the white path you were walking," Jolley told Houston, "and you turned your thoughts to my wigwam." So serious was the former governor about being with the Indians that he became a citizen of the Cherokee Nation on October 21, 1829.

An Indian woman caught his eye in the months that followed. She was the tall and gorgeous daughter of Captain John "Hell-Fire" Rogers, a Scotsman, and of an Indian mother. [She and Houston] were formally married according to the customs of the Cherokee.

During much of the three years Houston lived with the Cherokee the Indians called him "the Big Drunk." A Christian missionary would describe him as being, "vicious to a fearful extent . . . hostile to Christianity."

On more than one occasion Houston went to Washington, D.C., as the ambassador of the Cherokee Nation, once appearing at the White House in full Indian regalia.

On one such trip a member of the House accused Houston of dealing in a crooked way among the Indians. Houston thrashed the man with a hickory cane, then was tried by the entire U.S. House of Representatives, with Francis Scott Key as his counsel.

At the conclusion of the trial, when he received a mild reprimand, the defendant made a grand oration. Junius Brutus Booth, one of the great actors of America, whispered, "Houston, take my laurels."

Toward the end of 1832, the former governor of Tennessee began his first trip to Texas, riding a mustang with no tail. Some folks, both then and now, say he was Old Hickory's secret revolutionary agent.

[Once settled in Texas] Houston was elected as a delegate to the [Revolutionary] Convention of 1836 by the people of Refugio, being out of favor at the time with his hometown of Nacogdoches. Arriving at Washington-on-the-Brazos, he signed the Texas Declaration of Independence and two days later became the commander-in-chief of the Texas Army.

The Alamo and Goliad went under, and panic swept the civilian population, which followed Houston to the east in what is known as the Runaway Scrape.

Time after time Houston was ordered to stop and fight, but he kept on with his plan of drawing Santa Anna deeper and deeper into East Texas. Protecting his rear was Juan Seguin and his detachment of Mexicans, mostly born in Texas, who would fight alongside Houston at San Jacinto.

On the afternoon of April 21, 1836, the Battle of San Jacinto took place while Santa Anna was enjoying a siesta after having told his officers and men that the Texans would not attack.

A drum and fife began to play a love song, "Come to the Bower." Up and down the line Houston rode a white horse telling his men with itchy fingers: "Hold your fire, d——— you! Hold your fire."

Then he waved his hat: The Twin Sisters [cannons] fired their blast of broken horseshoes. In less than thirty minutes the battle was over: 640 Mexicans killed, 730 captured, nine Texans killed.

Houston was badly wounded. As a surgeon began to remove broken pieces of bone from his leg, the old man had April flowers brought to him. He made the flowers into a garland for a lady friend: "To Anna Rouguert, Nacogdoches, Texas: These are laurels I send you from the battlefield of San Jacinto. Thine, Houston."

The old soldier and lover became the instant hero of Texas; soon he would be Sam Houston, president of the Republic. . . .

"Houston's Name Lives in the Heart,"
June 24, 1979

Time after time during the fourteen years he served in the U. S. Senate, Houston opposed the extension of slavery to the newly acquired parts of our country, such as the Oregon Territory. In the process he earned the hatred of John Calhoun, Stephen A. Douglas and Jefferson Davis, whom he described as being "ambitious as Lucifer and cold as a snake."

Repeatedly he was attacked as a turncoat to the South. It became such a lonely experience for him, he quoted a poem to the members of the Senate in 1854:

> *I feel like one*
> *Who treads alone*
> *Some banquet hall deserted,*
> *Whose lights are fled,*
> *Whose garlands dead*
> *And all by he departed.* . . .

[In 1857, as] the prospect of civil war began to stalk our country, Sam Houston decided to leave the Senate, return to Texas, and run for governor. If Texas insisted on seceding, then let it become a republic again. But first he had to say his farewell.

All over the city of Washington the news spread. Sam Houston was to make his farewell address; the Senate galleries were packed.

It was a long address; the spectators especially cheered his conclusion–"I wish no prouder epitaph to mark the board of slab that may lie on my tomb than this: 'He loved his country, he was a patriot; he was devoted to the Union.'"

The *Washington Star* editorialized: "This distinguished man left Washington yesterday afternoon for Texas. . . . No public man ever made more sincere friends. . . ."

In 1857, Houston was defeated for governor by Hardin Runnels. In Brenham he was not permitted to speak in the county courthouse. In Lockhart he tried to speak, but people in the crowd called him a traitor.

The old man stared at the audience. "Sam Houston a traitor to Texas?" he thundered. "I, who in defense of her soil moistened it with my blood!" Limping on his San Jacinto leg, he asked: "Was it for this I rode into a bullet to be branded in my old age a traitor?"

Sam Houston wept that day in Lockhart in front of the crowd who called him a traitor. Soldiers in the audience who had fought with him at San Jacinto wept with him. But old Sam lost the election.

In 1859 Houston ran again for governor and won over Runnels by a vote of 33,375 to 27,500. Throughout the campaign he denounced the reopening of the African slave trade.

Time and time again he told the people that if they left the Union it would be at a price paid in blood. "Dear Heavenly Father," he would pray at night, "I beseech [you to] cast out of my mind the dark forebodings of the coming conflict. . . ."

[Then,] on March 16, 1861, Sam Houston went to the floor of the Secession Convention as the delegates screamed out his name to take the oath of loyalty to the Confederacy. "Sam Houston! Sam Houston!" they thundered in the old man's face.

Governor Houston left the convention and returned to his office. He knew that a delegation would shortly call on him seeking his resignation. By a handsome margin the people of Texas had decided for secession, but sixteen counties had voted with the governor. . . .

It was the people of German descent who mostly stuck with Sam Houston: Later on they would pay for it with their blood. In San Antonio he had spoken at San Pedro Springs against secession; Bexar with a large German vote nevertheless went with the secessionists by the narrow vote of 827 to 708.

The delegation from the convention arrived at Houston's office and received his resignation. To Edward Clark, the lieutenant governor of Texas, a man he had just put in office, Houston asked: "What is your name?" Later he would describe Clark as having all the qualities of a dog except gratitude. . . .

When he was forced to resign by the Secession Convention, Houston went back to Huntsville, but as a private citizen he continued to speak out against the Civil War. . . .

As Sam Houston lay on his deathbed, he was asked only hours before he died if he recanted his opposition to the Confederacy. "My views," he replied, "to the propriety and possibility of the success of this wicked revolution have undergone no change."

He fell into a deep sleep. Reverend Samuel McKinney, his Baptist preacher, prayed as Houston began to slip off into death. His wife, Margaret, by whom he had eight children, read the Bible to him. Jeff Hamilton, his black friend, was at the foot of the bed.

Mrs. Houston heard Sam murmur "Texas, Texas," and then he said, "Oh, Margaret." General, president, governor, senator, Sam Houston died at sunset on July 26, 1863, and was buried in a coffin built by a Yankee sailor, a prisoner of war and ship's carpenter, who had been captured aboard the *Harriet Lane*, a federal ship, at Galveston.

Some personal reflections. One's pulse quickens with the mere mention of Houston's name. Defender of the Union and of racial minorities, one-time alcoholic, genius, Baptist convert, libertarian, lover, fighter, wild horse rider, he was all those things and more.

I can see the delegates at the Secession Convention taunting him, degrading and bullying him if they could, calling out his name. "Sam Houston! Sam Houston!" What a moment of agony it must have been.

The old lion lives in our hearts, this greatest of Texans. Yes, by God, Sam Houston! Sam Houston! ★

JOHN COFFEE "JACK" HAYS: TEXAS RANGER
"Fearless Jack Hays, Texas Ranger,"
April 7, 1991

Jack Hays came from Tennessee to Texas just after the Battle of San Jacinto, and when he came to San Antonio . . . he was appointed a deputy surveyor. The surveying parties frequently had "brushes" with the Indians, and it was on these occasions that Hays displayed such rare military skill and daring, that very soon by consent of all, he was looked upon as the leader, and his orders were obeyed and he himself loved by all. In a fight he was utterly fearless and invincible. . . .

From Memoirs of Mary A. Maverick,
University of Nebraska Press, 1989,
Rena Maverick Green, editor.

This is [about Texas Ranger] Jack Hays, for whom Hays County was named. . . .

As an Indian fighter, Hays was such a heroic figure that his name became a household word throughout Texas and especially in San Antonio. This because of the battles of Uvalde Canyon, Plum Creek (near Lockhart), Llano, Enchanted Rock, and Bandera Pass, among several others.

Mary Maverick came to San Antonio in 1838 from Tuscaloosa, Alabama, and was at least twice, maybe three times, nearly killed by what she adamantly called "savage Indians."

One such occurrence took place on the banks of the San Antonio River opposite what is now the Southwest Craft Center. . . .

[The] truth is that although Jack Hays was astonishingly brave, he also had something the Indians didn't have: the six-shooter.

The idea of the six-shooter originated on the high seas when a sixteen-year-old boy named Samuel Colt carved in wood the model for a gun with a revolving cylinder that would shoot six times without reloading.

The Indian with his bow and arrow (or single-shot rifle) was no match for a six-shooter—especially when in the hand of the one and only Jack Hays.

The more I study the history of Salado Creek, the more I find it ought to be close to my heart. In February 1842, Mary Maverick and other women of San Antonio fled east fearing an invasion from Mexico.

The first night was spent in a cold rain on the east bank of the Salado. The feared invasion came some months later with General Adrian Woll, a French soldier of fortune, in command of some one thousand Mexican soldiers. Woll was defeated and began his retreat to south of the Rio Grande.

About that event Mary Maverick writes in her memoirs:

> September 21st [1842]. General Woll evacuated San Antonio. Col. Caldwell [Old Paint] with 650 men pursued them, and at night came upon their camp on the Medina. . . . He commanded Hays with twenty picked men to make a diversion on the enemy's left. Hays, with his usual dash and gallantry, entered vigorously into the spirit of the hour.

He charged with boldness into the ranks of the enemy and immediately captured the artillery. . . .

One of the best fellows in town before World War II was a retired colonel named Martin Crimmins. He quit medical school to fight with Teddy Roosevelt and after retirement became one of San Antonio's top historians. About Jack Hays he wrote in the *Frontier Times*:

> Colonel Jack Hays had a home at La Villita. . . . Hays was about five feet nine inches tall and weighed 145 pounds. He had black hair like an Indian and deep blue eyes. He did not order a charge. He simply said, "Follow me, men." During the war with Mexico Hays' services were outstanding while in command of a regiment of mounted Texans along the Rio Grande, at Monterrey under General William Jenkins Worth, and in the battlefields near the city of Mexico.

(Did you know that Ulysses S. Grant in his memoirs described our invasion of Mexico as an outrage and that he was politically ashamed of his participation in it?)

In April 1847, in Seguin, Hays married a Miss Susan Calvert, a direct descendant of the first Lord Baltimore. . . .

A couple of years later, "Miss Susan" and about twenty other people in San Antonio joined the Gold Rush and went with Hays to San Francisco. . . .

"Jack Hays Electrified the West,"
April 14, 1991

Is Jack Hays the greatest ranger of all times? That's like saying Babe Ruth is still the greatest baseball player. Either claim will get you an argument, but certainly Hays remains one of the three or four top rangers in the history of Texas. He was so adept with a six-shooter that the Indians thought bullets came out of his fingers. . . .

When that dude would take a stroll out of his home at La Villita, he was the most exciting person in San Antonio, but to the Indians he was a ruthless killer.

And he was equally exciting in California [where he went in 1849].

When the first election for sheriff of San Francisco County was held during 1859, there were three candidates. A man named Townes was the Whig Party nominee. J. J. Bryant, the richest man in town, was the Democrat. Hays ran as an independent.

Excerpts from a California book I found tell in flowery language what happened the day before the San Francisco election. Watch:

> Bryant arrived with a procession of mounted men and carriages filled with musicians. . . . But in the midst of the excitement Colonel Hays, mounted upon his noble animal, a fiery black charger, suddenly appeared, exhibiting some of the finest horsemanship ever witnessed. The sight of the Texan hero . . . took the people by surprise and called for the admiration and patriotism of the vast multitudes of spectators. Shout after shout rent the air . . . deadening the sounds of the trumpets. . . . Men crowded around him on every level . . . loud huzzas at every step. The next day a vast majority of the votes [were] given in favor of the Texan Ranger.

Brothers and sisters, I'm telling you, Jack Hays was a high stepper who electrified the people of San Francisco and before that the folks of old San Antonio.

I'd like to think that Jack Hays, who could "ride a horse like a Mexican and shoot like a man from Tennessee," would want you to love La Villita, where he lived for a few years, and protect it from overcommercialization. Why not say hello to the ghost of Jack Hays the next time you visit La Villita? Swear before whatever gods may be that you will protect La Villita! ★

GRIFFIN: A BRAVE BLACK

"Forgotten Slave a True Hero,"
June 23, 1991

> **M**averick*: Reverend Black, this is a delicate matter, but my great-grandparents, Sam and Mary Adams Maverick, owned a black slave by the name of Griffin, a forgotten hero of the 1842 Dawson Massacre, which was fought near the western boundary of present-day Fort Sam Houston. He was killed in combat by Mexican soldiers under the command of Colonel J. M. Carrasco while defending the city of San Antonio. My cousins and I want to erect a historical plaque in his honor and memory. Do you think we could do that in a way black people in San Antonio would accept it as an honor to Griffin and as an acknowledgment of the dignity of black people?*
>
> The Reverend Claude Black*: It could be a fine thing, but before black people will accept it in the spirit you say you intend it, you Mavericks must first say slavery was morally wrong.*
>
> A recent conversation between this columnist
> and the Reverend Claude Black, pastor,
> Mount Zion Baptist Church.

Slavery was morally wrong. Let me say it again: Slavery was morally wrong. On June 22, 1991, at Raymond Russell Park, some four hundred of us Mavericks celebrated 156 years in San Antonio. That's nothing compared to Mexican-Americans with an Indian ancestry, but pretty good for a gringo.

Thanks to the research of Dr. Donald Everett, retired history professor from Trinity University, and our cousin, Ellen (Mrs. Frank) Dickson, Jim Maverick's daughter, we made initial plans to erect a plaque in honor of a black man named Griffin.

Griffin is a forgotten hero of the Texas Revolution. Our great-grandfather, Sam Maverick, wrote: "I feel [Griffin's] death as the hardest piece of fortune we have suffered in Texas. . . . I owe him a monument and a bitter tear of regret for thy fall. I mourn [him] as a true and faithful friend and a brother, a worthy dear brother in arms."

When I was a little boy my father used to take me to the Alamo and say, "Maury, Jr., not all right was on one side in the battle of the Alamo. The Anglo Texans wanted freedom and land for themselves, but they had black slaves in the Alamo. After the battle we Mavericks were the first to bring black slaves to San Antonio. Don't be a bully about the Alamo."

According to the *Handbook of Texas*: "From the first, the Negro has shared and shaped Texas history." Some historians claim that the first black in Texas was a man named Estevanico, a Moorish slave. By 1791 blacks numbered 24 percent of the population of Texas.

The Institute of Texan Cultures has a booklet entitled *The Afro-Americans* [that states] Moses Austin first came to San Antonio with a slave. The Austin colony, later run by Stephen F. Austin, could not have survived without the blacks, all slaves, yet history does not give those blacks the credit they deserve. Some of their descendants live in San Antonio.

On December 7, 1837, my great-grandparents left Tuscaloosa, Alabama, with a group of slaves under the command of Griffin and with "a large carriage, a big Kentucky wagon, and three extra saddle horses and one blooded filly."

At Cibolo Creek, just before they reached San Antonio, Indians threatened an attack, but the blacks, armed with rifles, beat off the Indians. I thought about that . . . at the family reunion and speculated on the thought that we would not have had a family reunion if it had not been for the blacks' saving our ancestors.

Griffin was killed by Mexican soldiers in the Dawson Massacre, which occurred during the invasion of San Antonio under the command of General Adrian Woll.

Nicholas Mosby Dawson had assembled a group of fifty-three men in La Grange to go to the aid of Matthew "Old Paint" Caldwell and Jack Hays, who were to fight and win at Salado Creek. But en route to the Salado, Dawson's men were intercepted by the Mexicans under the command of J. M. Carrasco.

As for Griffin's heroism at the Dawson Massacre, Everett wrote about that by quoting Colonel Carrasco this way: "Mexican Colonel J. M. Carrasco later testified to Samuel A. Maverick as to the feats performed by that 'valiant black man.' Carrasco described Griffin as 'the bravest man I have ever seen.'"

In her memoirs, Mary Adams Maverick wrote this of Griffin the day he was killed: "He was a man of powerful frame, and he possessed the courage of the African lion. . . . When his ammunition became useless because of the proximity of the enemy, he fought with the butt end of his gun and when the gun was broken, he wrenched a limb from a mesquite tree and did battle with that until death closed his career. He received more than one mortal wound. . . ."

Even when it is friendly, it is hard for a white person to write about blacks without being accused of being patronizing. I admit to a guilt complex, but not [to] being patronizing.

The truth is that blacks have been my teachers from the late state representative G. J. Sutton, who was my client for twenty-five years in my lawyer days, to the Reverend Black. Don Albert, the East Side trumpet player, was another teacher and so was state representative Lou Nelle Sutton. And there were others, such as the nearly hundred-year-old John Inman, the radical of the East Side in his youth who goes back so far he was once the chauffeur of George Brackenridge.

I called retired Chief Justice Carlos Cadena, who in his lawyer days with Gus Garcia was responsible for the *Hernandez* case giving Mexican-Americans the right to sit on juries. Cadena told me: "We relied heavily on cases black people had won. In fact, before the blacks won their civil rights cases, Alonzo S. Perales and M. C. Gonzales repeatedly lost their civil rights cases for Mexican-Americans, and so we ride significantly in the stirrups of those black people." ★

LOUIS SCHUETZE: GERMAN-TEXAN UNIONIST

"Murdered Germans Loved U. S.,"
August 28, 1988

"Mr. Maverick, my name is Thelma Cade Perdue. My eighty-four-year-old mother, Wilfred Schuetze Cade, is the granddaughter of Louis Schuetze, a pro-Union German immigrant, who was taken out of his home in Fredericksburg and hanged....

"Mr. Maverick, you told the truth about the way the pro-Union German immigrants were treated in Gillespie and Kendal counties during the Civil War. Would you like to talk with my mother?"

A telephone call from Thelma Cade Perdue.

Thelma Cade Perdue and her mother, Winifred Schuetze Cade, are both talented artists. They know their onions about what happened in the Texas Hill Country to the [Civil War] pro-Union German immigrants. I couldn't wait to talk with Mrs. Cade about her murdered grandfather, Louis Schuetze. Here's part of what she told me:

My paternal grandfather, Louis Schuetze, was hanged near the town of Fredericksburg on or about February 24, 1864. He was dragged from his home in Fredericksburg, near the church which today is known as the Coffee Mill Church. He was a schoolteacher, a man of culture and education. In 1851, he founded a school in Indianola but later was hired to open a school at Live Oak, a town no longer existing, but then near Fredericksburg. Then he opened other schools in Gillespie County. Louis Schuetze's wife was Emelia Ritter Schuetze. In Germany they spelled it "von Ritter." After her husband was hanged, she put on a widow's cap and wore it until the day she died [in 1891]. . . . [The] thing people need to understand is that [before the Civil War] the German immigrants had . . . taken an oath of allegiance to the United States. They wanted to keep their word. They were proud of being Americans. Because of the persecution, the German immigrants became Republican, and I am a Republican in part because of what was done to my grandfather. My grandfather's brother was Julius Schuetze, who started the German-English school in Austin. He taught Sam Houston's children piano in the Governor's Mansion. He also taught the children of Governor Pendleton Murrah, who became governor in 1863.

(Murrah was loyal to the South, but he knew it was a hopeless war. He did not like the arbitrary way Confederate General John Magruder treated civilians. In 1865 Governor Murrah fled to Mexico and died that same year in Monterrey. He was a South Carolinian.)

What follows are comments of Julius Schuetze taken from family papers, German newspapers, and the recordings in the inquest:

.... there are hundreds still living and residing in Fredericksburg and its environs before whose eyes passed the terrible events of that time. . . . Like nineteen out of twenty Germans I was a Union man. . . . I was in 1860 music teacher to the family of Sam Houston. . . . In 1864 I also gave instructions in Governor Pendleton Murrah's family. . . . Murrah was an amicable, clever companion, a man of thirty-five years, brim full of humor and wit. He was also very liberal in his views . . . and opposed to the court-martials [of civilians by the Confederate military]. Then one day in Austin I was told that a band of twenty men had seized my brother, Louis Schuetze, taken him from his home, and murdered him.

With that news, Julius Schuetze rushed to Governor Murrah and secured from him a letter of safe conduct and then left immediately by horse for Fredericksburg. Down the road that night he slept at the home of George Hessner and discovered that all German immigrants were terrified. The next morning, as he neared Fredericksburg, he saw a man plowing a field and tried to talk with him.

At first the farmer would not talk. Julius asked in English: "Do you know Louis Schuetze?" Again the farmer would not talk, but finally said, "He has been hanged."

Now watch what happens as taken from the papers of the Schuetze family. It's enough to fill a brave man's eyes with tears.

"Mein Gott! Mein Gott!" I cried out of horror, involuntarily speaking in German.

"Are you German?" the farmer hastily questioned me.

"Oh, yes. I am Louis's youngest brother, Julius, from Austin."

"What! You are the Schuetze from Austin?" he exclaimed and immediately jumped over the fence and stood beside me. "Yes, you are. I can see the resemblance. Louis was my best friend."

We wept together.

During that encounter Julius Schuetze was told that four other people had been hanged: Peter Burg, H. Kirchner, W. Feller, and John Blank. With that parting information, Julius then rode his horse to the Nimitz Hotel, where Captain Charles Nimitz (the uncle of the then-unborn Admiral Chester Nimitz) directed him to where the inquest was being held.

The inquest papers describe a savage betrayal of due process and of all concepts of common decency. They set out that Louis Schuetze was found, "with a rope around his neck, hanging from a bough of live oak. His hands were bound behind his back. On the left side of his forehead a wound was found. His pockets were turned inside out."

Louise Schuetze, the murdered man's daughter, testified she saw [the mob] take her father from the house and then, "I heard a blow, and my father cried out 'Mr. Waldrip' and then 'Louise, come here.' I tore myself loose and hurried to my father. 'My Louise,' he said, 'they are going to hang me.'"

Louis B. Engelke wrote in the January 3, 1954, *Express* magazine:

> Gillespie County records show that Captain J. P. Waldrip's entire gang was known as 'Waldrip's Wolfpack,' and was indicted for mob murder. . . . For a period of four years, the proslavery Waldrip gang had killed one antisecessionist German after another.

In 1867 Waldrip came back to visit Fredericksburg. As he

was about to enter the Nimitz Hotel, one Henry Langerham killed Waldrip "like a turkey" with a shot between his eyes. Then the German immigrants "buried Waldrip with his black beaver hat," according to Engelke. . . . ★

J. FRANK DOBIE: FOLKLORIST

"Poetry Teachers Sneaky Petes of Morality,"
September 7, 1980

The late folklorist J. Frank Dobie, or Old Pancho, once wrote a poem about liberty in terms of the wild horses that roamed the American West. He called it "The Mustangs." As a preface to the poem, he reminded us how we Americans showed our affection [for] those magnificent animals by naming so many places after them: Mustang Island, Mare Island, Broomtail Flat in Oregon, Wild Horse Diggins in Montana.

"The Mustangs" is my favorite poem, a poem full of allegories about freedom. When I read it, I see James Madison fighting for the free speech amendment in our Bill of Rights and Jefferson striving for separation of church and state. I see Homer Rainey standing up for academic freedom at the University of Texas, and my old legislator friend, blind Jim Sewell, now dead in a cold and narrow grave, telling the blacks of Corsicana that he is with them in their quest for dignity. I see people wanting to be left alone, tired of big governments, big unions, big corporations.

I see the wildflowers of the German Hill Country north of San Antonio and the dogwoods in bloom about the Piney Woods. I see the good Texas soil we came from and the soil we will go back to some day. But most of all when I read "The Mustangs," I think about freedom.

Gentle reader, let's you and I do a trick. Let's conjure up Frank Dobie from the grave and have him read his own poem. All together now: Abracadabra! Look–there he comes, walking to the lectern, bowlegged as ever.

Dobie mutters under his breath: "Just strolled across the UT campus in Austin for the first time in twenty years. I told you it would look like Detroit before the regents and architects got through with it."

"Come on, Mr. Dobie," we tell him, "we agree with you, but that's off the point. Read your poem about the mustangs."

A silence comes over the room. You and I know in our bones it is a special moment. Old Pancho Dobie begins to talk:

I see them running, running, running,
From the Spanish caballadas to be free,
From the mustanger's rope and rifle to keep free,
Over seas of pristine grass, like fire-dancers on a mountain,
Like lightning playing against the unapproachable horizon.

I see them standing, standing, standing,
Sentinels of alertness in eye and nostril,
Every toss of maned neck a Grecian grace,
Every high snort bugling out the pride of the free.
I see them vanishing, vanishing, vanished,
The seas of grass shriveled to pens of barbwired property,
The wind-racers and wind-drinkers bred into property also.

But winds still blow free and grass still greens,
And the core of that something which men live on believing
Is always freedom.

So sometimes yet, in the realities of silence and solitude,
For a few people unhampered a while by things,
The mustangs walk out with dawn, stand high, then
Sweep away, wild with sheer life, and free, free, free
Free of all confines of time and flesh. ★

I. H. "SPORTY" HARVEY AND JOE LOUIS: FIGHTERS

"Beyond the Ring a Knockout,"
January 3, 1988

The Yankees hold the play,
The white man pulls the trigger;
But it makes no difference what the white man say,
The world champion's still a nigger.

A street song that black people sang after Jack Johnson,
the "Black Menace," defeated James J. Jeffries for
the heavyweight championship of the world.

The case of *Sporty Harvey v. Morgan,* in which Carlos Cadena and I had segregated boxing in Texas declared illegal, gets top treatment in Jeffrey T. Sammons' *Beyond the Ring: The Role of Boxing in American Society,* University of Illinois Press.

It is the case that had a lot to do with knocking out Jim Crow in rings all over the South.

What is especially pleasing is that Sporty Harvey, then a San Antonio black, is given a photograph in the book of equal dignity as that given Jack Johnson, Jack Dempsey, or [Muhammad] Ali. . . .

Here's only part of what Sammons wrote about the Harvey case: "Harvey sought relief via state legislator and liberal lawyer Maury Maverick . . . [who] . . . enlisted the support of Chicano lawyer and future judge Carlos Cadena. . . . Maverick defied convention and confronted the local courts, not the federal courts . . . ."

"Joe Louis, Sporty Harvey Nudged U.S. Along,"
May 10, 1981

In the early 1950s, [Joe] Louis, among others, had his black hand on my shoulder when I, then a young legislator, introduced a bill in the Texas House of Representatives repealing the law prohibiting professional boxing between blacks and whites. At that time, mixed boxing was illegal due mostly to the hatred that existed in the South against Jack Johnson when he became the heavyweight champion of the world.

The bill was co-signed with me by about half a dozen legislators, one of whom was Charles Lieck, later the district attorney of Bexar County. At the committee hearing where the bill was killed on the spot, rude remarks were made about black people, all reported by the press.

After the legislative session was over, Sporty came to see me, a huge man with a fifth-grade education but with plenty of street smart between his ears.

"I'm a professional heavyweight boxer who can only fight preliminary fights with other blacks. Every champ of every weight division is white," he told me. Harvey was a frank but pleasant guy, and I liked him immediately.

What was I to do? Well, I took a page from the late Gus Garcia's book and got myself the same brains he did: Carlos Cadena. Carlos can be as slow as molasses dripping on a cold winter morning, but finally he came up with pleadings and a legal brief. We filed suit in Austin; the case was called *I. H. "Sporty" Harvey v. M. B. Morgan.* Morgan was the boxing commissioner of Texas.

We had plenty of heartbreaks, but there was some unexpected humor as well. While investigating the case, we found that Sporty had boxed white men in Mexico but had been denied that right in his own country. That had all the makings of a dramatic point, and so Cadena and I brought it up in this exchange while Sporty was on the stand:

Question: Sporty, isn't it true you fought a white man in Mexico?

Answer: No, I didn't fight no white man in Mexico, I fought a Spaniard.

223

The "Spaniard" sitting next to me, Carlos Cadena, fell out of his seat laughing. This trial judge, Jack Roberts, tried to maintain his dignity but couldn't keep a straight face. We had to stop the trial and have a little recess.

The attorney general of Texas insisted that, if blacks were permitted to box whites, there would be race riots. Sports writers like Dick Peebles, then of this newspaper but later of the *Houston Chronicle*, and the late Harold "Pop" Scherwitz of the *San Antonio Light* testified for Sporty. Pop was plenty far to the right in his politics, but he went down the line for racial justice in sports.

We lost the case at the state district court level, finally winning before the Austin Court of Civil Appeals. It is one of the relatively few constitutional law victories in a state court of Texas that a black or brown person has won on the basis of race.

At first, the NAACP, Dallas chapter, was furious with me because I had filed the case in a Texas court instead of a federal court. You couldn't blame the NAACP because the historic record of most state judges [was then] outrageously bad in the area of racial justice. . . .

The most exciting thing about the Harvey victory is that a black person gave the state of Texas a whipping in a state court! I believe in the James Madison concept of federal and state governments where there is a vibrant balance of power. But state governments will waste away that balance if state officials always abandon those hard questions to Uncle Sam. . . .

"Bertrand Russell insisted that boxing came dangerously close to real fighting and war and appealed to our sadism and lust for cruelty," Sammons writes in his concluding chapter and then asks if boxing should be outlawed.

"Deaths and serious injury suffered in boxing contests reveal only a small percentage of the potential danger. Unfortunately, the damaging effects of the sport are cumulative and often difficult to diagnose," Sammons points out.

Only a few [boxers] get to the top, the purses of boxers are eaten up by taxes and handlers, and always in the big time there is the threat of the mob.

Thousands of dollars, even millions, paid to this or that famous black athlete detract from the general uplifting of minorities in our country.

We give blacks (and browns and poor whites) an illusory moment in the sun when they entertain us catching footballs, dunking basketballs, tap dancing, playing Mexican guitars and Harlem saxophones.

Boxing has indeed opened a few doors for minorities, but if they can be superb fighters, why not superb teachers or brain surgeons?

No kidding, *Beyond the Ring* is a knockout reading you won't put down. The sweat, the agony, some of the greatness, and much of the evil of our country are there. Don't miss out on this book. ★

ELEANOR ROOSEVELT: FIRST LADY

"Lessons in Courage Outlive Mrs. Roosevelt," October 28, 1984

You gain strength, courage, and confidence by every experience in which you really stop to look fear in the face. You are able to say to yourself, "I lived through this horror. I can take the next thing that comes along."
You must do the thing you think you cannot do.

Eleanor Roosevelt.

Born October 11, 1884, Eleanor Roosevelt would have been one hundred years old this month, something I had forgotten until friends gave me and my wife a delightful print of Mrs. Roosevelt by Ceci Casebier.

As Geoffrey C. Ward points out in the [October 1984] *Smithsonian,* Eleanor Roosevelt was more than the "eyes and ears" of her crippled husband those twelve years she spent in the White House; she was his "conscience as well and sometimes his goad, reminding him of the needs of people otherwise without access to him."

There was much sadness in her life. Her father, Elliott, younger brother of Teddy Roosevelt, was an alcoholic. As a child she was shunted from governess to governess and told by relatives, who did not want her around, that she was an ugly girl.

During World War I, she discovered that her husband (and fifth cousin) was having an affair with her social secretary [Lucy Mercer Rutherfurd]. From that point, some historians claim, there was no deep emotional attachment between Franklin and Eleanor.

Women generally did not seek a divorce in those days, and when she became the First Lady, it was a question of doing one's duty to country. Always, Eleanor Roosevelt was the good soldier.

She had her enemies, the two most famous being Westbrook Pegler, the columnist, and Francis Joseph Cardinal Spellman.

To Pegler she was "LaBoca Grande." Her father, he proclaimed with a meanness that knew no limits, was "a dissolute drunkard." What's more, she was a "coddler of communists."

Only once she answered Pegler, calling him a "gnat on the horizon." In the end she won, for the Hearst newspapers dropped Pegler's column. At the last he was writing for the John Birch Society.

Eleanor Roosevelt had thousands of friends among working and poor Catholics, but a significant part of the hierarchy hated her, especially Cardinal Spellman.

In those days, before [Pope] John XXIII and Archbishop Robert Lucey came along, the Catholic Church was more conservative than liberal. She was for Loyalists in Spain, against public funds for all parochial schools–Catholic or Protestant–and for separation of church and state.

She signed a statement criticizing the New York bishops for forcing the public schools to remove *The Nation* magazine from its libraries. It was then that Spellman called her an "anti-Catholic" and "unworthy of an American mother."

The lid blew off everything. Thousands of Americans of all faiths wrote to Mrs. Roosevelt wishing her well, and Archibald MacLeish gave Spellman a skinning by writing this poem:

> *Have you forgotten, Prince of Rome,*
> *Delighted with your Roman title,*
> *Have you forgotten that at home*
> *We have no princes?*
> *Prince of the church, when you pretend*
> *By rank to silence criticism*
> *It is your country you offend,*
> *Here man's the faith and rank's the schism.*

Eleanor Roosevelt was a friend of the working Catholic priests who identified with the poor.

I remember standing as a boy with her on the West Side when Father Carmelo Tranchese told her that San Antonio had America's highest infant death rate due to diarrhea and that we needed slum-clearance projects.

"Help us with the president, Mrs. Roosevelt," the Jesuit asked. She did.

In 1940, according to Arthur D. Morse in his book *While Six Million Died*, a ship carrying Jewish refugees had been turned away from Mexico although the passengers had visas. To return to France would have meant certain death.

The ship made a stop at Norfolk, Virginia, for coal. It was

then that a delegation of Jews rushed to the office of State Secretary Cordell Hull, who denied all relief.

At the last minute Hull let the passengers have sanctuary, but only because of the intervention of Eleanor Roosevelt.

Although she was born with a silver spoon in her mouth and reared with the attitude that blacks should be dutiful servants, Mrs. Roosevelt rose above her elitist background. She identified not only with great black artists, such as Marian Anderson, against the Daughters of the American Revolution, but also with down-and-out blacks.

She went among working people, even to the bottom of mines in West Virginia, to make speeches for greater industrial safety.

During World War II, Mrs. Roosevelt put herself on the side of G.I. Joe, going throughout Europe and the Pacific.

Former marines drink to the time when the control of Guadalcanal was in doubt. Japanese destroyers, only yards offshore, fired at the marine foxholes.

When there was a lull, a marine sergeant ran up and down the line crying out: "Don't worry, boys, it's only Eleanor Roosevelt coming in to trade with the natives."

After Harry Truman became president, he presented Mrs. Roosevelt's name to the Senate to be a delegate to the first meeting of the United Nations. Her name cleared the Senate with only one dissenting vote, which was cast by Senator Theodore Bilbo of Mississippi. He stated at the time she had been too friendly with black people.

Her appointment met with considerable dismay in Republican circles, but after John Foster Dulles saw her in action against the Soviet delegate over the rights of people in refugee camps, Dulles said, "I feel I must tell you that when you were appointed I thought it terrible, and now I think your work here has been fine."

With that compliment Mrs. Roosevelt noted in a letter home: "So against odds, the women inch forward, but I'm rather old to be carrying on this fight."

There are those who claim that her insistence that the United Nations pass a declaration of human rights was her greatest contribution to mankind. Pope John XXIII, in his encyclical *Pacem in Terris,* called the declaration "an act of highest importance," according to Joseph Lash in his book *Eleanor: The Years Alone,* W. W. Norton, 1972.

At seventy-eight she was afflicted with what doctors had privately diagnosed as a rare bone-marrow tuberculosis. She gracefully accepted death, but not before her favorite Democrat, Adlai Stevenson, came by for one last visit. What a touching moment that must have been.

Mrs. Roosevelt was a friend of my parents, especially my father, who was in charge of all [war production in] federal prisons . . . during World War II. One day during the war, Franklin Roosevelt turned to his secretary, Grace Tully, and asked: "Where's Eleanor today?" The secretary responded: "She's in prison with Maury Maverick." FDR, not so much as looking up from the paper he was reading, replied, "I'm not the least bit surprised." ★

LIZ CARPENTER: AN OLD FRIEND

"'Grandma Whiz' Hits Home,"
February 2, 1986

I was born a Texan with five generations before me. I am a pre-Alamo, pre-San Jacinto, pre-Civil War, pre-Republican Texas. All of these talismen murmur to me as my mother did: "Remember who you are. Make something of yourself." So I never lacked confidence, and I never had an identity problem. I knew who I was: a Texan born of pioneer stock.

Liz Carpenter in *Texas Monthly.*

I wrote home [1942] with girlish enthusiasm about my visits [in Washington, D.C.,] with Maury Maverick, the unorthodox Texas Democrat. . . . His son, Maury, Jr., was an old friend . . . well, really a serious boyfriend. . . . One time I wrote my mother, "I think I will marry Maury, Jr." Back came the letter of warning:

"I've found it a good idea never to make final decisions till you are at home and in normal surroundings . . . . The Mavericks may be all right, but they have been termed by conservatives as 'extremists' and by those more outspoken as 'crackpots,' and I want you to think long and hard before you align yourself with anything but the best.

"The qualifications you mention of an old Texas name and being a Southern gentleman are fine and much to be considered, but I have known people with both of those who were about as congenial to live with as a Bengal tiger with a tin can tied to his tail."

Liz Carpenter, *Getting Better All the Time*, Simon & Schuster, 1987.

"My God, Maury, do you realize how close we came to getting married?" Liz Carpenter asked me at lunch . . . in Austin, where I had gone to interview her [in 1986]. Then she read from a letter she had written to her mother in June of 1942: "I think I'll marry Maury, Jr. In fact I am going to have to if his father doesn't quit introducing me to all the Maverick relatives and newspaper columnists as Maury's fiancee. He is the politest boy I have ever known."

"Maury," Liz continued, "you were such a nice young man. How in the world did you turn out the way you did?"

My Polish wife, the former Julia Orynski, sitting at my side taking it all in, without so much as looking up from her plate, interjected, "Liz, I can tell you from personal experience that you lucked out. . . ."

Liz is the first woman ever to be elected vice-president of the University of Texas student body, and although she has always denied she had anything to do with it, I remember pre-World War II campaign posters in her behalf stuck up around the campus that read: "If you would vote against me for vice-president of the student body solely because I am a woman, you are a son of a . . . ."

She is one of the most famous people in America when it comes to fighting discrimination because of sex. All her life she has deeply resented women being treated as second-class citizens. . . .

"Liz," I asked, "who are the women that touched your life the most?"

"Lady Bird Johnson, my best friend. She taught me how to be a widow. Like Eleanor Roosevelt, she made the office of First Lady into something other than social."

"Oveta Culp Hobby, who was head of the WACs during World War II and who fought for the rights of women soldiers."

"Esther Van Wagoner Tufty, a great woman journalist known as 'the Duchess,' who hired me to cover the White House for $25 a week when I first went to Washington."

"Eleanor Roosevelt, because she fought for women journalists. In those days the wire services and the *New York Times* would just about hire only men, so Mrs. Roosevelt ordered that no one but women could come to her press conferences. We wore white gloves and hats, and Mrs. Roosevelt always served tea. By discriminating and insisting that only women could come to her press conferences, she eliminated a lot of discrimination."

"Shirley Hufstedler, who was secretary of education for Jimmy Carter. I was the assistant secretary. She would have been the first woman on the Supreme Court if the Democrats had won."

"Frances Perkins, known as Madame Perkins, who was secretary of labor for Franklin Roosevelt. She was the cutting edge for liberalism of the New Deal. Most working men today do not know it, but the really great legislation requiring such things as safety on the job came from her."

"Fannie Lou Hamer, a Mississippi black woman for whom I campaigned when she ran for the Mississippi state senate more than twenty years ago. She was the person most responsible for getting the delegation from Mississippi with blacks on it seated in the 1960 Democratic convention. She taught me some things about black dignity. . . ."

Whatever our political differences, and especially those that existed during the Vietnam War when Liz was at the White House, she never quit me as a friend, although I became one of the few lawyers in the country (along with a kid named Gerry Goldstein) representing war resisters.

One time in the worst of the Vietnam War, Liz called me to meet Air Force One at Randolph Air Force Base. I wouldn't have won any popularity contests in those days around the president and his assistants, but Liz walked up to me, gave me a hug, put her arm through mine, and stood there in full view of LBJ.

Liz's great-great-grandfather, Sterling Robertson, for whom Robertson County was named, signed the Declaration of Independence of the Republic of Texas and, as empresario, established Robertson Colony with folks from Tennessee. The Robertsons were close allies of Sam Houston.

Liz's great-great-uncle, Dr. John Sutherland, was the one Travis sent on horseback to scout the approach of Santa Anna's army, while [an early] cousin William D. Sutherland, a seventeen-year-old boy, died at the Alamo. "Bill had gone there to learn Spanish. That was a h--- of a way to take a foreign language lesson," Liz insists.

On top of all that, there are her Menefee ancestors who

equally figured in the Texas Revolution. . . .

Funny, smart as a whip, tough as a boot, and with a noble face worthy of being engraved on Mount Rushmore, Liz Carpenter is a friend of the women of this country, and of mankind.

No one has fought harder for the dignity of women than Liz Carpenter. . . .

"To Liz: No Crackpot Mavericks!"
July 26, 1987

[On the "crackpot" claim, surely] there is not a single reader, friend or foe of this column, who thinks for a minute the Mavericks are "crackpots." Extremists, maybe, but crackpots, never! I defy Liz to find a single person in San Antonio who would agree with that "crackpot" evaluation. . . .

Liz's [*Getting Better All the Time*] is about a lot of things, like her roots, which include her great-great-uncle, George Childress, a journalist, who wrote the Texas Declaration of Independence. . . .

There is one funny story after another regarding famous personalities, like the one about Betsy Cronkite, wife of Walter Cronkite, the famous television personality. The Cronkites spent much of their honeymoon at a particular hotel in Mexico City. On that occasion Mrs. Cronkite is quoted as saying she went in the bathroom and cried. Forty years later they decided to celebrate their marriage by going back to the same hotel. That second time, Mrs. Cronkite insists, "Walter went in the bathroom and cried."

I love Liz's story about the late U.S. Senator Paul Douglas, a hero of mine. Retired Colonel Fritz Knust, U.S. Marine Corps Reserves and a moss-back Republican lawyer of San Antonio, can get tears in his eyes when he talks about his old liberal pal, Paul Douglas, who, although a famous forty-two-year-old economics professor, joined the Marine Corps as a private. . . .

Late in life Douglas suffered a stroke. One day, reaching for something, he fell out of his wheelchair, and his wife, Emily, once a member of the U.S. House of Representatives, had no one to help her lift her husband back to the chair or to the bed. Mrs. Douglas immediately told her husband: "Paul, we haven't had a picnic in such a long time." With that she went to the kitchen, made some finger sandwiches, brought in a few potted plants to simulate a country scene, opened a bottle of wine, and then the two old lovers read poetry to one another until help came. . . .

I have one serious criticism of Liz's *Getting Better All the Time*, and it's the same one I had of her first book, *Ruffles and Flourishes*, Doubleday, 1969. In those two books she keeps throwing one softball after another. She knows better because I knew Liz when she was young, mean, lean, ambitious, and full of knowledge about the skeletons of the District of Columbia. I am waiting for her third book when she takes off the gloves.

Her skimpy treatment of the Vietnam War in her latest book is offensive to me.

Oh, dear me, Vietnam was such a burden to Lyndon and Bird. But what Liz does not mention is that the massive enlargement of the Vietnam War came from the lies and deceit of Lyndon Johnson's Tonkin Gulf resolution, an absolute frame-up.

I am particularly sorry about Lady Bird, my favorite First Lady after Eleanor Roosevelt, but Mrs. Johnson's suffering does not equal that of the Mexican-American mothers on the West Side of San Antonio whose sons did not come home, while the "well-born" sons remained in college, a gift of the Democratic Party, "the friend of the little people." (That's a rough thing to say, but when authors don't talk turkey, critics must.)

But personal loyalty is deeply important to Liz, and even I was the benefactor of that part of her thinking. . . .

I owe Liz this much: Her latest effort is a fun book of easy reading and of laughter and happiness. Understanding that, and forgetting the pain that I hope she will write about in her third book, I unhesitatingly urge you to buy *Getting Better All the Time*, but with the sure and certain knowledge that the Mavericks are not crackpots. ★

SAM JOHNSON, JR.: LYNDON'S DAD

"Sam Johnson, Jr., Stood Tall and Courageous,"
January 30, 1983

Robert A. Caro, in his first volume on Lyndon Johnson, *The Path to Power*, Knopf, 1982–a book well worth having–has convinced me that historians have not given Lyndon's father, Sam Johnson, Jr., his due.

Sam had the "Bunton arrogance" from his mother and the "Johnson strut" from his father, but, Caro insists, both characteristics were "open and friendly."

You folks in Fredericksburg, Comfort, Boerne, and throughout the Hill Country, gather around the campfire and let's talk about Lyndon's father, who is mostly remembered for ending up in life a financial failure with too great a love for the bottle. But Caro seems to contend that when it comes to kindness and honesty, Sam was a better man than his famous son, LBJ.

In 1904, Sam Johnson, Jr., was elected to the Texas House of Representatives. As a populist he demonstrated his concern for drought-stricken ranchers and farmers of West Texas by authoring a bill that would provide $3 million in assistance, a staggering sum for those days. A historian, he was author of the Alamo Purchase Bill appropriating $65,000 for the purchase of the Alamo. In 1905 the *Gillespie County News*, which had opposed Johnson, came out with an editorial describing the new representative as "one of the most active and influential members of the House and an ideal Representative."

Caro gives his highest marks to Representative Sam Johnson, Jr., for not abandoning the people of German descent in 1918 when anti-German hysteria was rampant in Texas. It was a time when "Germans" were "publicly horsewhipped."

Sam was faced with House Bill 15, that made the slightest criticism of America's entry into World War I a crime with a sentence of two to twenty years.

This was the same hysteria which ran my great-uncle James Slayden out of the U.S. House of Representatives. His district included Gillespie County, and when he opposed our country's entry into World War I, Woodrow Wilson wiped out Slayden. Slayden had earlier given Chester Nimitz an appointment to the Naval Academy. Ellen Maury Slayden, my blood aunt, had known Wilson at the University of Virginia and dated him. A pacifist, she loathed Wilson after 1918 for destroying her husband the congressman.

"But Sam Johnson," as Caro puts it, "standing tall, skinny, and big-eared on the floor of the House, made a speech remembered with admiration fifty years later . . . urging defeat of House Bill 15." Austin's German newspaper editorialized: "At a time when hate propaganda was at its worst, Sam Johnson, Jr., showed courage. . . ."

Years earlier, in 1907, Sam had made what was his first brave fight on the floor of the House by opposing Senator Joseph Weldon Bailey.

Bailey "to this day may be the greatest orator in the history of Texas," former Senator Ralph Yarborough told me over the telephone last week. He was, for a long time, an overwhelmingly popular political figure, as evidenced by the hundreds of men, black and white, who, even until the present have as their first two names "Joe Bailey." This is especially true around the Bible Belt near Waco. . . .

From one end of Texas to the other, Bailey would denounce the "selfish corporations." But it finally came out that Bailey was taking huge sums of money from those "selfish corporations"–including a $100,000 "retainer" from Standard Oil.

There was an investigation of sorts begun in the Texas legislature, which the lobbyists countered by arranging for what amounted to a vote of confidence for Bailey, a vote they wanted unanimously in his favor.

On the day of the vote in the Texas House of Representatives, the galleries were packed with sweet-smelling lobbyists who, the night before, had poured the booze and, some claim, provided "the blondes."

"Mr. Speaker! Mr. Speaker!" one of Bailey's men on the floor of the Texas House cried out, and then he brought up for consideration the confidence vote of Joe Bailey.

Of the nearly 150 members of the House, only seven had the courage to vote against Bailey. Sam Johnson, Jr., was one of those seven, once again standing tall, courageous, and big-eared, according to Robert Caro. Afterward the House chaplain called Sam "a quiet worker," and the saying became widespread in Austin that Old Sam as "straight as a shingle. . . ."

Near the end of his life Sam Johnson went broke, couldn't pay his bills, drank too much, and became a bad joke around the Texas Hill Country. He died in grinding poverty, and a good question is–did this experience in Lyndon's life cause him not only to want money, but all the money?

On October 23, 1937, Sam Johnson, Jr., died. The times he failed in life are remembered more today than the times he stood alone. Having served six years myself in the Texas House of Representatives during the Joe McCarthy period, I knew brave men, the blind Jim Sewells of Corsicana and the D. B. Hardemans of Denison and Goliad, and so, thanks to Caro, I have a new regard for Lyndon's father.

In my mind's eye I can see the bullies of World War I persecuting the people of German descent while Sam Johnson, Jr., stood up for them. I can see the lobbyists, always smirking, calling for a favorable vote on Senator Joe Bailey, a vote that gave credence to corruption, and Sam, "skinny and big-eared," once again standing virtually alone. Now I know Sam helped save the Alamo.

All my adult life I have heard Hill Country jokes about Sam Johnson, Jr., but the record suggests he was a better fellow than I was led to believe. This, then, is to right a wrong and to give the man his due. ★

"TIGER" JIM SEWELL: DEDICATED LEGISLATOR

"Sunsets Warmed Tiger Jim Sewell,"
May 6, 1979

It happened during World War II in the Pacific when one of our planes, back from a combat mission, was coming in for a landing on the carrier USS *Hornet*.

On deck waiting for the plane was Chief Petty Officer James Sewell, who had come out of the oil fields of Texas, a highly skilled, two-fisted, hell-raising roughneck.

As the plane landed, a bomb freakishly dislodged and exploded. Jim was knocked unconscious. When he came to, the doctors told him he was going to be blind for the rest of his life, and he was.

The blind sailor came home from the seas to Corsicana and sent a wire to his girlfriend, Janet Hoover, telling her that their marriage was off. Janet caught the next plane to Texas. "You are not going to get out of marrying me because you're blind," she said to Jim. Three days later they were husband and wife.

The couple moved to Austin, where Jim earned his undergraduate degree and then applied for law school. Law Professor Clarence Morris told him he couldn't make it. There was just too much to read, but Jim won a law degree with high scores. Professor Morris, who had been his friend all along, offered Jim a job with his father's business in Philadelphia.

But the new lawyer went back to Corsicana. [He was] elected to the Texas House of Representatives at about the same time I was, [and] we got to be friends over a resolution calling for the impeachment of Justice William O. Douglas. Only eleven members voted against it, Sewell and I among them.

He came to my desk on the floor of the House, introduced himself, and let me know he liked Judge Douglas, his eyes following my eyes all the time we talked. It was instant friendship. Then Jim walked away unaided. I didn't know he was blind as a bat until a week later. "A blind person has to work at making sighted people comfortable around him," Jim finally told me.

Afterwards the Gas House Gang was formed, a name the press gave some thirty-five of us when we first got together for the purpose of placing a tax on natural gas. We asked Sewell to be our leader. He accepted and around then the blind representative became known as "Tiger Jim."

He was a tiger about a lot of things. A tiger against Joe McCarthy legislation. A tiger against antiblack legislation. A tiger for country hospitals and for farm-to-market roads. A tiger for public schools.

Retiring from the legislature, he became the county judge of Navarro County and later the district judge. Martin Luther King, Jr., and the blacks were marching then; strong racial prejudices began to emerge in that part of Texas. . . . But the tiger was still a tiger with teeth and stood with the blacks and for the Constitution of the United States.

He was such a cheerful person who put you totally at ease about his blindness. To young girls and old girls he would say,

"You look so nice today. Where did you get that lovely dress?" Women liked him. Many times around sunset he would say to me, "Maverick, just look at that sunset. Isn't it pretty?"

Jim's wife died, and about two years later he began dating Kathleen Voigt, a widow and the one-time Democratic Party she-devil who scandalized her affluent Alamo Heights neighbors thirty years ago by inviting black people to her home for supper.

Kathleen went up for a dinner dance halfway between Dallas and Corsicana. She and Jim were dancing when it happened. Suddenly Sewell fell to the floor and died in minutes. The orchestra was playing "All of Me."

Who goes to a funeral tells of the dead. Those at Jim's covered more than fifty years of Texas politics. A few of the remaining lieutenants of Jimmy Allred, the last liberal governor of Texas (1936-1939), were there, half blind and crippled. Some old women schoolteachers sat off to the side; they had been hounded for standing with Homer Rainey, once the president of the University of Texas, who was destroyed over academic freedom.

New Dealers and Fair Dealers and folks who loved Adlai Stevenson were all over the place. Former Senator Ralph Yarborough, who has suffered more abuse than any politician in the history of Texas outside Sam Houston, was a pallbearer, and so was William Wayne Justice, the lonely and brave U.S. district judge from Athens, Texas. Colleagues from legislative days were on hand, as were blacks, plenty of them, who remembered the Tiger who couldn't see with his eyes, but could with his heart. Astonishingly, the funeral service was lackluster. I wanted a preacher of the type Abe Lincoln preferred for sermons—one who looked like he was fighting bees. If that preacher had known his onions as he looked at those battered Democrats next to Jim's casket, he could have well read a particularly appropriate passage from Shakespeare's *King Henry IV*:

We few, we happy few, we band of brothers;
For he today that sheds his blood with me
Shall be my brother; be he ne'er so vile
This day shall gentle his condition,
And gentlemen in England now-a-bed
Shall think themselves accurst they were not here;
And hold their manhoods cheap while any speaks
That fought with us on St. Crispin's day.

Late some afternoon I am going to drive up to Corsicana and Jim's grave and have a little visit. When it's time to leave, chances are I'll hear that voice again. "Maverick," it will say, "just look at that sunset. Isn't it pretty?" ★

SAM RAYBURN AND HENRY B. GONZALEZ: HONEST POLITICIANS

"Rayburn's Honesty Saluted,"
June 23, 1985

There is no terror, Cassius, in your threats;
For I am armed so strong in honesty
That they pass by me as the idle wind,
Which I respect not.

Shakespeare, *Julius Caesar*, IV, iii.66.

A few weeks ago I obtained a copy of the inventory and appraisal filed in the estate of Speaker Sam Rayburn with the county clerk at Bonham. It is an astonishing document; let me tell you about it. After more than half a century in political office, forty-eight years of which were in the U.S. House of Representatives, Speaker Rayburn, the beloved "Mister Sam," had only the following cash on hand at date of death: "(a) Checking account in the First National Bank, Bonham, Texas,

$4,192.13. (b) Checking account in the Bonham State Bank, $4,596.80. (c) Checking account in the First National Bank, Bonham, in the name of the Rayburn Brothers, wholly owned by Sam Rayburn, $404.05. (d) Checking account in the name of Rayburn Brothers, Bonham State Bank, $928.12. (e) Checking account with the Sergeant-at-Arms, House of Representatives, Washington, D.C., $16,153.44."

Add that all up and it comes to $26,274.54 owned by the third most powerful person, politically speaking, in the country.

Rayburn also owned 1,194 acres of land that Louis Bogey, a San Antonio podiatrist who comes from that neck of the woods, probably would call "some of the sorriest land in Texas" and that Rayburn bought at about ten cents on the dollar during Depression times.

His debts at death came to a total of $5,642. They include such items as: "Baylor University Medical Center, balance of medical bill, $921.12; Rev. H. G. Ball, funeral services, $100; Drs. Short and Balla, doctor bills for last illness [cancer], Dallas, $1,300.00; and Chesapeake & Potomac Tele. Co. to disconnect telephone, $2.12."

Donald C. Bacon . . . a person I would describe as middle-of-the-road leaning to civilized conservative, completed a biography of Speaker Rayburn [*Sam Rayburn: A Biography*, Texas Monthly Press, 1987] that was first researched and in part written by D. B. Hardeman. I wrote to Don Bacon and asked him to tell us what he recalled about the old man's honesty. Here's most of the reply letter from Bacon.

About Rayburn's honesty, you'll notice he died after a lifetime of public service with only a modest estate, most of which was real estate. The home place he built for his parents when he was a second-term congressman (1915-1917) with money he saved by serving as his own secretary.

The farm he bought with a little cash that came to him as a windfall. Most congressmen voted to cut their own pay during the Depression, but when the Depression was over, the congressmen voted to give themselves the money which had been withheld. That was the money used by Rayburn to buy the farm. He later bought two smaller pieces of land. The 1947 Cadillac was a car given him by his Democratic colleagues when he stepped down from the speakership in the two years when his party was in the minority. He had to give up the speaker's chauffeured limousine, so Democratic members of the House chipped in and bought him a Cadillac. The car, incidentally, is still garaged at the home place. Rayburn was scrupulously honest and maintained a strict code of personal ethics. He refused to invest in stocks and bonds because he was concerned about a potential conflict of interest. He was, as you know, the author of the legislation to regulate the sale of securities. The only stock he owned was one thousand shares in Kirby Petroleum stock. But being from a major oil-producing state he worried about the stock constantly and soon sold it. He would be far out of step in today's Congress—he refused to accept honorariums. The only two he ever accepted that I know of were a $200 payment for a speech in Roanoke, Virginia, and $25 for a speech in San Antonio. The Roanoke money he gave to the Robert E. Lee Foundation. The San Antonio money was given to a Rayburn staffer without Mr. Sam's knowledge. He was furious when told of it. . . .

The interesting thing about old man Rayburn is that he never called himself a "liberal," a word that has taken on a wimpy meaning. Time and time he would tell his assistant, D. B. Hardeman: "Call me a progressive conservative or a conservative progressive, but put the word 'progressive' in there."

Whatever the old man really was philosophically, he was first of all honest. Liberals who are crooks offend me more than conservatives who are crooks and this is so although liberals steal less than conservatives. . . .

It is true that the Great Society, and John Kennedy before that with the "beautiful people," did much for the poor, aside from sending them to Vietnam, but in the end a significant number of the Democratic leadership, including some of my own personal friends, took off their hairshirts and went instead for the $75 lobbyist luncheons, while smirking, giggling and winking over "one-liners" that were carefully placed in the various gossip columns of the District of Columbia.

Republicans, especially self-oriented yuppie Republicans, instinctively love money more than injustice to the poor, and, having that reputation, are less resented for it than self-righteous liberal Democrats shinning their rinds around fancy eating joints while not risking the old-fashioned, patriotic, red-white-and-blue radicalism of a Tom Paine that it is going to take for our country to survive in a rampaging, revolutionary world.

[This, therefore,] is a salute to honesty and in particular to Sam Rayburn. Born Samuel Taliaferro Rayburn near the Clinch River in eastern Tennessee on January 6, 1882, he came to Texas as a small child under the most dire circumstances of poverty. "Mister Sam" loved Texas and our country more than he loved money.

Postscript. A contemporary parallel can be made when it comes to a public official and money. Here are shortened extracts from the report Henry B. Gonzalez filed with the House Committee on Standards: Honoraria accepted, none. Interest from savings accounts, two such accounts each earning less than $1,000. Source of all gifts of $100 or more, none. Interest in a trade or property worth $1,000 or more, none (other than home). Money owed to any creditor exceeding $10,000, none. Any purchase of stocks, bonds or realty exceeding $1,000 or more, none.

Then Gonzalez makes one last statement in his own handwriting. It is in that archaic language Henry B. loves to invoke. . . . Here it is: "Neither I nor my wife . . . have any corporeal or corporeal hereditaments through gift, device or descent, nor do I own bonds, stocks, or real or personal property directly or indirectly or other benefits other than those enumerated above."

Gonzalez has a reputation of immediately denouncing journalists who write something nice about him, and so I'll get mine on the floor of the House next week, but like him or not, he appears to be as clean as a hound's tooth on money matters.

"Mister Sam" can move over; he's got a Mexican-Scottish-Italian buddy with the mark of Cortes and Montezuma on him. ★

JOHN HENRY FAULK: FIRST AMENDMENT FOLK HUMORIST

"When the Owl Called Johnny,"
April 29, 1990

John Henry Faulk's wife, Liz, was calling from Austin: "Maury, John Henry will be dead in a few days. Come up and hold his hand and tell him good-bye. He wants his old friends around him."

I drove to Austin the next day, but by then Johnny was in a coma. Never mind that, so I held his hand, told him I loved him, and thanked him for his defense of constitutional liberty and especially for the way he stood up to the Joe McCarthy crowd in the late 1950s when CBS Radio ran out on him. That betrayal destroyed what a lot of folks thought was going to be a superstar career in show business.

Three days later the owl called Johnny's name, as the Indians of British Vancouver say will happen when the time comes to die. "Hoot, hoot, hoot, John Henry Faulk, come with us," I heard the owl say in my heart. Johnny was gone. . . .

"Come Celebrate Johnny,"
August 18, 1885

When Johnny's mother was carrying him, she used to pray every night that she would have a son and that he would be a Methodist preacher. There is no family in South Texas more Methodist than the Faulks.

But when Johnny got to be a grown man, his mother told him: "From the language you were using at the age of ten, I prayed to God every night that if he just kept you out of the penitentiary, you could be anything you wanted. . . ."

In 1940 Faulk did his master's thesis at the University of Texas, entitled, "Ten Negro Sermons," the bibliography for which was one book, the *Bible*. With a grant from the Rosenwald Foundation, he also went with members of the Lomax family to record blacks working the fields and crying out for freedom. You see a lot of dignified Negro humor and grief come out in Johnny's book. Sometimes I think Johnny is an inside-out Oreo cookie: white on the outside, black on the inside. Two sermons by black preachers are included in the [thesis], word for word. . . .

"When the Owl Called Johnny,"
April 29, 1990

Unable to join the military because he was blind in one eye, John Henry first sailed with the merchant marine in World War II, then was with the Red Cross, and finally talked the U. S. Army into letting him join its ranks. From there he went with CBS Radio, where he had the network show "Johnny's Front Porch."

After being called a "Red," John Henry won a $3.5 million libel judgment but could never fully collect. [He got about $150,000.] Ed Murrow, the famous newscaster, mortgaged his home to raise money so Johnny could hire the famous lawyer, Louis Nizer. Others who helped were folks such as Norman Lear, creator of *All in the Family*, and Ozzie Davis, the black Broadway actor. But there is more: Years ago Johnny told me that Jewish friends, grateful for his defense of constitutional liberty, especially helped him eat three meals a day.

That was a lonely time. In the worst of it, when Johnny would walk into the famous Toots Shor restaurant in New York, where he was once a rising celebrity, friends would get up and walk out, not because they thought he was disloyal, but because they were afraid to be seen with him.

On April 21, 1990, there was a memorial service for John Henry at the University Methodist Church in Austin. The Reverend Charles Merrill welcomed the standing-room-only audience, and then Cactus Pryor took over as master of ceremonies.

Black people of Austin's Wesley Choir sang like nothing I had ever heard before in my life. "Come on up to glory!" they sang for Johnny, who had fought for black people in his life.

Bobby Bridges played the guitar and sang, and so did Jerry Jeff Walker, whose last piece was his famous "Mr. Bojangles. . . ."

I was one of the four who gave the eulogy, and here's part of what I said:

> After I left the Texas House of Representatives in 1956, Dr. Walter P. Webb, my future stepfather, invited me to meet John Henry at his country place, Friday Mountain. . . . On that night about fifteen of us sat around a campfire and talked the cause of liberty. I remember that Dr. Webb, J. Frank Dobie and Roy Bedichek were seated next to Johnny, lending him aid and comfort like fighter planes of World War II bringing in a crippled bomber from an air raid over Berlin. When [U.S. Justice] Hugo Black wrote in one of his opinions that mankind has had to fight its way

past the cross, the stake and the hangman's noose, he was in effect describing Johnny, who was handed a hangman's noose at CBS.

In the Jeffersonian sense, Johnny understood this world in revolution. When Third World countries seeking independence cried out the words of Jefferson as our American government or its surrogates bombed them into near oblivion, John Henry, the old-fashioned, indigenous American radical, more Tom Paine than Adlai Stevenson but some of both, made his objections known. The point must be made again: It is not enough to call Johnny a liberal. Part of him was on the radical left, like Sam Houston standing in San Pedro Park at San Antonio calling on the people of Texas not to secede from the Union. The morning after John Henry died CBS had the good grace to play a tape of Johnny's voice saying that perfectly decent people had run out on him, thus illustrating something that [historian] Arthur Schlesinger, Jr., wrote, and that Johnny in pain understood better than Schlesinger—that the threat of liberty comes not so much from the hard-faced person as it does from the faceless person, not so much from the person who would deny freedom to others as from the person who does not want freedom for himself. Historians claim that John Locke talked to Jefferson and Madison, who talked to Lincoln, who talked to Franklin and Eleanor Roosevelt. Well, they all talked to John Henry Faulk, and now Johnny talks to us from the grave. ★

MAURY MAVERICK HUEY: RESTAURATEUR

"Ding How for America,"
January 22, 1989

Today [January 1989] I am sixty-one years old, but on that day in 1942, I was fourteen living with my mother, Lui Cho Wan, in the village of Kun Yick, Toi Shan District, Kwantung Province, China. My father, Kok An, was in San Antonio running his Chinese restaurant, Hung Fong, on Broadway. The Japanese bombers began to fly over three abreast in wave after wave, dropping bombs. My older brother and I ran to the fields, but my mother refused to leave our home. After we saw the bombers depart we returned to find that the home had been blown to bits. We tore at the rubble until our hands were bleeding, but did not find our mother until years later when the miracle happened in Hong Kong, British crown colony. I thought my mother had been killed. For the rest of World War II it was hard for me. I barely survived, eating one meal a day at best. Sometimes no meal at all. Then Maury Maverick, Sr., the former mayor of San Antonio, went to court and won for me before Judge Ben Rice. Because of that court decree I was able to come to San Antonio and join my father in 1953.

Maury Maverick Huey, whose Chinese name
was Kok Kon Jong.

Maury, Jr., listen to me. It took years to get Maury Maverick Huey out of Hong Kong. If and when you bring his wife and children here be sure that the children have an education. Tell Maury Huey to send them to the University of Texas. Don't let anybody hurt those Chinese-Americans.

Maury, Sr., to Maury, Jr., Nix Hospital, San Antonio,
days before Maury, Sr., died on June 7, 1954.

Close friends of mine claim that when you add up all the

stories I insist my father told me as he lay dying in the Nix Hospital, it would have been impossible for him to have had the time to die. Sometimes they call me the biggest liar in town. Well, I might be stretching the blanket here and there on minor details. After all, Uncle Charlie [Charles Kilpatrick, publisher of the *Express-News*] didn't hire me to be a bore in this column, but my old daddy cared deeply about the Huey family, and he honest-to-God laid it on my back to look after the Hueys right up until the day before he died.

In 1964, the result of a hearing I sought as a lawyer before Immigration and Naturalization, Maury Huey's three children came to San Antonio. They are Maury Maverick Huey, Jr., today thirty-nine years old, a graduate of the University of Texas with a wife and four children; Maurice Huey, thirty-five, graduate of the University of Texas with a wife and four children; and Helen Huey See, mother of three sons who, with her electrical-engineer husband, owns and operates the Jade Fountain, a prominent Chinese restaurant in Austin.

The three Huey children who came here from Hong Kong were proclaimed U. S. citizens on November 6, 1964, by Chief U. S. District Judge Adrian Spears. . . .

Today the Hueys own three popular restaurants in San Antonio: Hung Fong on Broadway, Ding How on Northwest Interstate 410, and Casa Mauricio on San Pedro. The grandchildren are going to private Catholic schools. ("Mr. Maverick, we are Buddhists, but the Catholics have the best discipline for children.") They live in fine homes and drive fine cars.

If my father were alive today and dying, he would call in the Hueys and tell them to look after me. . . .

I thought up the name "Ding How" for the restaurant, its being a slang expression used by "China marines" of the U.S. Marine Corps before World War II. Roughly translated it means: "Everything is going good." I thought it a good name because it would bring back memories to the old birds of my generation who served in the Pacific.

But Lord God above, I have put the cart in front of the horse. Let's back up to 1916 as a Japanese ship, the *Nippon Yunan*, slides past the whistling buoy and the fog of San Francisco to drop anchor and discharge its passengers, who include one Kok An, master Chinese cook, who, on a return visit to China, would become the father of Maury Maverick Huey. (Because of Chinese exclusion laws, Chinese males in this country would live here a while, go back to China, marry, have children and then return to the United States.)

Kok An, the grandfather, cooked at the finest Chinese restaurants in San Francisco, Chicago, and New York City, but then a friend wrote him that San Antonio's weather was much like it is in Kun Yick, the village Kok An had left. So he came to San Antonio where in 1938 he opened Hung Fong on Broadway, today San Antonio's oldest Chinese restaurant.

But now it is time to tell you about the miracle, a needle in the haystack when you consider China has about one-fifth of the world's population.

In 1955 in a part of Hong Kong to which people from the Toi Shan District, Kwantung Province, China, gravitated, Diana Huey, by then the wife of Maury Maverick Huey and the mother of his three children, was in a store talking to a salesclerk.

An elderly woman recognized that the younger woman was talking in the dialect of her native village of Kun Yick. Back and forth the two women exchanged information until they realized that the older woman was the mother-in-law of the younger woman!

Some ten years later Diana and her three children arrived in the United States, and shortly thereafter Judge Adrian Spears decreed that the three Huey children were citizens of this country. That, too, was the result of a long legal fight in which I was

251

the attorney.

In 1967, the old grandmother, Lui Cho Wan, arrived in San Antonio. What a happening it was when she stepped off the airplane. Dennis Hevesi, writing in the San Antonio *Express* of May 26, 1967, described the moment this way: "The older Huey stepped up to the boarding ramp and escorted his wife off the plane. A moment later, a tear-filled man [Maury Maverick Huey] was at his mother's side, for the first time in twenty-five years."

Later there was a grand banquet at Hung Fong. The grandfather and grandmother, husband and wife, sat side by side, which reminded me of some testimony in an earlier court hearing when I had asked old Mr. Huey [the grandfather, Kok An] if he recalled the day he married his wife. It was then that Huey testified: "In the custom of China they carried the woman to me I was about to marry in a red sedan chair with long bamboo poles."

At the banquet cigars were passed around. Toasts were made to love, adversity, the blood of a family, and one in Chinese and then in English to my father.

There were laughter and tears, and as I looked at those Chinese-Americans, thinking back on some twenty-five years of legal effort, I said in my heart: "Thank you, Judge Ben Rice and thank you, Judge Adrian Spears." And in my heart, I saluted Old Glory.

That night the melting pot that is America took on a new people with a different culture, a different language, and a different religion. The grandfather and grandmother had a few years together in San Antonio and today are side by side in death. Now their grandchildren are graduates of the University of Texas and hard-working, law-abiding citizens.

By God, this can be a fine country, a shining light to the world when we are considerate, civilized, and gentle to one another.

Ding how for America. Ding how! ★

JOHN NANCE GARNER: "CACTUS JACK"

"The Cat's in John Garner's Bag,"
January 12, 1986

The thirty-second Vice President of the United States, John Garner, was born on November 22, 1868, in a log cabin in Red River County, Texas, 30 miles from Indian territory . . . died quietly of a coronary occlusion on November 7, 1967, 15 days short of his 99th birthday. Services were conducted in St. Philips Episcopal Church, and he was buried in the Uvalde Cemetery.

The Handbook of Texas Supplement.

As vice-president to Franklin Delano Roosevelt, John Nance Garner opposed FDR's attempt to reorganize the Supreme Court, was against recognizing the Soviet Union, and thought his president too generous with organized labor during the sit-down strikes of 1937.

Having told you old things that, what bubble-headed, goofy liberal in American politics was most responsible for the income tax? Henry Wallace? No, it was John Garner.

What good-for-nothing "socialist" did the most important legislative groundwork resulting in the law whereby the federal government, not free enterprise, guarantees bank deposits up to $100,000?

Norman Thomas, leader of the American Socialist Party?

No, it was John Garner. In the book, *Mr. Garner of Texas*, Bobbs-Merrill, 1939, by Marquis James, the point is made that Garner, at the beginning term of his some thirty years in Congress, introduced one of the first graduated income tax bills ever in the history of our country. In fact, James writes that Garner "fought to a standstill Andrew Mellon's income-tax ideas that favored the rich."

The proposed Garner income tax had a spread that ran

from a tax of 1 percent on incomes of less than $1,000 per year to a tax of 5 percent on annual incomes in excess of $100,000. The final form came out with modifications, but Garner won over Mellon.

The fifteenth Congressional District from which Garner was first elected, bigger than the state of Pennsylvania, ran 150 miles along the Gulf Coast and then four hundred miles up the Rio Grande from its mouth. It was a district with political bosses who did not cotton to a fair and square income tax.

There was the original Archie Parr of Duval County, which was known as the Free State of Duval; James B. Wells of Brownsville, attorney for the King and Kenedy ranches; Judge John Valls of Laredo; Robert J. Kleberg of Kingsville; Manuel Guerra of Starr County; Tom Coleman of Dimmit; and Pat P. Dunn of Nueces County, principal owner of Padre Island. These men of immense power backed Garner, but how he got away with his income tax ideas is a mystery to me.

Maybe the answer to the mystery of why Garner was elected from the fifteenth Congressional District is in part the result of an even bigger mystery. It involves the question: Was Garner ever defeated for office in Uvalde County?

The Handbook of Texas, ordinarily as reliable as the good Lord in his heaven above, mentions no political defeat in Uvalde County. Marquis James implies that Garner was never defeated there.

But I have another story from an old-timer, a Rock of Gibraltar whose name is a household word in West Texas, but he will not let me use his name.

This is what he told me: "When Garner was county judge of Uvalde County, the schools were run by that office. That was around 1895, and Garner stated even in those days that Mexican-American children should go to school with Anglo children. That, plus the fact he drank whiskey and played cards, which got him in trouble with the Baptists, defeated him for reelection as county judge, but the main thing was his stand for integration in the public schools."

I asked my source: "Did Mr. Garner in some way use this to his advantage when he ran for Congress?" To this I was told: "Yes, he did use it to his advantage for if you consider the geographical limits of his congressional district, it is immediately obvious that it was populated in a rank-and-file way by discriminated-against Mexican-Americans who knew of Garner's stand for racial justice. After that he had trouble getting reelected in Uvalde County, but as the votes came in from the counties to the south, he always won big."

Garner, as even his enemies admit, was a shrewd politician who had both the plain people and the power brokers with him. In Uvalde, where he was known as a "money lender," he had his troubles, but he knocked 'em dead in places like Nueces County.

If some of you Uvalde historians can prove or disprove the "school integration" legend, and I have heard it time and time again for years, then invite me out and let's examine the records. Shame the devil and tell the truth!

If your research proves the legend wrong, then maybe my sister-in-law, Elizabeth Woodward, principal of the Uvalde Episcopal School, will pray for my soul and seek forgiveness for me. She's a good-hearted woman, and I call upon the fine people of Uvalde, including Janey Briscoe, not to blame Elizabeth for her little sister's marrying me.

But Garner—backer of the graduated income tax—that's a cat out of the bag.

And Garner—backer of a school integration plan for Mexican-Americans around 1895—that's one h— of a cat out of the bag, if true.

Meow! Meow!

There are more cats to let out of the bag. Holy tamale,

255

Uncle Dudley done quit preaching and gone to meddlin'!

A few years before Garner died, I went to Uvalde to interview him. He wouldn't talk about his falling-out with Franklin Roosevelt, but he did tell me about the day he left the District of Columbia to return forever to Texas.

"I was standing by the train," Garner related, "and the newspaper boys asked me when I'd come back to Washington. I told them I would never come back, and so the newspaper boys gave me a big 'ha ha' but the 'ha ha' was on them. I never went back." When Garner told me that, he was in his nineties, and he was wearing pajama pants and a soft felt frock-tail coat, the very coat he was wearing when sworn in as vice-president of the United States.

Whatever his resentment of the New Deal, Garner never quit the Democratic Party.

Item. At the urging of Dolph Briscoe, a former governor and [a man] with whom I served in the Texas House in the early 1950s and [who] I remember as a first-rate legislator, Garner had a breakfast for Harry Truman when it looked like Truman didn't have a chance in 1948.

Item. He had another breakfast that time for Adlai Stevenson. Again Dolph Briscoe had a hand in this. I was there and remember Garner offering Adlai a drink of bourbon just as he was about to leave so that Adlai could "strike a blow for liberty."

Item. He backed Ralph Yarborough for statewide political office. . . .

Because I grew up in a fervent New Deal family, John Garner was one of the villains of my childhood, and I still disagree with him on opposing such programs as federal housing projects, which in Garner's mind threatened a balanced budget. I believe in things like Social Security, aid to farmers and ranchers, pensions for retired colonels, and other good democratic socialist programs like tax write-offs for oil men.

But on the subject of money John Garner was simply tight as a frog's backside, and that's watertight. He was that way in his own personal life, and he was equally that way about government spending. Ronald Reagan's deficit spending would have blown his mind.

If, however, John Garner really fought for legislative reform and went with the plain people instead of the rich on an income tax, if he laid the groundwork for federal guarantees for bank deposits, and especially if he made a fight for racial justice way back around 1895 by helping down-and-out Mexican-American schoolkids, all of which I believe to be true, then he was a better fellow than I was told.

You cats get back in the bag. Especially that school integration cat!

Uncle Dudley ain't going to get caught in Uvalde County after the sun goes down. (Don't take it out on my sweet sister-in-law, the Uvalde school principal.)

Meow! ★

THE NEWTON BOYS: OUTLAWS

"Newton Boys Were Gentle Bandits,"
February 27, 1994

The most successful bank and train robbers in American history, the Newton Boys (of Uvalde) still have not made it into the pantheon of famous outlaws, despite their having robbed more than sixty banks and six trains in four years . . . their career culminated with the biggest train robbery in U. S. history at Rondout, Illinois, on June 12, 1924. By their own accounting, they made out with more loot in those four years than Jesse and Frank James, the Dalton Boys, Butch Cassidy, and all the other famous outlaw gangs put together.

Claude Stanush, *The Smithsonian,* January, 1994.

257

I wanted something . . . and I knew I would never get it fol-
lowing a mule's ass and dragging cotton sacks down them middles.

Willis Newton, *The Newton Boys*, by Claude Stanush and
David Middleton, State House Press, 1994.

The thing that most attracted [Claude Stanush to] the Newton brothers–Willis, Jess, Doc and Joe . . . was their claim that in all their robberies, they never killed anyone.

Willis told Stanush: "We wasn't gunfighters, and we wasn't thugs like Bonnie and Clyde. All we wanted was the money. We was just businessmen like doctors and lawyers and storekeepers. Robbin' banks and trains was our business. . . . When we went on a job I told the boys, 'If you have to shoot, don't shoot to kill.' In fact, we loaded our guns with bird shot a lot of times to make sure we didn't kill nobody. We never did."

Those distinguished Newton capitalists, who stole less than savings and loan officials and bankers during the last ten years, spent a fair amount of time in various prisons about the country.

The most innovative of the Newton brothers during their convict days was Willis, who pulled off the slickest trick in the history of Huntsville. He wrote the judge and sheriff who had a lot to do with sending him to the penitentiary and asked that they join in a request for [his] pardon. They both wrote back saying they would not help.

Willis then forged their signatures to a pardon application and had about sixty of his buddy convicts sign the application as if they were upstanding citizens. The warden told Willis it was the finest pardon application he had ever seen, and with that Governor William Hobby granted Willis his pardon. . . .

The Newton Boys includes a fourteen-page prologue and an eight-page epilogue that Stanush and Middleton wrote together. The rest consists of conversations, mostly with Willis, which begin at page one with this comment: "I'm Willis Newton, and I live in Uvalde, Texas. I was born in Callahan County near the town of Cottonwood southwest of Dallas, January 19, 1889. . . . In my time I robbed over eighty banks and six trains. On most of these jobs Jess, Doc, and Joe was with me . . . we was just quiet businessmen."

Now and then there is an editor's note, such as this one at page 267: "The Newtons' successful career as robbers came dramatically to a climax on the night of January 12, 1924. The four of them . . . held up the Chicago, Milwaukee & St. Paul mail train . . . about twenty-five miles northwest of Chicago. . . . Approximately $3 million was seized, making this, in the words of the *Chicago Tribune*, June 15, 1924, 'the biggest of all mail robberies.' That's when they went to Leavenworth."

Folks in Uvalde remember the Newton Boys in a good-natured way. I called former Governor Dolph Briscoe. . . . I asked Dolph: "Is it true the Newton Boys never robbed your Uvalde bank because that's where they kept their money?" Dolph laughed at that, but would neither affirm nor deny the rumor. He did say: "The brothers borrowed money from us and always paid it back on time. Their word was good at First State Bank in Uvalde."

I mentioned U. S. District Judge Darwin Suttle to Dolph, who told me: "Judge Suttle when practicing law in Uvalde was one of the finest and most able lawyers I ever knew. He represented John Garner and he represented First State Bank."

Suttle explained: "I slightly knew the Newton Boys, but the one who was my friend was Joe, who sold me the best horse I ever had. Joe was always completely honest with me." Margaret Rambie, in a *Uvalde News Leader* column, described Joe as "my favorite bank robber." ★

D. B. HARDEMAN: SOFT-HEARTED STORYTELLER

"D. B. Hardeman: Soft-Hearted Storyteller,"
in D.B.: Reminiscences of D. B. Hardeman,
Larry Hufford, editor, 1984

D. B. and I served our first term together in the Texas House of Representatives in 1951.

John McCully, then a newspaperman and a partner of Stuart Long, came to me and said: "You're going to meet a man named D. B. Hardeman. He will talk conservative at first but will vote liberal. He's smart as a whip and a good fellow. Don't run him off because of what he says at the outset."

As we liberals began to discover one another–John Barnhart of Beeville, Bob Mullen of Alice, Doug Crouch of Denton, Jamie Clements of Crockett, Edgar Berlin of Port Neches, Jim Sewell of Corsicana, and Bob Wheeler of Tilden, among others–D. B. would tell us: "Now let's give Governor Allan Shivers a chance to do right. He was one of my campaign managers when I ran for editor of the *Daily Texan* at the University of Texas."

But Shivers turned more and more to the right, and D. B. began to turn more and more to the left, although he never called himself a "liberal" because he didn't like the term. He used the term "progressive." Whatever term you prefer, Hardeman, according to the AFL-CIO, had a perfect voting record for both of the terms he served in the house.

On a long-range, day-in, day-out basis, D. B. was the most important member of the Texas House of Representatives I ever served with in my six years as a legislator. He was not important in the sense of power or committee assignments because he was not then the speaker's man. In those days he fought the speaker. But he was important as an intellectual and as a high-minded person. Above all he was important because he brought the liberals together, taught them how to count votes, and even persuaded them to be polite to one another.

We gathered at least three nights a week at D. B.'s apartment and plotted floor fights for the next day, sometimes drinking too much and on occasion making fools out of ourselves. As an aside, I could always tell when it was the end of the month and D. B. was broke—he started drinking cheap whiskey and lived off brussels sprouts.

But at those nightly meetings, usually around midnight, D. B. would be in his baggy shorts—a libation in one hand, a book in the other—and deliver a stirring oration, urging us to go out on the floor of the House the next morning and fight the honey-money lobbyists.

D. B. had a quality of kindness about him that was his strength but also his weakness and the reason, I think, he never held high office, such as U. S. senator or even higher.

He just couldn't hurt anybody. In politics, figuratively speaking, one must on occasion plunge a knife into an adversary. D. B. understood this, would talk about it late at night, advocate it, and promise to personally do it the next morning. But he never would, and with those of us who loved him it became an affectionate joke.

When the time came for D. B. to retire, my wife, Julia, and I had a significant hand in getting him to make his home in San Antonio. In less than a year he had made more friends than you can shake a stick at. Especially young people.

About two years before D. B. died—his middle name was Barnard—I began efforts as a lawyer to bring to Texas the remains of his great-grandfather, Dr. Joseph Henry Barnard, "the surgeon of the Goliad Massacre," as he is known in Texas history books.

Dr. Barnard, a hero of the Texas Revolution, had unexpectedly died on a visit to Canada in 1861. On the same day that

D. B. died in the Nix Hospital in San Antonio, the remains of Dr. Barnard arrived at the funeral home in Austin.

After former Governor Dolph Briscoe gave the eulogy for D. B., who had been Dolph's best man, we buried D. B. and his great-grandfather next to one another midway along the west fence of the state cemetery in Austin, a stone's throw from Stephen F. Austin, Big Foot Wallace, and D. B.'s favorite history professor, Dr. Walter Prescott Webb.

Then we went over to the home of Jean and Russell Lee– Russ was one of the New Deal's great photographers of hungry people during Depression days–and had a few drinks and told D. B. Hardeman stories. . . .

"D.B.: A Knockout Book and Man,"
March 18, 1984

D. B. was the greatest storyteller I ever knew. When he died, a "tombstone committee" was established made up of myself, Don Bacon, an important editor of *U.S. News & World Report*, and Jamie Clements, legal director of Temple's Scott-White Hospital. Each member had a right of veto, and Clements vetoed the idea that the word "raconteur" be on the tombstone because a hundred years from now people from the Piney Woods might think D. B. was a "French coon hunter."

But Clements will tell you no one could spin a yarn like D. B. More than 95 percent of Larry Hufford's editing of *D. B.: Reminiscences of D. B. Hardeman*, AAR/Tantalus, 1984, consists of interviews with him. Here are some excerpts:

I was born the first year of World War I [in Goliad] and remember the Al Smith-Herbert Hoover presidential race. The most bitter part was the anti-Catholicism. We were told that the Catholic Church basement was filled with arms and ammunition and that if Al Smith was elected, the pope would immediately catch a ship to Washington and give orders for an uprising.

Dr. Homer Rainey became president of the University of Texas about 1939 or 1940. . . . He was born over in East Texas, and he went to Austin College and pitched in the Texas Baseball League. . . . Rainey got into a fight with his board of regents and was fired. . . . He ran for governor in 1946. . . . It was an extremely vicious campaign. . . .

That 1941 senatorial election was the one that [Lyndon] Johnson lost. It was stolen from him, I always thought. . . . What happened, and this is my gut feeling, Jim Ferguson didn't give a damn about [Pappy] O'Daniel. He had great contempt for him. But Ferguson wanted Coke Stevenson, who was then lieutenant governor, so he wanted to kick O'Daniel upstairs—get him to Washington—so Coke would become governor. There were still some Ferguson machine counties in East Texas, over generally in the Lufkin area. They held the count out in about ten of those counties.

In 1952 [Adlai] Stevenson was coming to Texas [running for president]. Our Democratic politicians had run off. So Sam Rayburn just had to run the campaign [but needed a manager]. When Maury Maverick, Jr., gets an idea about something he runs his friends absolutely to the asylum and his enemies over the wall. Maury decided that Mr. Rayburn should have [blind] Jim Sewell as campaign manager for Stevenson. Mr. Rayburn had never heard of Sewell. But Maury sent telegrams. He sent oversized post-cards. He sent special-delivery letters. He just drove the old man out of his mind until Rayburn finally said: "Well, let's talk to this fellow Sewell." Rayburn fell in love with Sewell, like the rest of us, and asked Jim to be campaign manager. . . .

Rayburn was not impressed with [John] Kennedy until the first television debate with Nixon. He said, "Kennedy was in the House here, and he made absolutely no impression on us. Rumpled suits and hair hanging down in his face. He was running around after the girls all night long." But Rayburn watched the first television debate. They say he turned off the set and said, "My God! The things that boy knows."

I've often thought that if LBJ had listened to Lady Bird's judgment more often on things, he might have avoided some of the headaches he had. She has what Sam Rayburn loved so much: She has common sense. Rayburn said, "When you've got common sense, that's all the sense there is. . . ." ★

RALPH YARBOROUGH: DEDICATED LIBERAL

"Ralph Yarborough: Great Texan,"
September 25, 1988

Because I want to honor eighty-five-year-old Ralph Yarborough, I decided to ask him to reflect on his life. His answers were edited by me for reasons of space. Listen now to the "old populist lion" from the Piney Woods [who would later die in 1996].

Q. What are some of your childhood memories?

A. I was born at Chandler, Henderson County, Texas, on June 8, 1903, the seventh in a family of eleven children. My home, in which I was born, was one mile from the Neches River. I could go to the river and fish or hunt. We lived on the edge of town with a population of five hundred. Few boys in this nation at this time have the privilege that I enjoyed watching the birds and animals. I went to the local school, graduated valedictorian from Chandler High in 1918 [ten grades] and then salutatorian from Tyler High School in 1919.

Q. What about law school days at the University of Texas-Austin?

A. I worked my way through law school waiting on tables. As a drill sergeant in the National Guard I received $43 every three months and from that got my spending money for clothes and books. . . .

Q. You have mentioned to me on a number of occasions your days as an assistant attorney general of Texas under Governor Jimmy Allred. Why is that time of your life so dear to you?

A. There were only seventeen assistants in the office to represent all the departments of the state. I represented the Land Office, the State Superintendent of Public Instruction, and all of the colleges in Texas. It was a dream world for a young lawyer. In *Magnolia Petroleum Co. v. Walker* . . . I won a landmark case of the oil and gas bonus interest in over six million acres of land, the fruits of which resulted in over a billion dollars in the Permanent School Fund to date. I also was responsible for an opinion that put $433 million in the Permanent University Fund.

Q. How did you get to be a district judge?

A. When Allred became governor, a vacancy arose in a district judgeship in Austin, and he appointed me. It paid only $4,000. I served from January of 1936 to January 1941.

Q. But, Judge Yarborough, you were no spring chicken when World War II came along. What did you do about that war?

A. I did not run for reelection for the judgeship because I felt the war was coming. I volunteered and was commissioned a captain and asked for service with an infantry division. I was assigned to the Ninety-seventh Infantry Division, commanded by General Louis Craig, one of the finest commanders of World War II.

A vivid memory was the concentration camp at Flossenberg, which our division occupied in eastern Bavaria, not far from the Czech border. The bodies of the starved people were stacked like wood in regular rows. They were stacked before the crematories, waiting to be burned.

I remember seeing a German corps commander walking to our division headquarters to surrender with ragged and hungry and dirty German soldiers all around him. But he had on his immaculate uniform and shiny boots.

Q. What about your military duty later on in Japan?

A. In Japan it was a different story. The Japanese were a people in shell shock. Japan had never been defeated or occupied by foreign troops. They were resigned and disciplined. No obscene gestures. I became the *de facto* governor over one-seventh of the people of Japan.

As I stood behind our American generals and watched the Japanese generals surrender, the most amazing thing about them was how the stunned Japanese watched the Nisei [Americans of Japanese descent] who were a head taller than the native Japanese. They served with us unarmed, did not take part in combat, and saved many casualties. They stood behind our generals and translated their surrender orders . . . .

"Three Heroes, Battered But True,"
February 25, 1990

Ralph Yarborough was thirty-nine years old with wife and child when he gave up a district court bench to join the army, serving first in Europe and then in Japan on General [Douglas] MacArthur's staff.

During his thirteen years in the U. S. Senate he did much for the country.

Item. He was the one most responsible for the establishment of Guadalupe Mountains National Park, the Big Thicket National Preserve, and Padre Island National Seashore.

Item. He did more to help libraries than any senator in the history of our country.

Item. He was the lead author of the Cold War G. I. Bill that helped millions of young people get a college education.

Item. He had a lead in raising the minimum wage and expanded the law as never before to include women.

Item. He was a lion in the Senate by getting funds to fight cancer.

Item. With Senator John Kennedy he was co-lead in launching community health services.

Item. He was the chief sponsor of the Endangered Species Act to protect rare animals.

Yarborough was defeated for reelection to the senate because the Lloyd Bentsen campaign reflected on his love of country. [Yarborough] had begun to question the unconstitutional Vietnam War. Those who are devoted to Ralph Yarborough will never forget the attacks on his patriotism.

At eighty-five, with a bright mind but in poor physical health, there is no greater patriot than Ralph Yarborough. No one loves Texas more. . . .

I was especially touched when the old man said to me: "Maury, I love Texas and was proud to serve her and have had a good life. You come from a great and historic city. God bless the good people of San Antonio." ★

DANA X. BIBLE: FOOTBALL COACH

"The Eyes of Texas Were Upon Coach Bible,"
April 17, 1983

The Bible years were over, but the legacy of the man and his system remained. . . . D. X. Bible poured the foundation for what was to become a football dynasty. . . .

James W. Pohl, *Southwestern Historical Quarterly*, October 1982.

"What kind of a man was D. X. Bible?" I asked my cousin, Jack McGarraugh, who, in 1933, [set] the high school state low hurdles record of 220 yards in 23.8 seconds. After that Jack went to the University of Nebraska on a track scholarship and came to know Bible. "I used to go to Coach Bible's home on Sundays and eat Mexican food, since his wife had a San Antonio background. I knew what a good coach was before I went to Nebraska, having met Doc Sowell of Mark Twain [Junior High School] through Bubba Reeves and having played under Joe Ward at Edison [High School]. As for Bible, there was nothing in the world like him. I don't know of any coach who grieved more when one of his athletes got hurt. None of this modern stuff of shooting a kid full of so-called medicine and then sending him back on the field to be permanently injured," said Cousin Jack.

Born in Jefferson City, Tennessee, and a graduate of Carson-Newman College in 1912, Dana Xenophon Bible studied coaching at the feet of A. A. Stagg, Pop Warner, Fielding Yost, and Bob Zuppke. His lifetime won-lost-tied record was 209-64-19 in thirty-five seasons.

The Aggies insist that Bible's greatest halftime performance came in 1922 when, as their coach, he drew a line and reminded the players of [William] Travis' having done the same thing at the Alamo. That day the Aggies scored their only Austin win between 1909 and 1956 with a 14-7 victory.

But University of Texas folks claim Bible's all-time locker room performance came at Madison, Wisconsin, when, in 1939, the Longhorns finally cast aside their reputation as a hick football team and took on the aura of a national contender. It began when the team left from the Missouri-Pacific station in Austin on a Thursday and rode continuously until it reached Chicago Friday night where a short workout was had at Soldier Field. Then back on the train for another all-night ride with no time for rest as the buses took the players straight to the Madison football stadium.

Warming up on the field, the Longhorns heard a wild roar as the incomparable song "On, Wisconsin!" broke out. Bible asked to take his team back to the locker room and then, according to Professor Pohl, "conjured up images of Texans, of gnarled old men and lithe-limbed lads, of affectionate mothers and worshipful sisters and girlfriends, all of whom were gathered about radios, straining to hear of the epic words that told of heroic deeds and final victory. . . . Wisconsin was big, but Texas had the emotional surge and the speed; and when the game was over, Texas had won it, 17-7. . . ."

Dr. James Dolley, chairman of the UT Athletic Council, was the one who suggested that Bible be brought to Texas from Nebraska. The campus went into an uproar when Bible demanded a ten-year contract at $15,000 a year with the alumni to pay his income tax. . . .

Dr. H. Y. Benedict, president of the university, was making only $8,000 a year, while associate professors hired out for $3,500. The *Daily Texan* came out with an editorial asking: "Can we afford Mr. Bible?" But UT did afford Bible, and the man who finally cut the deal with him was my friend, University Regent Major J. R. Parten.

Most folks thought that Bible would bring his staff with him from Nebraska, but Coach Bible had other ideas. He would get the best Texans he could find, and he did: Bully Gilstrap of Schreiner Institute in Kerrville, Blair Cherry of Amarillo, Clyde Littlefield, already on board, and Ed Price.

Then the new coach set up "the Bible Plan," which divided Texas into fifteen sections pretty much along the lines of congressional districts. There the alumni went to work; Bible had agents all over the state doing recruiting for him.

Grades were important to him, and so he established the system of a "brain coach" where players would have tutorial help. The first brain coach in the history of UT was David Kaine, then a petroleum engineering student with top grades who, in his last year, won his letter as a football player.

[He is] a successful contractor today in San Antonio. I asked David to search his memory about Bible and to evaluate the man. "Among the top ten coaches in the history of the country and as a human being at the very top. He had tremendous respect from the players," David said.

Then Kaine repeated what Jack McGarraugh told me [about] how Bible worried about his players being hurt. "Coach Bible used to send me in to play with specific orders to watch an all-conference center named Jackson who was injury prone, but who would hide it from the coaches. Bible would tell me that if Jackson appeared hurt to send word to him and he would take

Jackson out. Coach Bible always cared about young people not being maimed over sports. He was a considerate person."

In January 1980 D. X. Bible, eighty-three years old, winner of fourteen major conference titles, died in St. David's Hospital at Austin. He gave me and my old pal, Liz Carpenter, once of White House fame, the only football hero we ever had: Jack Crain, who, in the final thirty seconds of the 1939 game with Arkansas and after Bible called time out for the band to play "The Eyes of Texas," ran a dazzling sixty-seven yards for the winning touchdown. What a moment that was!

So a round of cheers for D. X. Bible. There is no stone-and-mortar memorial to him . . . at Austin. Why not? It seems to me that we old tea sippers, with the eyes of Texas upon us, ought to do something about that. ★

NAOMI NYE: POET

"Hoot Toot for Poet Naomi Nye,"
July 10, 1988

"West Side"

In certain neighborhoods
the air is paved with names.
Domingo, Monico, Francisco,
shining rivulets of sound.
Names opening wet circles
inside the mouth,
sprinkling bright vowels
across the deserts of
Bill, Bob, John.
The names are worn
on silver linked chains.

271

Maria lives in Pablo Alley,
Esperanza rides the
Santiago bus!
They click together like charms.
O save me from the
boarded-up windows,
the pistol crack in a
dark backyard,
save us from the leaky roof,
the rattled textbook
that never smiles.
Let the names be verses
in a city that sings.

"Rebellion Against the North Side"
[first stanza]
There will be no monograms
on our skulls
You who are training
your daughters to check
for the words
"Calvin Klein" before
they look to see if
there are pockets
are giving them no hands
to put in those pockets. . . .

Naomi Shihab Nye, *Hugging the Jukebox,*
National Poetry Award, 1982.

Naomi Shihab Nye, the poet, graduate of Trinity University, is a handsome woman with a rich, resonant voice and laughing eyes.

From my grave I see her thirty-five years from now, internationally famous, an interesting old woman . . . wearing a brown derby, a pigtail, and a long blood-red skirt with a silver belt from Santa Fe, where she spends the summer.

On a shelf above her head will be a photograph of her then-late husband, Michael, next to a bowl of oranges.

On her paternal side Naomi has a Palestinian grandmother living on the West Bank. From her mother she is of German-Swiss descent. Half of her high school days were spent in Jerusalem where her father was an editor for the *Jerusalem Post*; the other half in San Antonio.

Her husband, Michael Nye, is a lawyer who practices law a few months a year to make beans but then for the rest of the year turns into an excellent photographer. He is the . . . son of Chief Justice Paul Nye of the Corpus Christi Court of Appeals. . . .

All over the world Naomi and Michael have traveled, year after year: Latin America, the Middle East, Pakistan, India, and Europe—she writing poetry, he photographing. They go dirt-cheap, living and talking with local people, edging away from the image of the ugly American. Of this couple Barbara Stanush, herself a poet and writer, says: "Naomi is a pied piper. She has taught in schools all over the country, including San Antonio, for over a decade, exciting young people about words. The young follow her. She and her husband are role models for higher ideals, for a spirit of unselfishness not found in the yuppie mentality."

Naomi began writing poetry at the age of six.

A childhood hero was Carl Sandburg, the one-time Chicago newspaperman, who wrote of the plain people pushing on, "In the night, and overhead a shovel of stars for keeps."

That's pretty good going for a little girl from the West Bank who remembers that her grandmother "blessed me with whispered phrases in the old way. Mohammed this, Mohammed that, circling my head with her silver ring in a kind of prayer."

During her San Antonio high school days Naomi was in the

Pegasus Society, one of the oldest poetry clubs in the country. . . .

In Greek mythology Pegasus was the winged horse of the Muses, born of the blood of the decapitated Medusa.

In its flight to heaven and while kicking its way free from an oppressor, Pegasus created the fountain of Hippocrene, the source of all poetic inspiration.

The poets, the truly good ones . . . grab all of us with any sensitivity. A winner of a number of prestigious national awards—I mean big league stuff—Naomi does that.

Plato feared poets and banished them from his utopian state. But Wordsworth was more generous claiming: "Poetry is passion." Shakespeare linked poets with "lunatics and lovers" in his *Midsummer Night's Dream*, while Coleridge insisted, "the poet brings the soul of man into activity."

Naomi does poetry readings from one end of America to another including San Antonio.

She loves to do poetry readings and told me that one of the most moving experiences she had was reading poetry about peace by Israeli and Palestinian women to the sisterhood of Temple Beth El.

Vachel Lindsay's poem, "The Kallyope Yell," somehow reminds me of Naomi's going about tooting hope with poetry. It is written in the manner of what poets call "onomatopoeia," a Greek word that signifies the making or forming of a word by imitating a sound. Fasten your seat belts, pals. Here's "The Kallyope Yell" for Naomi:

> *Music of the mob I*
> *Circus day's tremendous cry.*
> *I am the Kallyope,*
> *Kallyope, Kallyope!*
> *Tooting hope, tooting*
> *hope, tooting hope;*

Hoot toot, hoot toot,
hoot toot!

Willy willy willy
wah Hoo!

For gentlemen like myself I urge you to read *The Pursuit of Poetry* by Louis Untermeyer, 1969, Simon & Schuster. It is one of my favorite books. ★

O'NEIL FORD: ARCHITECT

"Heaven Won't Be the Same with O'Neil Ford,"
August 8, 1982

Our play begins at the Induction Center, just inside the Pearly Gates of Heaven.

An architect from San Antonio, O'Neil Ford, is walking around, pointing his cigar at this and that, giving everybody a lot of free advice. Captain Tim O'Hara in charge of the night shift, can't cope with the situation. O'Hara places a call to St. Peter.

O'Hara: St. Peter, help me with this new guy from San Antonio. He's been up here only two weeks, and he thinks he is running the place. Wants to know who designed the Induction Center. Says it's the worst architecture he ever saw.

St. Peter: I knew we would have trouble once O'Neil arrived and so I tried to placate him with a welcoming committee of New Deal folks. You know, O'Neil got his start under Franklin D. Roosevelt at La Villita.

O'Hara: What was that, a musical group at the Pearly Gates?

St. Peter: Those were his old jazz buddies who came up from San Antonio before he died–Jim Cullum, Sr., on clarinet, Don Albert on trumpet, Bert Etta Davis on sax, George Pryor on bass fiddle and Claytie Polk on piano. Jim Cullum, Jr., did the funeral down on earth with the Happy Jazz Band and Herb Hall out of Boerne. I tell you, O'Hara, when Herb let loose with a wail on his clarinet we heard it all the way up here. . . .

[At the funeral service for O'Neil, Maury Maverick, Jr., son of the mayor who accomplished the restoration of La Villita in the thirties, along with humanist Amy Freeman Lee and folk humorist John Henry Faulk, were some of Ford's friends who spoke at the ceremony. The following is a text of Maverick's remarks, reprinted in the September 1982 newsletter of the San Antonio Conservation Society:

Only months before he died, Oliver Wendell Holmes quoted a Greek poet: "Death plucks at thy ear and says, Live for I am coming."

O'Neil knew that death had plucked him on the ear, and, as he readied himself for it, he lived and lived and lived until the last moment.

What a sad occasion this would be if O'Neil Ford had never lived at all. The saddest thing in all the world is an elderly person who, when the time comes to die, knows he or she never lived.

Some deaths we understand, some we do not. We ought to understand this one in good grace, in good spirit, even in joy—yes, even with some laughter in our hearts.

I first met O'Neil at La Villita when I was fifteen years old trailing behind him and Dave Williams, the regional architect for the National Youth Administration. It was Williams who had recommended that O'Neil be the on-site architect. You can't imagine how proud we were later on when Eleanor Roosevelt came to town and bragged on La Villita. Hungry kids in the worst of a depression had been put to work, and they, with O'Neil, had created something of beauty.

O'Neil stood up to the enemy as defined by Gilbert Murray, a British classical scholar: "The enemy has no definite name, though in a certain degree we all know him. He who puts always the body before the spirit, the dead before the living; who makes things only in order to sell them; who has forgotten that there is such a thing as truth, and measures the world by advertisement or money; who daily defiles the beauty that surrounds him, and makes vulgar the tragedy."

In his architecture and in his life O'Neil stood up to those who would destroy beauty, who would make vulgar the tragedy. He was a world-class architect and a good citizen.

Only O'Neil Ford could say better what he wanted said at his own funeral. Along with the instructions for his service, he wrote: "I don't know how to say there must not be any great ceremony—no weeping. I have gone away for pretty long trips before—and besides, does anyone have any choice about dying? Why fear the inevitable? Why scorn the natural ending?" ★

DUNCAN BORLAND: COURAGEOUS PASTOR

"Illness Gives Pastor His Ministry,"
March 25, 1990

"Maury, my multiple sclerosis (MS) has worsened since you did your column on me in April of 1988. Then I could dress myself, take a bath and drive a car. No more. My vision is worse. You do not know how much I love those dear nurses and attendants at Morningside Manor for keeping me going and how much I love the people of the First Presbyterian Church of San Antonio for giving me a chance to have a mission in life."

The Reverend Duncan Borland upon being ordained as a
Presbyterian minister at the First Presbyterian Church of
San Antonio on Sunday, March 11, 1990.

After watching Duncan Borland be ordained I went away with good feelings about Presbyterians. And I was an outsider!

As a pantheist [I have as] my cathedral a sunset; my preachers, to list only a few, are purple martins, hoot owls, and Naomi Nye, the poet, with whom I have lunch now and then and who brings along as a chaperone her three-year-old son, Madison Cloudfeather Nye. Any mother who would give her son the middle name of "Cloudfeather" has got to have a touch of pantheism in her. . . .

We pantheists, all at the same time, are Jews, Christians, Hindus, and Moslems, but only after rejecting any claims of religious superiority of those religions above named, which we think suggest a stingy God in spreading his (her?) love.

Our heroes include such folks as Baruch Spinoza (1632-1677), a seventeenth-century Dutch metaphysician; the ancient American Indian holy men who respected the soil and the rivers; the late J. Frank Dobie, and his pal John Henry Faulk. . . .

Anyway, I first explained all these religious warts of mine to young Borland, who solemnly advised me that Presbyterians are understanding people and so I could interview him, my shortcomings and all.

I expected the best because I had a Presbyterian chaplain in the U. S. Marine Corps by the name of Jack Lewis who, on the Solomon Islands, used to sing "Minnie the Moocher" in a way that would have made Cab Calloway green with envy. Retired now in the state of New York, Lewis is one of the good guys.

[In 1988 Borland] stated to me regarding his seminary experiences: "One class I loved was a course in evangelism taught by three pastors from the First Presbyterian Church in San Antonio. Their Texas church sounded like a special place, and I got up my courage to ask [Reverend] Louis Zbinden if I could do an internship with them. He said it might work, and amazingly enough it has."

With the help of Zbinden and others, Borland spent a one-year internship in San Antonio, returned to the Virginia seminary for his last year, and then upon graduation was invited by the First Presbyterian Church to return to San Antonio, where his ministry today involves working with the elderly at Morningside Manor Meadows and with retarded youngsters at Mission Road Development Center.

Duncan and I had an exchange. Watch.

Q. What do you have to say about the First Presbyterian Church?

A. I am incredibly grateful to them. I love that church and feel at home there.

Q. What about your work as a minister?

A. The elderly help me as much as I help them. I tell the elderly not to compare their lives with the way it was when they were young. We all have to understand that often when we cross bridges in life we cannot go back.

As for the mentally retarded young people at the Mission Road Center, they see the shape I'm in and are impressed with the fact that I am still going, so far keeping my head above water. It gives them strength to cope with their own problems.

Q. You keep telling me God is wonderful. If he is so wonderful, why did he let you have MS?

A. Because through my disease God has given me a ministry, a purpose in life. I think of that line in the old song which goes: "When you ain't got nothing, you got nothing to lose." For people in my shape I would change that line to read: "If you ain't got nothing, you better love God because that is all you got."

The ordination service could not have been more touching. Down the center aisle came Borland on his new battery-driven chair, the first of its kind in Texas, and on which he can stand up straight after the machine lifts his body.

As the choir sang, Borland did a circle in front of the altar and faced the congregation which included a contingent of the elderly from Morningside Manor Meadows and about twenty-five mentally retarded youngsters from Mission Road watching their friend have a rare taste of honey.

The Reverend Louis Zbinden spoke for Borland's courage. Then Borland's father, David Borland, a medical doctor from Williamsburg, Virginia, told the congregation of his son's body being "a total wreck" but his inner body so full of hope and spiritual depth. That's when I saw some wet Presbyterian eyes.

The ceremony over, back up the center aisle came the Reverend Duncan Borland to the outer foyer of the church.

Cheers for Louis Zbinden for his lead in all this; cheers for the members of First Presbyterian Church for making it possible, but most of all cheers for a young man terribly crippled but full of good cheer and hope, reaching out for tomorrow. ★

WILLIAM O. DOUGLAS: JUDICIAL MAVERICK

"Justice William O. Douglas, 'This Man of Freedom,'"
September 16, 1979

When retired U. S. Supreme Court Justice William O. Douglas passed through those Pearly Gates, folks fearful of Big Brother (Uncle Sam) bid a friend farewell.

Through the years Judge Douglas and I corresponded a bit; he's a hero of mine. . . .

"Farewell to Justice William O. Douglas,"
February 3, 1980
[As Douglas stated in his autobiography *Go East, Young Man*, Random House, the] judge's Republican mother was Julia Fisk Beckford, who was born in 1872 at the town of Maine, Minnesota. His Presbyterian Douglas ancestors came to Nova

Scotia from Scotland in 1773 and did not migrate to the United States until the 1890s.

His father, William Douglas, was ordained a Presbyterian preacher at Crockett, Minnesota, on May 6, 1898, and never made more than $600 a year. The cat is out of the bag. Now we know why Bill Douglas raised so much hell all his life. (Preacher's kid!)

Most of the judge's childhood was spent at churches in Minnesota, California, and finally in the state of Washington. It was the latter experience that caused him to claim Yakima as his hometown.

He remembered going with his father to Dot, Washington, a spot on the road where Reverend Douglas was to make his first sermon in a new community. Only one person was in church, a cowboy. Reverend Douglas offered to put off the sermon, but the cowboy said: "If I had forty horses and a load of hay and went out to feed them and could find only one horse, I don't think I'd let that one horse go hungry."

The sermon lasted for a full hour. When the service was over Reverend Douglas shook hands with the cowboy and asked how it went. "Well," said the cowboy, "if I had forty horses to feed and went out looking for them with a load of hay and found only one horse, I don't think that I'd give the whole load to that one horse."

Douglas was, I think, a religious man, depending on how "religious" is defined, but he had a profound distrust of the abuses of organized religion. Here are some thoughts he expressed on the subject:

"As I started to move around the world, I discovered that the church—whatever faith or creed it espoused—was usually aligned with the establishment. Few clergymen were relating the teachings of their church to the marketplace. . . ."

At the lower grades of school, Bill Douglas was taunted

because of his skinny, almost deformed legs, the result of a brutal bout with polio.

"In retrospect, I see that this period," he would later write, "is when I became a loner." As a child he climbed mountains to gain strength for his legs. Mother Nature befriended him, and he never forgot her.

He was a high school teacher, a graduate of Columbia Law School (where he made the *Law Review*), a professor of law at Columbia and Yale, and later chairman of the Securities and Exchange Commission, where he came to know as much about corporate finance as any businessman in the country. Then FDR put him on the High Court, where he remained longer than any person in the history of our country.

Even as a young law professor he was an iconoclast. When Nicholas Butler appointed a dean of the Columbia Law School without consulting the faculty, Douglas resigned in protest and went to teach at Yale.

Always he had a high regard for good college professors and sometimes tried out their theories in his dissents. One of the most delightful concerned a USC law professor who developed the theory that the trees, birds, the underground water, the air about us, and all the wonders of nature were not inanimate nothings but had "lives" of their own that could be respected in courts of law through you and me as "Next Friend." . . .

I last saw Douglas in San Antonio when I introduced him to the local bar association. After the luncheon we walked back to the Menger Hotel. As we came to the Alamo, he gave me a lecture on courage and liberty.

"That took courage, Maury," he said as he pointed to the Alamo, "but there's all kinds of courage. The [Joe] McCarthy period and the Vietnam War all go back to the old-time China hands in the State Department who were destroyed for courageously telling the truth about the then-coming revolution in

China."

As we shook hands in the hotel lobby, he said as a parting shot: "Stick with the kids who are dissenting under the First Amendment against the war."

Later he would try to have the Vietnam War declared unconstitutional because, among other reasons, there had been no formal declaration of war approved by the Congress, as required by the Constitution of the United States.

Douglas was right in standing up for law and order in the face of three presidents—Kennedy, Johnson, and Nixon—running out on the Constitution. We, the people, share in the guilt for we let those presidents get away with it. . . .

Like his Scottish ancestors, this important jurist went to his grave according to the rites of the Presbyterian Church, with a song of Woody Guthrie's thrown in for good measure. I bet Woody would have liked that.

Good-bye, Justice Douglas. ★

JIM LEHRER: NOVELIST

"Hometown Boy Does Great,"
June 19, 1988

June 1, 1988
Maury:

I am not sure I have involved memories of my youth in San Antonio. They're mostly just simple and straightforward. We came to San Antonio from Beaumont in the summer of 1950. I graduated in 1952 from Jefferson High School, where I received an excellent education and a good whetting of my appetite for journalism. My father managed the Continental Trailways bus depot. Our family had many friends among the people who worked at the depot and the drivers who drove in and out. They were important to all of us—not just to Dad.

My mother worked at the National Bank of Fort Sam Houston among another group of nice people. My brother, Fred, who is two years older, attended Trinity University for one year and then San Antonio College before going on to the University of Texas.

I left San Antonio for college and then the marines and then to newspaper work, but my mother and father stayed there until Dad died in 1970. He died in the Nix Hospital following complications from cancer surgery. The last time I was in San Antonio I stayed at La Mansion Hotel, and my room looked out on the old Nix building to the room where my father died. It was all I could do to keep from crying. Even though I have spent little time there since 1952, I have always looked upon San Antonio as my home. It was where I longed to go when I was in school or in the service. It was where my heart always was and where a part of it will always be.

Jim Lehrer, "The MacNeil/Lehrer News Hour," author of
Kick the Can, G. P. Putnam's Sons, 1988.

[In 1985] I visited Washington, D. C., to make a pilgrimage to the Vietnam Memorial. While there Nick Kallison Kotz invited me to have supper with Jim Lehrer at a Vietnamese restaurant in which Nick owns a small interest. In about five minutes of talking it became clear to me that Jim's Texas roots go deep and that they are important to him. His wife is from McKinney. He attended a junior college in Victoria after leaving Jefferson High School. For years he was a reporter in the Dallas-Fort Worth area, and then went to Austin to cover the legislature.

Lehrer can visit any city room of any big daily in Texas and find an old buddy. Although internationally famous, he remembers his Texas friends with affection and puts them at ease.

That night we had supper he went on endlessly about San Antonio, bringing up landmark after landmark. On his list was the Nix Hospital. Why would anyone mention a hospital? But when he did I said: "That's where my father died." Jim came back: "My father died there, too." That was a handshake between two strangers. Anyway, it was a delightful evening for me and the beginning of a new friendship. . . .

But now to Jim's book *Kick the Can*. (He also wrote *Viva Max*, the satire about the Alamo.)

After reading *Kick the Can*, I know why Jim had heart surgery. The book is so full of laughter, sadness, and deep emotion that Jim has to be a person of profound feelings. It's his TV program that's dangerous to his health.

Watch the way Jim keeps a poker face on the "McNeil-Lehrer News Hour," bottling up his feelings. . . .

Kick the Can is a book about a nineteen-year-old country boy, the son of a Kansas state highway trooper, who runs away from home to be a pirate on the Gulf of Mexico. If you know Kansas, Oklahoma and Texas, this book will have a special meaning to you because all the action takes place in those three states.

The trooper's son calls himself "the One-Eyed Mack." Some years before, a child he was playing with kicked a can and knocked out his eye, hence the title of the book. One-Eyed Mack had planned all his life to be a Kansas trooper, but a trooper has to have two eyes. Pirates can have one eye and wear a black patch.

On the way to Galveston our hero has a sexual encounter with a prostitute at the rear of a nearly empty bus, the details of which I cannot give you in this column. My God, but it is nasty. (I didn't dream Jim Lehrer could be so nasty.)

Mack falls in with an ex-convict by the name of Pepper, who is an experienced hobo obituary writer for any newspaper that will give him a job. Mack and Pepper can't get in enough trouble. They burglarize a store, but Mack is so guilt-ridden he goes back, burglarizes the store a second time and returns the merchandise.

All over Texas they go from one "Holy Road" church to another, getting saved time and time again. Then they head for Adabel, Oklahoma, since the name "Adabel" sounds so good. They get there by going through Coffeyville, Kansas, where there's more trouble. Once they hit Oklahoma, the mud turns red and the rollercoaster ride gets wilder until the law catches up with Pepper, who is given the option of joining the marines and fighting in Korea or going to the penitentiary.

Pepper goes off to Korea, leaving a pregnant wife. He is killed by throwing himself on a hand grenade, thereby saving his squad, and wins the Medal of Honor. One-Eyed Mack marries the widow and in time becomes an Oklahoma county commissioner.

Kick the Can is wacky, silly and dippy, but before it is over with, Lehrer will make a tear slide down your face when Pepper's remains are brought back from Korea. In the end, although it is obvious Lehrer has teased Baptists, Methodists, and Holy Roaders, it is also clear he has honored them.

If you're a big intellectual whose timbers don't shiver when you think about Sam Houston, or can't say "thank you" in your heart to Sam Rayburn and [former Democratic Texas Governor] Dolph Briscoe for farm-to-market roads, or don't care that Jim is writing about the kind of country folks, warts and all, who died at the Alamo, then this is not your book.

But if it's the other way around, and you can do a little toe tapping when a country band gets going on "Ida Red, Ida Green, prettiest girl I ever did seen," then this book is for you. Silly? Oh, lordy, it is silly, but there are lots of laughs and at the end a good cry. ★

RONNIE DUGGER: MAVERICK JOURNALIST

"Dugger: An Asset to Liberty,"
January 25, 1987

About once every year and a half I like to give you old things a status report on Ronnie Dugger, publisher of the *Texas Observer,* who lived his childhood in San Antonio, graduating from Brackenridge High School. From there he attended the University of Texas at Austin and became the editor of the *Daily Texan,* the campus newspaper.

[In 1986] Ronnie and I had a debate in the *Texas Observer* regarding the Sandinistas of Nicaragua. He came down harder on them than I did. The debate must have had some merit because the *Washington Post* gave our growling at one another prominent space.

As always, prophets are without honor in their own home-town, but the truth is that Dugger is among the top ten investigative reporters in our country. . . .

"Ronnie Dugger is 'Genuine Article,'"
May 27, 1979

[I asked Dugger:] "Of all your teachers in Brackenridge High School, which one touched your life the most, Ronnie?" "It was Miss Christine Lawrence," he replied, "because she was a superb English teacher. We would diagram sentences together. I don't think they teach that anymore. And she taught me about art and literature."

I first knew Ronnie when he was a student at the University of Texas. In those days he was Hollywood handsome.

Today, a grandfather with ample girth and beard, he looks like Orson Welles. That's also Hollywood, but not the early Hollywood.

287

Academics, except for the University of Texas, which treats him with continuing rudeness, has been a part of his life. In the last ten years he has held prestigious teaching positions at such great universities as UCLA, Amherst, and, his favorite, because of the influence of Thomas Jefferson, the University of Virginia.

In his salad days Ronnie had the tendency to use the longest words he could find. Mostly that came from the influence of high-tone intellectuals he was then running with, such as . . . Dr. John Silber, a one-time San Antonio boy [and former administrator at the University of Texas at Austin, president of Boston University and Massachusetts commissioner of education].

It got so bad for a while that Dugger caught a rash called "multisyllabicism," but things have considerably improved since he started keeping better company. . . .

"Dugger: An Asset to Liberty,"
January 25, 1987

If he would write with shorter words, using shorter sentences and shorter paragraphs, and quit worrying over whether or not Harvard professors appreciate him, he could become the I. F. "Izzy" Stone of his day. When he is at his muckraker, Texas-porcupine journalistic best, he has few equals when it comes to honesty, brains, and courage. He's a marvelous citizen: indeed, an asset to the cause of liberty.

Well, I've said enough. Let's listen now to Dugger.

"I love San Antonio, my hometown and my city of permanent residence. My mother and other close relatives live here, and more of my friends than any other place. I'm here and in Austin, attending to *Texas Observer* business, a large part of the year."

"My sense of place has undergone a metamorphosis. I have always been a Texan, but living and working in and out of New York City. I don't feel as if I have lost Texas."

"It takes a while for our ideas to catch up with our inventions, and our idea of place is way behind. It's all one place, New York City, Minneapolis, London, San Antonio, Mexico City, Moscow, one place. Jet airplanes, instant communications and nuclear weapons mean we're all one people, which was always true even though we couldn't see it. . . .

"My wife, Patricia Baker, is a specialist on the Russian culture. She has edited five books on the works of the courageous dissident writers. Right now she is finishing a book for Random House on Svetlana Alliluyeva, Stalin's daughter. . . .

"My son, Gary, is a carpenter and tree surgeon in Austin. My daughter, Celia, is a reporter on the *Miami Herald.* Their mother, Jean Marshall, is a teacher in the Austin public schools. They are all doing well.

"I have some problems, but who hasn't? I'm fifty-six, healthy, strong as a horse, and happy. I like being a Texan at home in the world. I believe that I have done good work, but that I am on the threshold of my best work. When I think about the rest of my life, I feel a sense of experimentation. Like most of us, I have abilities I've never used. . . ." ★

For years Maverick has complained about being at death's door and even occasionally looks the part—sometimes becoming paranoid about his health. He even has become worried that some irate reader of his column might shoot him. That became evident when several years ago this editor was to meet him at the *Express-News* building. I arrived first and watched him park and exit his old, run-down car. My quiet approach surprised the columnist, causing him to jump and exclaim: "Good God! I thought you were someone going to kill me!" To which I calmly responded: "You probably deserve it, but I won't be the one to perform the act."

Maverick claims he has become a pantheist and maintains: "I worship trees and sunsets and the earth and the moon and the sky. I don't believe all that was created just for Moses, or just for Jesus Christ, or just for Allah. The only definition of God that I accept is St. John's: 'God is love.' Beyond that, when we become Christians, Jews, Hindus, Muslims, or whatever, we go to killing one another, and I become suspicious of all organized religions."[1]

He has even planned his own funeral. He wants Naomi Nye to read some of her poems and John Barnett of National Public Radio to bring his harmonica and play "Toot, Toot, Tootsie, Good-bye." Initially, he planned to have the mourners sing "The Old Rugged Cross" but has decided instead to have those attending listen to a "good whorehouse song."

An extension of his thoughts on religious beliefs and death appeared in 1990 with a column entitled "Gaining Wisdom from the Owl," which follows. ★

WHEN IT ALL ENDS
July 8, 1990

A few years ago I decided to be a pantheist after nearly becoming a Quaker, and in the process took with me some of my Christian heritage. After all, the Reverend James Maury, my fairly close cousin, was Thomas Jefferson's first Episcopal priest.

Furthermore, when I was a student at the University of Texas I began negotiations to enter an Episcopal seminary, but, thank God, the Japanese bombed Pearl Harbor, which saved me and the Episcopal Church from a fate worse than death. . . .

The leader of my religion is a she-owl who sits on a sacred tree in San Antonio's Brackenridge Park. I talk with her every day when I go on my morning hike. That I would pick an owl is appropriate. Not only are owls wise, but they have been around a long time, beginning some forty-five million years ago in North America. During that period they learned how to rotate their heads three-fourths of a circle and even turn their heads upside down.

Episcopal bishops can do neither of those things, nor have they read as many books on Third World revolutions as the owl. What's more, my owl has not threatened Catholic office-holders with excommunication if they are soft on abortion.

The book I am here reviewing, *I Heard the Owl Call My Name*, by Margaret Caven, Dell, 1974, begins with the terminally ill young vicar, Mark Brian, being taken by boat to the Indian village he will serve far north of the Canadian city of Vancouver, British Columbia. No sales tax-financed, rich man's playpen Alamodome is the village, but there is something better as enviously described by the Anglican bishop to his young vicar: "The Indian knows his village and feels for his village as no white man for his country, his town, or even his own bit of land. . . . The myths are the village and the winds and the rains. The river is the village, and the black and white killer whales that herd the fish to the end of the inlet the better to gobble them. The village is the salmon who comes up the river to spawn, the seal who follows the salmon and bites off his head, the bluejay whose name is like the sound he makes—'Kwiss-kwiss.' The village is the talking bird, the owl, who calls the name of the man who is going to die, and the silver-tipped grizzly bear who ambles into the village, and the little white speck that is the mountain goat on Whoop-Szo."

I have earned my pay for this week by merely quoting such writing. Have you ever read anything more beautiful? It is pure poetry. Read it again, but this time out loud to your spouse, treating each word as a kind of a spiritual diamond. Then be nicer to Mother Nature and all her things such as the Edwards aquifer.

After about six months the vicar writes his bishop: "I have learned little of the Indians as yet. I know only what they are not. They are none of the things one has been led to believe. They are not simple or emotional, they are not primitive."

The Indians of the village seem to have an affectionate regard for the little church and good-naturedly accept the cross inside but on condition that the carved and painted totem pole just outside the church symbolizing ancestral spirits is given equal dignity. The vicar agrees to that and wonders if his bishop would be offended.

(His bishop would not be offended because he made the same agreement in the same parish years before. . . .)

One day the owl calls the vicar's name. Shortly afterward he is killed in a mountain slide. The men of the village carry his body to the church, "While the women sing to a Supreme Being whose existence had been sensed before the white man ever came to this land. . . ."

Little wonder I do my praying with an owl in Brackenridge Park. . . . ★

NOTES

PREFACE

1. Maury Maverick, Jr., quoted in Nelson Allen, "Maverick: Famous Name Lives in Writing," San Antonio *Express-News,* May 10, 1987, p. 12G.

2. *Ibid.*

3. Based on Dale A. Somers, "James P. Newcomb: Texas Unionist and Radical Republican" (master's thesis, Trinity University, 1964).

4. Maury Maverick, Jr., "Purple Prose for a Dandy Bird," San Antonio *Express-News,* January 8, 1989, p. 3M.

5. *Ibid.*

6. *D. B.: Reminiscences of D. B. Hardemann,* Larry Hufford, ed., Austin: AAR/Tantles, 1984, pp. 48-49.

7. Ronnie Dugger, quoted in Maury Maverick, Jr., "Dugger: An Asset to Liberty," San Antonio *Express-News,* January 25, 1987, p. 3L; Ellen Sweets, "Life as a Maverick," Dallas *Morning News,* July 8, 1995, p. 1C.

8. Willie Morris, *North Toward Home,* Oxford, Mississippi: Yoknapatawpha Press, 1967, p. 291.

9. Maury Maverick, Jr., quoted in Clara Tuma, "Last of the Red Hot Liberals," *Texas Lawyer,* October 15, 1990, p. 24.

10. Maury Maverick, Jr., quoted in Morris, *North Toward Home,* p. 296.

11. Richard B. Henderson, *Maury Maverick: A Political Biography*, Austin: University of Texas Press, 1970, p. 163.

12. Letter from Maury Maverick, Jr., to Allan O. Kownslar, August 31, 1989.

MAVERICK WRITES ABOUT ICONOCLASTIC RELATIVES

1. Based on Richard Henderson, *Maury Maverick: A Political Biography*, Austin: University of Texas Press, 1970, and Paula Mitchell Marks, *Turn Your Eyes Toward Texas: Pioneers Sam and Mary Maverick*, College Station: Texas A&M University Press, 1989.

2. Rena Maverick Green, ed., *Memoirs of Mary A. Maverick*, Lincoln: University of Nebraska Press, 1989, pp. 113-114, 115.

3. Marks, *Turn Your Eyes Toward Texas*, p. 252.

4. Henderson, *Maury Maverick*, p. 6.

5. *Ibid*, p. 7.

6. *Ibid*, pp. 13-14.

7. *Ibid*, p. 17.

8. *Ibid*, p. 22.

9. *Ibid*, p. 26.

10. *Ibid*, pp. 26-27.

11. *Ibid*, pp. xv-xvi.

12. Maury Maverick, Sr., quoted in *ibid*, p. 60.

13. *Ibid*, pp. 218-220.

14. *Ibid*, p. 272.

15. Maury Maverick, Sr., "The Case Against Gobbledygook," *New York Times Magazine*, May 21, 1944, p. 11.

16. Henderson, *Maury Maverick*, p. 30.

MAVERICK WRITES ABOUT RED SCARES AND LEGISLATIVE MEMORIES

1. George Norris Green, *The Establishment in Texas Politics: The Primitive Years, 1938 – 1957*, Norman: University of Oklahoma Press, 1979, p. 16; and James McEnteer, *Fighting Words: Independent Journalists in Texas*, Austin: University of Texas Press, 1992, p. 79.

2. Green, *The Establishment in Texas Politics*, pp. 16-17.

3. Henderson, *Maury Maverick*, pp. 275-276; and Green, p. 145.

4. Green, *The Establishment in Texas Politics*, p. 131.

5. Maury Maverick, Sr., speech to Town Hall Meeting, February 25, 1954; Maury Maverick Papers, "Speeches, 1952-1954," University of Texas at Austin.

6. Larry L. King, "Machismo and the White House: Lyndon B. Johnson and Vietnam," *American Heritage*, August 1976, p. 11.

7. Robert Davis, interview with Maury Maverick, Jr., April 30, 1985; videotape of interview in the Trinity University Archives, San Antonio, Texas.

8. *Ibid*.

9. Maury Maverick, Jr., quoted in Tuma, "Last of the Red Hot Liberals," p. 24.

10. Joe B. Frantz, *The Forty-Acre Follies: An Opinionated History of the University of Texas*, (Austin: Texas Monthly Press, 1983), p. 86.

11. Davis interview.

12. Letter of Maury Maverick, Jr., to Allan O. Kownslar, July 14, 1984.

13. Davis interview.

14. Maury Maverick, Jr., "Legislative Memories Both Bitter and Sweet," San Antonio *Express-News*, March 6, 1983, p. 3K.

MAVERICK WRITES ABOUT BASIC CIVIL LIBERTIES

1. Maury Maverick, Jr., quoted in Tuma, "Last of the Red Hot Liberals," p. 25.

2. *Ibid.*

3. Morris, *North Toward Home*, p. 298.

4. Maury Maverick, Jr., quoted in Tuma, "Last of the Red Hot Liberals," p. 2.

5. Maury Maverick, Jr., quoted in Don E. Carleton, *Red Scare! Right Wing Hysteria, Fifties Fanaticism, and Their Legacy in Texas*, (Austin: Texas Monthly Press, 1985), pp. 265-266.

6. Davis interview.

MAVERICK WRITES ABOUT WAR AND PEACE

1. Davis interview.

2. *Ibid.*

3. *Ibid.*

4. Maury Maverick, Jr., quoted in Tuma, "Last of the Red Hot Liberals," p. 25.

5. *Ibid.*

6. Maury Maverick, Jr., quoted in Allen, "Maverick: Famous Name Lives in Writing," p. 12G.

7. *Ibid.*

CONCLUSION

1. Tuma, "Last of the Red Hot Liberals," p. 26.

About the Editor

Allan O. Kownslar, who received the Ph.D. degree from Carnegie-Mellon University, is professor of history at Trinity University in San Antonio. A native Texan, Kownslar is the author of sixteen books and several articles on history and political science.